The Scottish Trusts Guide

The Scottish Trusts Guide

By

Yasmin Prabhudas

Additional research by

Nicola Eastwood

Julie Carlaw

Susan Robinson

Robin Tatler

A Directory of Social Change Publication

The Scottish Trusts Guide

By Yasmin Prabhudas

Published by the Directory of Social Change, 24 Stephenson Way, London NW1 2DP, from whom further copies can be obtained. (Telephone 0171-209 5151; Fax 0171-209 5049; e-mail info@d-s-c.demon.co.uk)

Printed and bound by Page Bros., Norwich

British Library Cataloguing-in-Publication Data

A catalogue for this book is available from the British Library.

ISBN 1 873860 82 X

The following trusts supported the research of *The Scottish Trusts Guide*

The Carnegie United Kingdom Trust

The MacRobert Trusts

The TSB Foundation for Scotland

We are very grateful to them for their support.

Contents

Foreword   **7**
By John Naylor, Carnegie UK Trust

Introduction   **9**

How to make an application   **17**
By Fraser Falconer, BBC Children in Need Appeal

How to use this Guide   **24**

National trusts   **27**

Local trusts   Aberdeen & Perthshire   **131**
                   Central   **141**
                   Edinburgh & Lothians   **145**
                   Glasgow & West of Scotland   **157**
                   Highlands & Islands   **173**

Index   **181**

Foreword

As a grant-maker, it is a pleasure to wholeheartedly welcome this guide!

In Scotland, grant seekers suffer as there is no readily accessible cheap central source of up-to-date information about charities and grant-givers. The only index is held by the Inland Revenue but that information is inadequate.

A recent survey has shown about 1,500 addresses and contact names on the Inland Revenue list are out of date. Even if there is a good contact, a charity's most recent accounts and annual reports do not have to be filed with the Revenue. They have to be sought from the charity itself. This can prove difficult. New SCVO (Scottish Council for Voluntary Organisations) research reveals 10,000 of 22,000 recognised Scottish charities failed to provide them with the basic information, bound to be given by law within one month on request. Charges for obtaining simple accounts can be as high as £60. Such obstacles place unmanageable administrative and cost burdens on grant seekers.

Legal and other changes are needed to establish an effective regularly updated register of charities with useful back-up information so that all grant seekers and charities can benefit. The present system favours the charities with the time, energy and resources to carry out effective research. A number of Scottish grant-givers feel strongly about this issue and are pressing for change. Sympathetic signs are emerging from the Scottish Office.

Until recently, this would not have been possible as Scottish grant-makers did not meet. Now there is a group which meets to consider issues relevant to their work. In fact, at the same time that the Directory of Social Change was beginning work on this guide, the group approached them for such a directory as they felt that existing information was so poor.

They recognised that effective grant-giving depends on a clear flow of information from trusts to applicants and open supportive relationships between the two. Not all trusts would share this view but such openness can reduce wasted effort by all.

The most common difficulty faced by major trusts is the number of applications which do not fit within guidelines. In the case of the Carnegie UK Trust, it is almost nine out of ten applications. This directory should help to reduce this figure. If in doubt, applicants should first establish the criteria for grants before spending time completing applications which will be instantly rejected.

Fraser Falconer of Children in Need Scotland writes in greater detail in this publication about approaching trusts for funds. His article is rooted in his experience of going out to local areas and offering training. This training now includes information about Scottish trusts. Staff from other trusts participate in the training from time to time.

There is more work to be done. Some trusts are very reluctant to give information on priorities and methods of application but significant steps are being taken towards more open and co-operative relationships between the grant-giver and receiver.

While this directory focuses on Scotland, Scottish charities do have opportunities south of the border. The Association of Charitable Foundations, the UK-wide umbrella body for charitable trusts and foundations, has a working group and one of its aims is to encourage more grant applications from Scotland to grant-givers in England. It is worth reading the Directory of Social Change's other directories to establish the appropriate trusts.

Such publications will prove particularly useful at this time when the funding environment is changing so significantly, particularly in Scotland. Key changes include local government reorganisation, the development of contracting and the advent of the lottery.

Many charities will be affected by the reorganisation of local government. At best, it is likely to mean applying to more authorities, with a consequent increase in the administrative burden and the uncertainty of outcome; at worst, it will mean a reduction, or even an end to funding as the small unitary authorities face reductions in finances. While many trusts, like the Carnegie UK Trust, will be reluctant to replace statutory funding, they do provide a source of funding at a difficult time.

At the same time as reorganising, local authorities may replace grants with contracts for services. For some who are flexible and already have experience of contracting this may even prove beneficial. For the smaller charities, it may prove an insuperable challenge.

Against this background, the advent of the Lottery provides welcome additional resources. While it is too early to identify the effect in Scotland, or in the UK as a whole, it would appear that the various Scottish-based lottery boards are proving sensitive to local need. Significantly, some of them have indicated that their greatest need is to receive improved applications. This directory gives you real help in doing this.

The Directory of Social Change, I know, has been surprised at the amount of research that was needed to produce this book. It is a milestone along the road of improved understanding in the voluntary sector. It could not have come at a more appropriate time.

C John Naylor

Introduction

Welcome to the 1st edition of *The Scottish Trusts Guide*. It is our first attempt at producing a comprehensive record of grant-making trusts which are based or are active in Scotland. The Guide contains details of 350 trusts giving a total of £60 million. Through the Guide we aim to help charities, especially those without experience or contacts in the trust world, to make well-directed applications and to raise money as efficiently and economically as possible.

The impetus for the Guide came from an approach by the embryonic Scottish Group of Charitable Trusts who argued that there was a need for comprehensive information on Scottish grant-making trusts along the lines of our established *Guides to the Major Trusts Vols 1 & 2*. As with all trusts guides we have published, especially 1st editions, we expected trusts to respond with varying degrees of warmth to our requests for information. However, we did not expect to experience as many difficulties in obtaining information as we in fact encountered.

Criteria for inclusion

The basic criterion for inclusion is that the trust must be able to give at least £500 to organisations in Scotland. Many give considerably more. We have included all such trusts that we could find which were based in Scotland. Details of many have never been published before. However, there remained a problem with those trusts based outside Scotland but which could give grants there.

If we had compiled a guide to all foundations which could possibly fund charitable activities in Scotland, we would have had to reprint much of *A Guide to the Major Trusts Vols 1 & 2* plus undertaking major new research to find all those trusts with an income under £45,000 (the bottom limit for Volume 2) but which are UK-wide in their remit. Not only would this have been a monumental undertaking, the resulting book would have been so big as to be unusable (and would have cost organisations a fortune to buy).

We therefore took the editorial decision to include only those trusts which give Scotland a meaningful priority in their grant-making. Therefore, major foundations such as the Tudor Trust, Henry Smith Charity and the various Sainsbury Family Trusts are excluded from the Guide, even though they can and do fund in Scotland. However, the Allen Lane Foundation and the P F Charitable Trust are included.

Scotland's Top 25 Trusts

❑	£21,845,000	**Cancer Relief Macmillan Fund**	Cancer
❑	£10,620,000	**Shetland Islands Council Charitable Trust**	General in Shetland
❑	£3,046,000	**Robertson Trust**	General, mostly in Scotland
❑	£2,394,000	**BBC Children in Need Appeal**	Disadvantaged children
❑	£1,407,000	**Gannochy Trust**	Youth, recreation, general, especially in Perth
❑	£1,141,000	**Carnegie Trust for the Universities of Scotland**	Scottish universities
❑	£1,141,000	**Scottish Hospital Endowments Research Trust**	Medical research
❑	£857,000	**Carnegie United Kingdom Trust**	Community service, amateur arts, restoration
❑	£753,000	**Unemployed Voluntary Action Fund**	Projects involving unemployed people as volunteers
❑	£687,000	**MacRobert Trusts**	Science and technology, services, disability, youth, education, social welfare
❑	£487,000	**Hugh Fraser Foundation**	General
❑	£480,000	**Chest Heart & Stroke Scotland**	Medical research and related areas

There is no hard and fast defence for such a policy; we simply wanted to survey the grant-makers who have a clearly-expressed interest in Scotland. We hope that as a result of campaigning activity and an increase in the quality and volume of applications from Scottish groups, we will be able to include a greater number of UK-wide trusts in the next edition of this Guide.

The layout of the book

The layout of the entries is similar to our established patterns in *A Guide to the Major Trusts Vols 1 & 2* (see also the typical entry

❏	£480,000	**Radio Clyde - Cash for Kids at Christmas**	Children in the Strathclyde area
❏	£317,000	**Northwood Charitable Trust**	General
❏	£316,000	**Souter Foundation**	Christianity, third world, social welfare
❏	£300,000	**Trades House of Glasgow**	Social welfare, general
❏	£250,000	**W A Cargill Fund**	General
❏	£242,000	**TSB Foundation for Scotland**	Education and training, scientific and medical research, social and community needs
❏	£219,000	**Aberdeen Endowments Trust**	Education
❏	£212,000	**J T H Charitable Trust**	Education
❏	£203,000	**Tenovus-Scotland**	Medical research
❏	£200,000	**D W T Cargill Fund**	General
❏	£196,000	**North British Hotel Trust**	Disability, elderly, medical aids and equipment
❏	£192,000	**Miss Agnes H Hunter's Trust**	General
❏	£188,000	**Hayward Foundation**	Social welfare, medicine

Note: We have omitted some trusts (eg. Save & Prosper Educational Trust, P F Charitable Trust, Network Foundation, Hoover Foundation) from this list, even though the grant total published in the Guide would indicate that they should be in. These trusts all give throughout the UK and the grant total figure quoted in the Guide is their UK figure, not a figure for Scotland. There may also be some very large trusts for whom we have been unable to obtain a grant total.

on page 25). We have printed any policy details supplied by a trust, plus our own comments - where appropriate - on the trust's grant-making pattern. We are very keen to establish what the trust actually does, rather than what it is in principle able to do. Wherever possible we include examples of beneficiaries and the grants they receive. Although this may only reflect one year's grant-giving it is helpful to potential applicants to see typical grants and amounts given.

The entries come under two broad sections:

- Firstly, all those trusts which can give throughout Scotland or to a significant part of it.

- Secondly, the trusts which limit their giving to a local area (or part of it). The layout of these is explained on page 24.

Availability of information

In our various trusts guides we always aim to include all publicly registered trusts of relevance. This stems from our strongly-held belief that grant-making trusts are public institutions not private ones. Furthermore, as public bodies we believe grant-making trusts should be brought into "the beneficial light of public scrutiny" (as Sir Philip Woodfield put it). We have argued this very strongly to the Charity Commission for England and Wales throughout the passage of the 1992 and 1993 Charities Acts. In practice, the issue comes down to two main points:

1. The requirement for trusts to give information on the grants they award

If charities are to be publicly accountable, they must give some detail on what they do with their money. For grant-making trusts, this inevitably means that they must publish details of the grants they give (clearly this disclosure only applies to grants given to organisations; we would never argue for naming individuals in grants lists). As we wrote to the Charity Commission in 1990:

"First, the only work of most of these trusts is to make grants. If it is not known what these grants are, the work of these charities is concealed and they do not benefit from what your Annual Report called, a couple of years ago, the "beneficial light of public scrutiny".

"Secondly, to quote from Lord Nathan, a charitable trust is not a private institution but a public one, and we believe that there must be a presumption against public institutions operating in secret.

"Thirdly, these charities are important both collectively, where they account for perhaps 15% of all voluntary income; and individually, where a single charity can have an income of £9 million, the use of which is almost entirely unknown [this charity happily now supplies admirably clear and full information on its grant-giving].

"Fourthly, we know that such disclosure is both practicable and does not prevent trusts from operating effectively. For example, in this country the Marble Arch group of trusts, though widely respected, give no details of which organisations they help. Their sister trust in New York, the Brencanda Foundation, successfully pursues similar objects while making the full disclosure that US law requires.

"Finally, operation in the public domain must greatly assist in deterring any misuse or misappropriation of trust funds.

"Some benefactors say that they wish to make 'wholly personal and anonymous donations'. They are of course free to do this, tax-effectively, at any time - but not in our view through the machinery of a public and perpetual trust. However, if they wish to establish a trust anonymously, they are free to do this as well, and I hope will continue to be so under any new arrangements."

A new accounting standard, the revised Statement of Recommended Practice (SORP), has recently been issued. It contains guidance for grant-making trusts on how they should report on grants awarded. It is unfortunately, in our view,

One trust that didn't make it into the Guide

John Jamieson's Trust - Objects of the trust

The Trust Disposition and Settlement dated 11th May, 1922 and registered in the Books of Council and Session on 6th October, 1923, directed the Trustees to hold the Trust Funds and to apply the annual income thereof in publishing standard works of Scottish History, and particularly, and without prejudice to the foregoing generality to Sir Walter Scott's "Tales of a Grandfather", and the Reverend James Mackenzie's "History of Scotland", and John Jamieson's "Bell the Cat" or "Who destroyed the Scottish Abbeys?"; The Truster further stated his earnest wish that these books be kept before the Education Authorities of Scotland and also before the School-Masters in order that children may be taught the history of their country, that the publication price may be one shilling per copy, or such sum as the Trustees may consider reasonable, and that any manuscript left by the Truster may be published at the Discretion of the Trustees. In addition, the Truster specified that these books may be edited and brought up-to-date but that the text ought not to be tampered with and that, if any explanation or correction of a passage is necessary, it should be done in notes throughout the respective volumes and, if so, the price may be increased: Finally, the truster directed his Trustees to publish standard works on Protestantism at such prices and at such times as they may in their absolute discretion think fit.

something of a victory for the secretive tendency among grant-making trusts. The new SORP requires trusts to disclose "material grants" (broadly those over £1,000 to organisations). It goes on to say: "This disclosure ... should be limited to the largest 50 grants, or such larger number as may be considered necessary to convey a proper understanding of the charity's grant-making activities". If this were applied to the largest 10 UK grant-making trusts it would mean that they would only need to disclose 500 of the 12,000 they collectively make. This is an issue of some concern to us.

Under Scottish charity law, grant-making trusts must send a copy of their accounts to anyone who asks for them in writing. These accounts must also include "details of any grant or grants paid which exceeds or exceed in aggregate the greater of £1,000 or 2% of the gross income from all sources for the financial year; separate disclosure shall not be required where the grant or grants is or are made on behalf of an individual; and grants made for the benefit of individuals should be aggregated and the total, number and range of grants shown". These requirements, clearly expressed, represent a legal requirement for openness and public accountability in grant-making. They should be sufficient for an organisation like ours to provide comprehensive information on all identifiable Scottish trusts. However, in practice there are ways round at least the spirit of the legislation, which brings us on to the second point.

2. The right of public access to trust accounts

In England and Wales, there is a Charity Commission. This holds details about all registered charities in England and Wales. Furthermore, there is a file for each of these charities containing details such as:

Charity address

Area of operation/benefit

Charity objects

Charity constitution

An annual set of accounts

To get details of any charity in England and Wales it is a simple matter of going to one of the three Charity Commission offices and requesting the relevant file. You can then glean most of what you need to know about the work of most charities.

In Scotland and Northern Ireland there is no publicly accessible information point on charities, rather the Inland Revenue simply holds a register of charities. In theory this is somewhat mitigated by the requirement to send out accounts. In practice, however, trusts can get round this by asking too high a price for members of the public (or, indeed, voluntary organisations) to pay. We were routinely charged upwards of £20.00 for accounts. One trust wanted to charge £100.00! We had to spend well over £2,000 on obtaining information relevant to the trusts in this Guide. This was a considerable overspend on our budget, but still left many trusts untouched. Trusts should only charge the cost of producing the extra set of accounts. They cannot offset the audit or other fees in this. In other words, we are essentially talking about photocopying and postage charges. Interestingly, the exemplary Shetland Islands Charitable Trust charges just £2.00 for a copy of their accounts; they are the second largest trust in this Guide.

If the aim of the legislation is to give the public the right of access to information on Scottish charities, in practice this can be thwarted by the levying of such charges. We would urge Scottish authorities to consider issuing guidance on what constitutes a reasonable charge for such information. We would urge even more strongly for a publicly accessible register of Scottish (and, indeed, Northern Ireland) charities to be set up. Without such measures, certain grant-making trusts could continue to operate in effective secrecy for years to come.

Research methods

Despite these difficulties, we contacted as many trusts as we found (over 1,500 in total). All the trusts in the Guide were sent a draft entry to comment on, update and supplement with further information. About 50% replied to this draft entry. The remainder were followed up by telephone, fax or letter. This pushed the response rate up to 85%. Where trusts resisted all our attempts to generate further information we stated this in the entry.

Unsolicited applications

Sometimes trusts state that they do not want to be included in our Guides. One of their standard lines is that they do not want to be inundated with a stream of irrelevant applications. Indeed, some state that they do not consider applications at all, rather the trustees simply decide which projects they would like to fund and then go ahead and give them money. We fully understand both points of view. However, our Guides are not just handbooks for fundraisers; rather they are also surveys of how much trust money is available and what is being done with it. Therefore, we include all trusts of relevance, although we try to give as much information as possible to cut down the number of inappropriate applications which, after all, waste both the applicant's and the trust's time and serve only to annoy.

The rather difficult issue remains, however, of what to do when an entry says: "Trust funds fully allocated; no applications will be considered", or "The trustees only give grants to projects known to them". We would never counsel an indiscriminate mailing of trusts, nor would we recommend that a charity ignore any part of an entry simply because it does not suit their situation. However, in the specific instance of trusts warding off applicants with the above wording (or when there is no real information to go on) we accept there is a problem. In some cases it is probably not true that trusts never respond to an unsolicited application, but how do you sort the wheat from the chaff?

When we think a trust will or will not consider applications we say so. However, often we have not commented because we are not clear either. This leaves the reader none the wiser! If the situation is not clear we suggest that if a trust clearly could **support your application** apart from the above health warning then send a **short** application with little or no supporting material. The application should recognise that the trust has said that it will not respond and should state clearly that **if this is the case the trust should not respond to your application** either (do not even enclose a stamped addressed envelope). Nor should you follow it up with a telephone call or further correspondence. Therefore, if a trust's policy is simply to ignore applications you have placed no burden on them to reply to you; if they do sometimes consider applications you have given them enough information to decide whether you will be eligible or not.

We would naturally ask readers to exercise great care when making such applications. Nothing makes our task harder or a grant-making trust's life more frustrating than when our readers send a series of ill-conceived and irrelevant applications to any trust which happens to take their fancy. This kind of indiscriminate mailing leads some trusts to make the above statements when previously they had been willing to consider and reply to relevant applications from any registered charity.

And finally ...

This Guide is the first attempt at a large and very difficult task. The research for this book has been done as fully and carefully as we have been able. We are very grateful to the many trust officers, trustees and others who have helped us in this. To name them all would be impossible and although drafts of all the entries were sent to the charities concerned, and any comments noted, the text and any mistakes within it remains ours rather than theirs.

We know that some of the information in this Guide is incomplete or will become out-of-date. We are equally sure that we have missed some relevant charities. We regret such imperfections. If any reader comes across omissions or mistakes in this Guide, please let us know so that they can be rectified in the thrice yearly *Trust Monitor* and in future editions of this Guide. A telephone call to the Northern Office Research Department of the Directory of Social Change (0151-708 0136) is all that is needed.

Thank you and good luck!

How to make an application

Putting an application in to a grant-making trust can be a daunting prospect. You basically have up to two sides of A4 in which to persuade the trust that they should give you a grant. Furthermore, there are often very few trusts local to your project. Many are in Glasgow, Edinburgh or even London and voluntary organisations are often put off by the apparent distance between their work and the trusts who might support them. "Why would a trust based in London be at all interested in what we are doing? They don't know our area; they never come here; they gets lots of applications from elsewhere." In practice this distance does not really exist, but somehow for a group in Alness to write to London is a major achievement, first in confidence, and then in determination.

It is my experience in having organised meetings in Scotland that many organisations think they can get a trust grant so they can just carry on with what they are doing at present. Many people were shocked to be asked questions which appeared to cast a doubt on why an organisation should exist! "It's obvious why we exist" is not a very convincing answer. Funders are not going to be particularly impressed with a plea to "remember their obligation to the local community" – they want something much more substantial than that.

You also need to be absolutely clear what you want a grant for. It's amazing how many applications I receive where I am not really sure what they actually want, even after reading it through three or four times. So, before any organisation applies for a grant, they must sit down and ask themselves: "Why do we need a grant?" You may need to have an internal discussion at Committee level and with the people who use or are members of the organisation. I am often surprised by how radical this idea appears to be.

In fact, you may not need to apply for a grant at all. Groups often assume that the best way of raising £1,000 is to write letters to funders. It is usually much easier for community groups to raise this money themselves through sponsored events or other public fundraising. Remember, some of the oldest ways of raising money are still some of the best! We live in a grants-obsessed culture; there are other very effective means of raising money.

However, assuming you are going to apply for a grant the key questions you will need to answer are:

◆ What is the need we are meeting and why is it important?

- What are we going to do to meet the need?

- Who are we and what have we achieved?

- How much do we need?

- What happens once the trust money is spent?

I would like to consider these points in more detail.

1. The background – what is the need we are meeting and why is it important?

Voluntary organisations exist to meet important needs (eg. elderly people being isolated and neglected; young people at risk of crime or abuse; disabled people being discriminated against; the environment being destroyed by overuse and pollution). Why is your work crucial to those who benefit? Why can nobody else do it as well as you? What would happen if you were not there?

Laziness is often the greatest vice here. I often see applications from organisations which presume so much of the reader. "We are a tenants group in Newton..." "We are a youth club..." "Our self-help group meets weekly". There usually follows a few statements about the need for a grant for running costs or for old equipment that needs to be replaced. Not much to go on!

Organisations must believe in what they do, enthuse about their achievements and what income they have raised. If you can't be clear and enthusiastic about the work you do, a possible funder certainly won't be. Fundraising is a "selling" process where you persuade someone to support you and your work. If you can't show why it is really important that your work

develops, you will not get the money.

Facts and figures can be helpful. Generalised statements like: "We work with young people who are excluded from school" doesn't really tell you very much. How many young people? Why are they excluded? How many will return to full-time education as a result of your work? What will happen if they do not? What will be the cost to society if they do not?

If the organisation undertakes a proper review of its services on a regular basis and knows what its purposes are, then it often applies appropriately. If it does not, the application often looks tired and pretty unexciting.

Having understood afresh what your purposes are, you then need to think about how you will meet these needs.

2. The proposal – what are we going to do to meet the need?

OK, you have convinced the funder that there is a real problem or need that you are meeting, and that it requires an urgent solution. The next question is: what are you going to do about it? As with showing what the need is, you need to be very clear about exactly what you intend to do.

It is not good enough simply to say: "We will work to reduce crime and petty vandalism in our community". How are you going to do this? Are you going to run a youth group to give young people something to do? If so, how are you going to make sure that those at risk of turning to crime actually come to the group? Are you going to set up football and basketball leagues for unemployed late teenagers? If so, how are you going to organise training and coaching sessions and make sure that people come along? Are you going to involve the local professional club?

Just because an idea seems good on paper doesn't mean to say that it will work in practice. However, by showing very clearly how you intend to go about meeting the need you have identified, you will go a long way to convincing the funder that yours is a good application.

3. Our credibility – who are we, how do we operate and what successes have we achieved to date?

By now, the reader of your application should be thinking: "Yes, I agree that this is a real problem and their solution seems very sensible. However, can they really deliver the goods?" So, the next stage is to show the funder why they can trust you to do the work.

There are plenty of ways of doing this. Here are just some ideas. Mention some of the successful projects you have run in the past. Get a quote from someone who the funder will respect, saying how good you are. Show how many volunteers are prepared to give you their precious time because of the important work you do. Talk about the excellence of the people involved in your project. Talk about the excellence of your management committee and its members. You will not be able to

---

A possible structure for a letter of application

Please note, there is no model good application letter (although there are plenty of model bad ones!). Write the letter in whichever way suits the individual application. However, here is one structure that usually works.

Dear ... (use the name of the correspondent if you can)

I am writing on behalf of ... seeking funding towards the cost of ...

... was set up in ... by ... to do ... Major initiatives have included ...

I am currently writing about ... project. The need we are meeting is particularly important because ...

We know the project will be effective because ...

We will actively monitor and evaluate the project by ...

We know we are the best people to do this work because ...

The project will cost £... We intend to raise the money as follows ... I am therefore writing to you for ...

At the end of the grant we expect the project will be funded by ...

If you require any further information or wish to discuss the application, please contact me on ...

Yours sincerely,

Don't forget: Use headed paper, include your charity number (if you have one) and sign the letter.

do all of this; in any case you may have some better ideas. All you are trying to do is assure the funder that you are a well-run organisation capable of doing the work you have identified.

4. The budget – how much do we need?

I always leave the money to the end. This is because the most important thing is the value of the work being done, not what it costs. However, it is very important that you are absolutely clear about finance. You need to do three things:

- State clearly how much the overall project will cost (eg. "We are looking to raise a total of £30,000").

- Give the funder a clear idea of how much you expect them to contribute. You can do this in one of three ways:

  (i) Ask for a specific amount (ie. "I am therefore writing to ask you for £2,000").

  (ii) Show how much other trusts have given (eg. "BBC Children-in-Need have already given us £2,000"). This will indicate that you expect a similar amount from the trust you are currently writing to.

  (iii) Show how many trusts you are writing to (eg. "I am therefore writing to you and eight other major trusts to ask for a total of £10,000"). This gives the trust a pretty good idea of how much you expect them to give (ie. around £2,000), but gives them the flexibility to give more or less than this.

- Show where the rest of the money is coming from (ie. "The overall project will cost £30,000. We expect to raise £15,000 from our members and supporters; £5,000 from other fundraising events and £10,000 from grant-making trusts. I am therefore writing to you and eight other major trusts to ask for a total of £10,000"). This will give the trust more confidence that you know what you are doing and you can raise the necessary money.

5. The long term – show what happens once the trust money is spent

Most grant-making trusts do not want to fund a single organisation indefinitely. You are highly unlikely to receive trust funding for more than three years for a single project. Therefore, the trust will want to know two things:

- If you are asking for revenue funding (ie. regular costs such as salaries, rents, rates), and you expect the project to carry on once the trust money has run out, where do you expect the future money to come from? Will the project become self-funding because you can charge for the services? Will you be able to charge a membership fee which pays for the service? Will you develop your community fundraising to cover the cost of the project? In other words, how will you ensure the project carries on long-term (if you want the project to be long-term, that is).

- If you want capital funding (ie. one-off grants for buildings, equipment etc.), how will you pay for it to be used? For example, if you ask the trust to help pay for a minibus, where will the insurance money come from? How will you service the vehicle? What about breakdowns? Even though you only have to buy an item once, it often costs money to use and maintain it.

What to include with an application

If the trust has an application form you must fill it out following its instructions. However, most do not, so you will need ...

1. An application letter stating:

Who you are

What you do

Why is it important

How much it will cost

Where the money is to come from

This letter should be two sides of A4 at the most, preferably less.

2. You should always enclose:

(a) A set of your most recent accounts, or a budget for the year if you are a new organisation.

(b) A budget for the particular project you are wanting support for, including estimated income and expenditure.

(c) An annual report (if you have one).

3. You can also enclose anything else that will support the application (eg. newsletters, press cuttings, quotes sheets, photos, drawings, letters of support from famous people etc.). However, don't rely on these extra bits to get you the money. Assume that the trust will only read your letter and the financial information (budget and accounts). They should be able to get the complete picture from these. If in doubt, ask yourself:

(a) Is this relevant to my application?

(b) Will it help the funder make a decision in my favour?

(c) Can I afford to send all this?

Remember everything you attach should be for a fundraising purpose. It is not a question of "never mind the quality feel the width", rather if it doesn't help the application don't put it in. The letter and financial information are the most important parts. Other bits are often never read.

The need to target applications

Increasingly today, in response to the deluge of requests for support, grant-making trusts have their own priorities for the work they would like to support. You will see in this book that some are very specific about what they give for. Indeed, nothing annoys a grant-making trust more than when applicants use a "scatter-gun" approach. In other words, they send off unspecific, wrongly-targeted applications to any trust that happens to take their fancy. This approach is a recipe for fundraising disaster.

However, it is also clear that a well thought-out proposal, which defines the overall budget, always has a better chance of consideration than an open-ended request for a grant. Most of the trusts in this book wish to make a difference to people's lives. As such they read hundreds of applications every year. A reasonable, well-written budget for a project which shows other possible sources of income and expenditure is always appreciated. The financial part of an application can be daunting for an organisation, but they have to remember the donor's or trust's perspective. Most trusts are conscious of how their funds are raised or donated to

The Trust Donor's Perspective

When considering your application, trustees will be asking themselves some or all of the following questions:

Grant policy

1. Does the application fit in with our published trust policy and guidelines?

2. Are we particularly interested in the problem area?

3. Is the approach to the problem the best way of spending our resources?

4. Have we funded anything similar recently?

5. Is there a geographical reason for or against it?

Your project

1. Will the project work?

2. Are the outcomes worthwhile and achievable?

3. Can the project organiser deliver?

4. What are the long-term goals and are they achievable?

5. Is the project of purely local significance or could it have a wider benefit?

6. What is the project's relationship with clients/community/other bodies?

7. What will happen afterwards?

8. What are the long-term funding implications?

9. Is the project organiser and organisation well thought of (what is the project's reputation, who is the patron, who sponsored them etc.)?

10. In general, have the organisation and its proposal got credibility?

Benefit to the funder

1. Is the project cost-effective? Is it more effective (better) and cost-effective (cheaper) than alternatives, or at least is it comparable?

2. Is the project well-presented and the budget well prepared?

3. Can we guarantee the organisation will handle the money well?

4. Will the organisation say thank you and keep in regular contact (have there been any problems in the past)?

5. Will there be any publicity/recognition for the donor?

6. In general, will it be the best use of present resources?

And

"Do we know, like and trust these people?"

them. They are often overwhelmed with applications and so they want their money to go to organisations who are well organised and demonstrate that they can handle money competently. They presume in such circumstances that it is up to the organisation to project itself in a competent and appropriate manner.

Most of the trusts will make decisions on the applications they receive based on their balanced assessment of this picture. Also my colleagues will often go on their intuitive feel for how this picture looks. The most disappointing applications we read are from small neighbourhood groups, with only a few hundred pounds of surplus per year, requesting £15,000 for a minibus, who have ignored the several thousands of pounds required for running costs each year.

It is possible to make a simple list of "do's and don'ts", but these could hide the real message that charitable trusts and foundations want to receive applications which are well thought out, concise and have a clearly-defined purpose.

Fraser Falconer
Regional Co-ordinator, Scotland
BBC Children in Need Appeal

I would like to acknowledge the invaluable help and advice given by Jim Hoeseason, a Community Education Worker in the Highlands of Scotland, in the production of this article.

How to use this Guide

The contents

The trusts are separated into six sections. The first is the **National** section, which contains all those trusts which give throughout Scotland or in more than one of the following five local areas listed below. This first section contains about 200 trusts in alphabetical order.

The other five sections are "regions" within Scotland and contain trusts which give specifically within that area. The "regions" are:

- **Aberdeen & Perthshire** (including Dundee and Tayside and the old Grampian region)

- **Central** (the belt north of and between Edinburgh and Glasgow, from Fife to Stirling)

- **Edinburgh and the Lothians** (also including the Scottish Borders Council region)

- **Glasgow and West of Scotland** (also including Dumfries & Galloway)

- **Highlands & Islands**

Within each "region" the trusts are in alphabetical order. Some will cover the whole region, others are restricted to single towns/cities.

Finding the trusts you need

Local organisations should first look in the relevant geographical section of the Guide to see if there are any trusts specifically for your area and that give to your type of work.

When looking at the National trusts section, it may be worth glancing at the summary of main activities (see typical entry opposite) and noting any that may be worth a second look.

Once you have identified enough trusts to be going on with, read each entry very carefully before deciding whether to apply. Very often a trust's interest in your field will be limited and specific, and may require an application specifically tailored to their needs – or indeed, no application at all.

Sending off applications which show that the available information has not been read antagonises trusts and brings charities into disrepute within the trust world. Carefully targeted applications, on the other hand, are welcomed by most trusts and usually have a reasonably high rate of success.

A typical trust entry

The Fictitious Trust

£100,000 (1993/94)

Welfare

The Old Barn, Main Street,
New Town ZX48 2QQ
0151-100 0000

Correspondent: Ms A Grant, Appeals Secretary

Trustees: Lord Great; D Good; T Rust.

Beneficial area: Scotland, with a preference for New Town.

Information available: Accounts for 1993/94 were supplied by the trust.

General: The trust supports welfare charities with emphasis on disability and homelessness. The trust had assets in 1993/94 of £1 million and an income of £110,000. Grants totalled £100,000.

35 grants were given ranging from £100 to £10,000, with over half given in New Town. The largest were to: New Town Disability Group (£10,000), Homelessness Scotland (£7,500) and New Town Family Support Agency (£7,000). There were seven other grants for £1,000 or more including those to New Town Mobility, Refugee Support Group and Tiny Tots Playgroup.

Smaller grants were given to a range of local charities, local branches of Scottish charities and Scottish welfare charities.

Exclusions: No grants for minibuses, to individuals or to non-registered charities.

Applications: In writing to the correspondent, including a brief description of the project and a budget. Trustees' meetings are held in March and September.

Name of the Charity

Grant total (not income) for the most recent year available.

Our summary of the main activities. We state what the trust does in practice rather than what its trust deed allows it to do.

Contact address and telephone number and fax number if available.

Contact person

Trustees

Geographical area of grant-giving including where the trust can legally give and where it gives in practice.

Sources of information we used and which are available to the applicant.

Background/summary of activities. A quick indicator of the policy to show whether it is worth reading the rest of the entry.

Financial information. We try to note the assets, ordinary income and grant total, and comment on unusual figures.

Typical grants range to indicate what most successful applicants can expect to receive.

Large grants – to indicate where the main money is going, often the clearest indication of trust priorities.

Other examples of grants – listing typical beneficiaries, and where possible the purpose of the grant. We also indicate whether the trust gives one-off or recurrent grants.

Exclusions – listing any areas, subjects or types of grants the trust will not consider.

Applications including how to apply and when to submit an application.

National Trusts

The Miss S E Adams Charitable Trust

£3,000 (1993)

General

c/o Maclay Murray & Spens, 151 St Vincent Street, Glasgow G2 5NJ
0141-248 5011

Correspondent: The Secretary

Trustees: Miss S E Adams; M Crichton; Vindex Trustees Ltd.

Beneficial area: Unrestricted.

Information available: Information was supplied by the trust.

General: The trust's annual income is about £2,000. In 1993, a total of £3,000 was awarded to charitable organisations. No grants were given in 1994.

Grants ranged between £200 and £500 and were awarded to organisations such as the City of London School (£200), Scottish Hospital Endowment Research Trust (£200), and Birmingham Contemporary Music Group (£500).

Applications: In writing to the correspondent.

The Adamson Trust

£35,000 including grants to individuals

Children's holidays

Messrs Drysdale Anderson WS, 14 Comrie Street, Crieff, Perthshire PH7 4AZ
01764-655151

Correspondent: Neil Drysdale

Beneficial area: Scotland.

Information available: The following information was provided by the trust.

General: Grants are given to groups organising holidays for needy children and individual children under the age of 16.

Applications: In writing to the correspondent, giving details of the organisation, the proposed holiday, and the number of children who will benefit.

The Age Concern Scotland Enterprise Fund

£33,000 (1994/95)

Elderly people

Unit 53, The Fountain Business Centre, Ellis Street, Coatbridge ML5 3AA
01236-427299

Correspondent: Mrs June Girolami

Trustees: Members of Age Concern Scotland Assembly.

Beneficial area: Scotland.

Information available: Guidelines for applicants, a general leaflet and an annual report are available.

General: The fund's income is dependent upon donations. Grants are awarded to charities concerned with elderly people only.

In 1994/95, these ranged between £500 and £1,000. New initiatives and developments in the field are funded and priority is given to Age Concern Scotland member groups. Support is given to a wide range of projects in all areas of Scotland. Most of the organisations which are funded are small, locally based voluntary groups.

Exclusions: Statutory authorities and individuals are not supported. No grants for major capital programmes or for running costs.

Applications: An application form and further details are available from the correspondent.

The Sylvia Aitken Charitable Trust

£99,000 (1992/93)

General

Hacker Young, Chartered Accountants, 4 Royal Crescent, Glasgow G3 7SL
0141-333 9515

Correspondent: Jim Ferguson, Trust Administrator

Trustees: Mrs S M Aitken; J Ferguson.

Beneficial area: UK with a preference for Scotland.

Information available: The 1992/93 accounts were provided by the trust.

General: In 1992/93, the most recent year for which accounts were available, the trust had assets of £1.3 million, generating an income of £129,000. The trust distributed £99,000 in grants to six beneficiaries.

The largest grant was given to the University of Wales which received £47,000. Other beneficiaries were: Respiratory Diseases Research (£12,500); Glasgow University (£14,354); Kind Charity and the Variety Club Children's Charity (£10,000 each) and Friends of the Lake District (£5,000).

Applications: In writing to the correspondent.

Edward Alexander's Trust

£5,000 (1992/93)

Medical research

1 Golden Square, Aberdeen AB9 1HA
01224-408408

Correspondent: Messrs Ledingham Chalmers, Solicitors

Beneficial area: Scotland.

Information available: The 1992/93 accounts were provided by the trust.

General: The trust accumulates about £5,000 annually for distribution to medical research establishments. In 1992/93, grants included £4,000 to the University of Aberdeen's Department of Renal Medicine for equipment and materials for specific renal research. Grants awarded in the past include £1,300 for a research project on the healing of wounds and a similar amount for research into computer applications in anaesthetics.

Applications: In writing to the correspondent.

The AMW Charitable Trust

£105,000 (1993/94)

General

KPMG, 24 Blythswood Square,
Glasgow G2 4QS
0141-226 5511

Correspondent: Campbell Denholm

Trustees: R W Speirs; C Denholm;
Prof R B Jack.

Beneficial area: Scotland.

Information available: Accounts are
available for 1993/94.

General: The trust's assets in 1993/94
amounted to £739,000 and grants totalled
£105,000.

Grants are awarded to a wide range of
projects and in 1993/94, ranged between
£5,000 and £10,000. Recipients of £10,000
were Alzheimer's Scotland, Boys Brigade,
British Red Cross, Crossroads Scotland,
Laurel Bank School, Salvation Army and
Scottish Motor Neurone Disease Association.

Recipients of £5,000 were East Park Home,
Erskine Hospital, Glasgow Cathedral,
Glasgow West Conservation Trust, National
Trust for Scotland, Riding for the Disabled
Association – Glasgow Group, and Scripture
Union Scotland.

Exclusions: No grants for individuals.

Applications: In writing to the
correspondent.

The James & Grace Anderson Trust

£25,000 (1993/94)

Cerebral palsy

c/o Scott-Moncrieff, 17 Melville Street,
Edinburgh EH3 7PH
0131-226 6281

Correspondent: J D M Urquhart

Trustees: Prof S P F Hughes; J Donald;
J D M Urquhart.

Beneficial area: Scotland.

Information available: Information was
supplied by the trust.

General: The trust was established in 1974
and currently funds research into alleviating
those conditions which arise from cerebral
palsy. In 1994, the trust had assets of £284,000
and a net income of £20,000.

In 1993/94, one grant of £25,000 was
awarded to the Gait Analysis Project as
ongoing funding. The same project received
£30,000 in the previous year.

Applications: In writing to the
correspondent.

Miss Agnes Anderson's Trust

£7,000 (1993/94)

Armed forces charities

c/o 43 York Place, Edinburgh EH1 3HT
0131-556 7951

Correspondent: John A Loudon, Solicitor

Trustees: J B T Loudon; J A Loudon;
D A Needham.

Beneficial area: UK.

Information available: Annual accounts are available from the correspondent.

General: In 1993/94, the trust awarded grants to the following organisations: Royal British Legion (£1,400), Earl Haig Fund (£1,400), King George's Fund for Sailors (£1,400), and RAF Benevolent Fund (£2,800).

Exclusions: Applications from individuals are unlikely to succeed.

Applications: In writing to the correspondent.

The John M Archer Charitable Trust

£13,700 (1994/95)

General

12 Broughton Place, Edinburgh EH1 3RX
0131-556 4518

Correspondent: Miss I C Archer, Secretary

Trustees: G B Archer; Mrs M C Archer; R Stewart; Mrs I Morrison; Mrs A Morgan; Mrs W Grant.

Beneficial area: Unrestricted.

Information available: Accounts for 1994/95 were provided by the trust.

General: The trust's income amounted to £14,500 in 1994/95 and 125 organisations benefited from grants totalling £14,000.

Edinburgh Common Purpose, which received a grant of £1,500, and the Princess Royal Trust for Carers, which received a grant of £1,000, were the only organisations to receive £1,000 or more.

Applications: In writing to the correspondent.

The Baird Trust

£161,000 (1994)

Maintenance and repair of churches and halls of the Church of Scotland

182 Bath Street, Glasgow G2 4HG
0141-332 0476

Correspondent: Angus Sutherland, Secretary

Beneficial area: Scotland.

Information available: The 1994 accounts were provided by the trust.

General: The trust supports the building and repairing of Church of Scotland churches and halls, endows parishes and generally helps the work of the Church of Scotland.

In 1994, the trust's assets were £4.3 million, generating an income of £235,000. Grants totalled £161,000. Over 60 churches and parishes throughout Scotland received grants ranging from £500 to £10,000 with most grants between £1,000 and £5,000. Grants are largely given for repairs and improvements to existing buildings.

Applications: In writing to the correspondent.

The Balcraig Foundation

£73,000 (1993/94)

Social welfare, third world

21 Auld House Wynd, Perth PH1 1RG
01738-634745

Correspondent: Linda Scott, Secretary

Trustees: Ann Gloag; David McCleary; Linda Scott.

Beneficial area: Scotland; third world.

Information available: The latest annual report and accounts were available from the trust but did not contain a detailed breakdown of grants made.

General: This trust's income increased dramatically in March 1993 with a gift of 500,000 ordinary shares in Stagecoach Holdings plc from Mrs Ann Gloag, one of the trustees. The foundation sold some of its shares for a net cash amount of £879,000 and its income totalled over £1.6 million that year.

The following year, income was £322,000 and after charitable donations a surplus of £249,000 was carried over. The foundation purchased a residential property in Blantyre, Malawi for £62,000 and intends to use rental income from the property to fund charitable projects in Malawi.

In 1993/94, grants were given to a hospital project in Malawi (£24,300) and an orphanage project in Kenya (£7,850). Five donations totalling £8,700 were for the benefit of individuals.

Exclusions: Applications from individuals are not generally accepted.

Applications: Applicants should apply in writing, setting out a brief outline of the project for which funding is sought. Trustees meet quarterly. All grants are made at the trustees' discretion.

The Balfour Aitnoch Charitable Trust

£2,000 (1991/92)

General

W & J Burness, 16 Hope Street, Edinburgh EH2 4DD
0131-226 2561

Correspondent: The Secretary

Trustees: Alasdair Laing; Colin Baxter.

Beneficial area: UK with an interest in Scotland.

Information available: The 1991/92 accounts were provided by the trust.

General: The trust makes grants for education, the relief of poverty, medical research, religious bodies connected with the Church of Scotland or England, relief of famine through UK based charities, and the care of disabled children.

In 1991/92, the trust's assets were £23,000, generating an income of £4,700. Grants to four beneficiaries totalled £2,000. The beneficiaries, who received between £250 and £1,250, were Save the Children Fund, Durley Parochial Church, UMDS Cancer Research Fund and Children's Country Holidays Fund.

Applications: In writing to the correspondent.

H D Balfour's Trust

£1,000 a year

Scottish Open Brethren Assemblies

58 Frederick Street, Edinburgh EH2 1LS
0131-225 8291

Correspondent: William Balfour

Trustees: Balfour & Manson Trustees.

Beneficial area: Scotland.

Information available: Information was supplied by the trust.

General: The trust has an income of about £1,000 available for distribution. The trust helps with equipment, special campaigns and new centres for Scottish Open Brethren Assemblies. Grants range between £250 and £500.

Applications: In writing to the correspondent.

The Kenneth Barge Memorial Trust

£10,000 (1994/95)

Local charities, disaster funds, third world, environment, military, religion

c/o Messrs McCann Fordyce, Solicitors, 53 High Street, Dumbarton G82 1JS
01389-730340

Correspondent: Charles Anthony Murdoch

Beneficial area: Worldwide, with a preference for Scotland.

Information available: The entry was compiled from the 1994/95 accounts provided by the trust.

General: In 1994/95, the trust had assets totalling £29,000. Grants totalled £10,000 and were awarded to local charitable organisations, third world charities, military organisations and charities concerned with the environment and ministry.

In 1994/95, recipients of £1,000 were the British Red Cross Society, Christian Aid, CRMF Macmillan Nurse Teacher Project, Crossroads, Helensburgh Branch of the British Red Cross Society, Kilfinnan Church, LEPRA, Princess Louise Hospital, Thistle Foundation and the World Society for the Protection of Animals.

£500 grants went to Friends of Loch Lomond, Royal Commonwealth Society for the Blind, Rhu Community Education Management Committee and Scottish Scripture Union.

Applications: In writing to the correspondent.

The Bartholomew Christian Trust

£4,000 (1994)

Christian, poverty

Calgary, Isle of Mull, Argyll PA75 6QT
01688-400240

Correspondent: J E G Bartholomew

Trustees: Commander I M Bartholomew; Mrs A Bartholomew; R P Bartholomew; Miss F A Bartholomew; D G Bartholomew; A J Bartholomew.

Beneficial area: Worldwide, England, Scotland.

Information available: The entry was compiled from the accounts for 1994 provided by the trust.

General: In 1994, the trust had assets totalling £26,000, generating an income of just over £4,000, virtually all of which was given in grants.

The trust awards grants to Christian organisations which promote the Christian faith, provide Christian education and work for the relief of poverty. Amounts rarely exceed £100.

Exclusions: Grants are only awarded to registered charities. Funds are not usually awarded to support building work.

Applications: In writing to the correspondent. Unsuccessful applications are not acknowledged.

The Ian & Margaret Baxter Charitable Trust

£2,000 (1991/92)

General

W & J Burness, 16 Hope Street,
Edinburgh EH2 4DD
0131-226 2561

Correspondent: The Trustees

Trustees: G Baxter; Ms M Baxter; W Baxter;
R Witheridge; W & J Burness Trustees Ltd;
W Henderson.

Beneficial area: Scotland.

Information available: Accounts for 1992
were provided by the trust.

General: In 1992, the trust's estate was
valued at £22,000 and grants totalling £2,000
were awarded to two organisations:
Leanchoil Hospital Benefits, Forres and the
Aberdeen and North East Society for the
Deaf. Both received £1,000.

Applications: In writing to the
correspondent. This entry has not been
confirmed by the trust. The address details
are correct.

BBC Children in Need Appeal

£2,395,000 in Scotland (1993/94)

Disadvantaged children

Broadcasting House, 5 Queen Street,
Edinburgh EH2 1JF
0131-469 4225

Correspondent: Fraser Falconer

Trustees: Sir Robert Andrew; Jane Asher; Sir
Kenneth Bloomfield; C Browne; Mark
Byford; D Carrington; J Clarke; Alison Reed;
Elaine Ross; M Stevenson.

Beneficial area: UK with a proportion of
grants made in Scotland.

Information available: Guidelines for
applicants are available from the
correspondent.

General: BBC Children in Need distributes
the funds raised by the BBC's annual
broadcast appeal which are between £10m to
£20m every year. Administration costs are
taken from the interest earned on banked
donations.

Applications are invited from good quality
projects which show a clear focus on children
and careful planning to bring about a
positive difference or change in their lives.

The children should be aged 18 years and
under. Their disadvantage may be through
mental, physical or sensory disabilities,
behavioural or psychological problems,
poverty, deprivation, illness, abuse or
neglect. Typical grants range from £100 to
£30,000 a year.

In 1993/94, 14% of the £17.2 million grant
total was awarded to organisations in
Scotland. Scottish beneficiaries include the
Oasis Creche in Edinburgh (£500) towards
toys and equipment, and the Ipswich Town
Boys Club in Blackhill, Glasgow, (£600) for an
annual football trip for the boys from a
disadvantaged area of the city.

One of the largest grants awarded in
Scotland was a three-year grant of £147,000
to the Scottish Child Law Centre which is
pioneering a new scheme to provide legal
assistance and advice to children and young
people in conjunction with the legal
profession in Scotland.

A total of £63,634 was allocated over three
years to the YMCA in Bellshill to expand
their youth service work.

Exclusions: Grants are not made for the
following: trips or projects abroad, medical
treatment or medical research, unspecified
expenditure, deficit funding or the
repayment of loans, projects which take place

before applications can be processed, projects which are unable to start within 12 months, and the relief of statutory responsibility.

Applications: An application form is available from the correspondent. There are two closing dates for applications: 30th March and 30th November.

The Beauchamp Trust

£7,000 (1993/94)

Relief of poverty, education, Christian

The Computer Centre, Benmhor, Campbeltown, Argyll PA28 6DN

Correspondent: G Beauchamp, Chairman

Trustees: G J P Beauchamp; H C P Beauchamp.

Beneficial area: Preference for Scotland.

Information available: Information was provided by the trust.

General: The trust makes regular grants to a small number of organisations involved in the relief of poverty, education and Christian work. A small number of one-off grants are made to similar organisations, or their staff, known to the trustees. Grants are usually for less than £200.

The trust has no asset base, relying on income from donations each year. In 1993/94, the income was £10,470 and grants totalled £7,150. Over £5,500 was carried forward for distribution the following year.

Exclusions: Individuals or organisations with which the trustees are not already familiar will not be supported.

Applications: Unsolicited applications are not supported.

Bell's Nautical Trust

£23,000 (1993/94)

Maritime education

Cameron House, Abbey Park Place, Dunfermline, Fife KY12 7PZ

Correspondent: William McDonald

Trustees: R S Salvesen; R A S Alexander; S J Boyd; F D Collen; C W Davidson; J MacNeill; B Parker; N J Purvis; R K Scovell; J W Sellars; N C Souter; C Hutton; Sir David Thomson; Captain A H F Wilks; G B Archer.

Beneficial area: Scotland with a preference for Leith.

General: The trust had assets of £350,000 in 1993/94. Grants totalled £23,000.

Grants ranged between £340 and £5,000 and were awarded to 16 maritime and nautical organisations. The majority of the awards were of up to £2,000, with larger grants to the Tall Ships Race 1995 (£5,000), Jewel and Esk Valley College (£3,000) and Glasgow College of Nautical Studies (£3,000).

Other beneficiaries included T S Condor (£1,000), Centre for Advanced Maritime Studies (£1,500), Royal Forth Yacht Club (£1,000), Dundee Heritage Trust (£1,600), Fort William Sea Cadet Unit (£550), Aberdeen and Stonehaven Yacht Club (£700) and North Carr Lightship, Anstruther (£500).

Applications: In writing to the correspondent.

The Bethesda Charitable Trust Fund

£100,000 (1992/93)

Christian churches, general

6 Albert Place, Aberdeen AB2 4RG
01224-626090

Correspondent: Jim Wilson

Trustees: J Wilson; B Wilson;
Mrs A R P Wilson.

Beneficial area: Scotland.

General: The trust fund had an income of
£112,000 in 1992/93, a substantial increase
from its income of £1,332 in 1991/92.

£100,000 was distributed in grants (£4,250 in
1991/92) ranging between £100 and £10,000.
Beneficiaries included Deeside Christian
Fellowship (£36,300), Doulos Trust (£50,750),
Abernethy Trust Ltd (£4,480), Poplars Church
Charity (£3,000) and the Romanian Relief
Fund (£2,500).

A number of smaller grants each under
£2,200 were also awarded.

Applications: In writing to the
correspondent.

The Mairi Bhan Trust

£800 (1994)

Disaster appeals, third world charities, wildlife and environment, local groups

The Anchorage, Shore Road, Carradale,
Campbeltown, Argyll PA28 6SH
01583-431629

Correspondent: Mrs Mary McMillan

Trustees: D McMillan; Mrs M McMillan;
A Conley; Mrs G McIntosh.

Beneficial area: Unrestricted.

Information available: Accounts for 1994
are available from the trust.

General: This small family trust had a total
of £74 in capital in 1994 (£877 in 1993). Grants
totalled £830 (£530 in 1993).

Grants are only made to local projects based
in Argyll and to groups working for the
benefit of the third world, wildlife and the
environment and to disaster appeal funds.
Grants range between £10 and £100 and
beneficiaries included the British Red Cross
Yugoslavia Appeal (£100) and Argyll Animal
Aid (£10).

Applications: In writing to the
correspondent. Circular letters do not receive
a response.

The Birnie Trust

£13,000 (1993/94)

General

Messrs Dundas & Wilson, Saltire Court,
20 Castle Terrace, Edinburgh EH1 2EN

Trustees: Lt Col E F Gordon; D A Connell;
Mrs E A G Gordon; Dr L J King.

Beneficial area: Worldwide with a
preference for Scotland.

Information available: Accounts for
1993/94 are available from the trust.

General: The trust was set up in 1986 to
award grants to Scottish charities and some
international projects. Its assets in 1993/94
totalled £227,000, compared with £100,000 in
1992/93.

Grants totalled £12,800 in 1993/94 (£19,500 in
1992/93) and ranged between £150 and
£4,000. The largest grants were £4,000 to
Stopover and St Andrew's Church, Madras.
Beneficiaries of smaller grants included the
Edinburgh Scout Council, Craigroyston
Community High School, Seagull Trust, and
the Eric Liddell Centre.

Applications: In writing to the
correspondent.

The Blackstock Trust

£20,000 including grants to individuals

Relief in need for elderly people

Messrs Pike & Chapman, 36 Bank Street, Galashiels TD1 1ER
01896-752379

Correspondent: William Windram, Secretary

Beneficial area: Scotland, particularly the counties of Roxburgh, Berwick or Selkirk.

Information available: No financial information was available.

General: Most of the trust's income is given in grants to individuals over the age of 60 who are in need. Grants total about £20,000 a year.

A small part of the income can be given in grants to any institution or charitable body in Scotland which provides care and attention for elderly, or disabled people.

Applications: In writing to the correspondent.

The Bourne-May Charitable Trust

£6,700 a year

General

Murray Reith Murray WS, 39 Castle Street, Edinburgh EH2 3BH
0131-225 1200

Correspondent: The Trustees

Trustees: J J S Bourne-May; J K Scott Moncrieff; Mrs J J Bourne-May; G G Bourne-May.

Beneficial area: UK, but with a preference for Scotland and Rutland.

Information available: Information is available from the trust.

General: The trust has assets totalling around £140,000, generating an income of around £6,700 each year. The trust's entire income is awarded in grants to organisations to whom funds have been committed long-term. Funding is awarded mainly to national charities – in particular to those concerned with medical research, the military, animal welfare and environmental work. However, local organisations based in Scotland and Rutland are considered. Grants rarely exceed £350.

Exclusions: No grants to individuals. Local charities are only considered if they are based in Scotland or Rutland.

Applications: In writing to the correspondent.

Miss Margaret Boyd's Charitable Trust

Not known

General

Biggart Baillie & Gifford, Dalmore House, 310 St Vincent Street, Glasgow G2 5QR
0141-228 8000

Correspondent: R I D Anderson

Beneficial area: UK.

Information available: No financial information available.

General: Grants are given to registered charities. No further information was available from the trust.

Applications: The trustees do not solicit applications.

James Boyle's Trust

£8,000 (1994)

Relief of human suffering

34 Albyn Place, Aberdeen AB9 1FW
01224-643573

Correspondent: Stronachs, Administrators

Trustees: G Cunningham; J E F Thomson;
G W Stevenson.

Beneficial area: Scotland.

Information available: Information was
supplied by the trust.

General: The trust was set up with funds of
£116,000 on the death of James Boyle.
Organisations are funded at the discretion of
the trustees and grants are awarded "for
general or specific purposes of named
charities". No further information was
available.

Applications: The trust states that there is
no application procedure. Contact the
correspondent for further details.

Miss Marion Broughton's Charitable Trust

£31,000 (1993/94)

Elderly people, disability, churches

Messrs Brodies, Solicitors, 15 Atholl Crescent,
Edinburgh EH3 8HA
0131-228 3777

Correspondent: E J Cuthbertson

Trustees: E J Cuthbertson; A M C Dalgleish.

Beneficial area: Scotland with a preference
for Lothian.

Information available: Accounts are
available from the trust.

General: In 1993/94, the trust's assets were
£319,000 and its income totalled £31,000.

Grants, which totalled £30,500, ranged
between £500 and £3,000 and were awarded
to 15 organisations. Recipients of £3,000 were
Alzheimer's Scotland, Edinburgh & Leith
Old People's Welfare Council, Multiple
Sclerosis Society and Salvation Army.

£2,000 each went to Age Concern, Drum
Riding for the Disabled, Mental Health
Foundation, Muscular Dystrophy, Royal
Scottish Society for the Prevention of Cruelty
to Children, St Mary's Cathedral Workshop
and Shelter.

Other grants were to Chest Heart & Stroke
Association (£1,500), and Marie Curie
Memorial Foundation, 5th Edinburgh
Amenities Group and Children's Hospice
Association Scotland (£1,000 each).

Applications: In writing to the
correspondent.

The Brown Charitable Trust

£1,000 (1993/94)

General

22 Meadowside, Dundee DD1 1LN
01382-201534

Correspondent: The Secretary

Trustees: Mrs A V U Brown; A H Brown.

Beneficial area: Scotland.

Information available: The information
for this entry was based on the trust's latest
annual report and accounts.

General: This trust makes donations
ranging from a few hundred pounds to
£3,000. No details are available of grants
awarded in 1993/94 but the previous year
the trust gave a donation of £3,000 to
Longforgan Parish Church.

Exclusions: No grants to individuals.

Applications: The trust states that no applications will be considered or acknowledged. It also stated that it did not wish to appear in this Guide.

The John J Calders Charitable Trust and Trust for Guides & Scouts

£6,000 (1993/94)

Guides and Scouts Associations, general

27 Braid Farm Road, Edinburgh EH10 6LE
0131-447 3966

Correspondent: R A Ferguson, Trustees Manager

Beneficial area: UK.

Information available: The following information was provided by the trust.

General: The Calders Charitable Trust has an annual gross income of £3,870 and awards the total amount in equal proportions to the Society of Vincent de Paul, Edinburgh Royal National Institute for the Blind and Imperial Cancer Research Trust.

The Trust for Guides and Scouts awarded its total income of £2,200 to the Scouts Association Scotland and the Girl Guides Association.

Applications: For further information about either trust, contact the correspondent. This entry has not been confirmed by the trust. We were unable to confirm the address details.

The Caledonian Foundation

No grants given yet

Undecided

18/19 Claremont Crescent,
Edinburgh EH7 4QD
0131-557 6490

Correspondent: Jane Salmonson, Secretary

Beneficial area: Scotland.

Information available: No financial information is available for this new trust.

General: This very new foundation was established in 1995 to help attract charitable funding to Scotland. The foundation was given a kick-start through an initial grant of £100,000 from the Baring Foundation before the bank's collapse. The foundation is to match this with other funds, with the long-term goal of raising £5 million annually for Scottish charities.

The foundation is currently drawing up guidelines, criteria and priorities for spending its income. Scottish charities have been included in a consultation process by way of a simple and short questionnaire asking for their views on where the foundation's money is most urgently needed. At the time of writing decisions had not yet been made about which areas would benefit from this very significant trust.

Further information will become available as the foundation becomes fully operational.

Applications: For further information and consultation questionnaires, contact the correspondent.

The Campagnat Trust

£4,800 (1991/92)

Care, education and development of young people

Kinharvie House, New Abbey,
Dumfries DG2 8DZ
01387-85433

Correspondent: A R McEwan

Trustees: A R McEwan; C Gay.

Beneficial area: Scotland.

Information available: The following information was provided by the trust.

General: In 1991/92, the trust gave £4,800 in grants, a substantial increase on the previous year when it gave £400. The trust makes funds available for work with young people "to develop their physical, mental, moral and spiritual capacities".

A grant of £4,800 was awarded to Kinharvie to help young people participate in the organisation's experiential programme. The organisation is committed to supporting Kinharvie. Other projects may be considered where they meet the trust's objectives.

Applications: In writing to the correspondent. Please note the trust's funds are currently fully committed.

The Cancer Relief Macmillan Fund

£21,845,000 (1993)

Cancer

Office for Scotland and Northern Ireland,
9 Castle Terrace, Edinburgh EH1 2DP
0131-229 3276

Correspondent: Mrs Catherine Duthie, Regional General Manager

Beneficial area: Scotland & Northern Ireland.

Information available: Accounts are available for 1993.

General: The fund's total income amounted to £33.4 million in 1993. Grants totalled £21.8 million and included awards to nurses, individual patients, medical and academic posts.

The fund is already committed to further grants totalling £40 million due before 1999; £20.5 million of these commitments are due in 1995.

Additionally, the fund supports the health service and other agencies in building and upgrading in-patient and day care units tailored to the needs of people with cancer. Grants are also awarded to four other cancer charities offering information and self-help to people affected by cancer: Breast Cancer Care, the British Colostomy Association, CancerLink and the National Association of Laryngectomee Clubs.

Applications: Contact the correspondent for further details.

The W A Cargill Charitable Trust

Around £75,000

General

190 St Vincent Street, Glasgow G2 5SP
0141-204 2833

Correspondent: Alexander C Fyfe

Beneficial area: Preference for Scotland.

Information available: Only very limited information was given by the trust.

General: The trust has assets of around £1.5 million, and gives around £75,000 in grants for general charitable purposes. No further information was available.

Applications: In writing to the correspondent.

The D W T Cargill Fund

Around £200,000

General

190 St Vincent Street, Glasgow G2 5SP
0141-204 2833

Correspondent: Alexander C Fyfe

Beneficial area: UK, with a preference for Scotland.

Information available: Only very limited information was given by the trust.

General: The trust's assets are around £4.5 million. In recent years, the trust has given around £200,000 in grants, with over 80% of the income distributed in Scotland.

No further information was available.

Applications: In writing to the correspondent.

The W A Cargill Fund

Around £250,000

General

190 St Vincent Street, Glasgow G2 5SP
0141-204 2833

Correspondent: Alexander C Fyfe

Beneficial area: West of Scotland.

Information available: Only very limited information was given by the trust.

General: The trust has assets of around £5 million, and gives around £250,000 in grants. No further information was available other than that the trust confines its giving to the West of Scotland.

Applications: In writing to the correspondent.

The Carnegie Trust for the Universities of Scotland

£1,141,000 (1993/94)

Scottish universities

Cameron House, Abbey Park Place, Dunfermline, Fife KY12 7PZ
01383-622148; Fax: 01383-622149

Correspondent: Professor J T Coppock, Secretary and Treasurer

Trustees: There are 14 appointed trustees. Ex-officio trustees comprise the Principals of the Scottish universities, the Lord Provosts of Edinburgh and Glasgow, the Provost of Dunfermline and the Secretary of State for Scotland.

Beneficial area: Scotland, but research may be undertaken anywhere.

Information available: Detailed guidance notes and application forms for both personal research grants and for assistance with fees are available from the trust. (See also Exclusions below.)

General: This trust was established by Andrew Carnegie to improve and expand Scottish universities, to help pay tuition fees for students of Scottish birth or extraction, and to provide research and similar grants.

The original endowment was of US $10 million (a then unprecedented sum: at the time, total government assistance to all four Scottish universities was about £50,000 a year). The demands on the trust have changed greatly and there are now thirteen Scottish universities in place of the original four in 1901. The trust assists the universities primarily by making capital grants and grants for research by its staff and graduates.

By its Royal Charter, one half of the net income of the trust is to be applied to the improvement and expansion of the Universities of Scotland and up to one half to help with the payment of fees of students of Scottish birth or extraction in respect of courses leading to a degree from a Scottish University.

In 1993/94, the trust's total assets had a market value of £32.6 million and the excess of income over expenditure was £1.5 million. Total expenditure on grants amounted to £1.14 million. The two largest items of assistance to the universities were the Block Travel Grants for staff travel (£330,000), and grants for research (£221,000). These research grants have a maximum value of £2,000 and are intended to support low-cost research in libraries and archives and in the field, to help with pilot projects which may form the basis of an application for major funding, or to assist research visits for discussions with others working in the applicant's field.

The Executive Committee has decided to restore the suspended capital grants made through quinquennial allocations, while the trust assesses the impact of the addition of five new universities. Capital grants were restored from October 1994, and Block Travel Grants discontinued. A category of larger grants has been introduced to help projects which are of benefit to Scottish universities as a whole.

Personal research grants in 1993/94 were for between £100 and £2,000, although two larger grants were awarded ranging from £9,000 to £24,000. The trust also gives a small number of Carnegie Scholarships (totalling £222,085 in 1993/94), which cover both fees and maintenance, "the latter fixed at a level that makes them the premier award in

Scotland". The trust also awards Vacation Scholarships designed to encourage undergraduate students of high academic merit to undertake a piece of research during their third summer vacation. These are competitive awards, and names are submitted by Deans of Faculties by 1st April.

The trust believes that their "policy of prudence is still appropriate", a view "reinforced by uncertainties over the future size and shape of higher education in the UK – in particular, the number of students which the Government is willing to finance".

Exclusions: Research grants can be made only to members of staff and graduates of Scottish universities. Costs of equipment, consumables, bench fees, radiocarbon dating and similar tests, and of secretarial, technical and other assistance are specifically excluded. The trust does not give grants to individuals for attendance at conferences, participation in expeditions, travel (other than for research) or attendance at institutions other than Scottish universities.

Assistance with fees is given only for degree or postgraduate diploma courses at Scottish universities; only those born in Scotland, or with a parent born in Scotland or with at least two years' secondary education in Scotland are eligible to apply, and the trust will not supplement awards made by other bodies.

For taught postgraduate courses, the trust will consider applications only from those with a first-class honours degree or who have achieved a similar level in a degree where honours are not available.

For research degrees, the trust will also consider applications from those with very good upper second-class honours.

Applicants for second 'first' degrees will be considered only from those achieving first-class honours in their first degree, except for dental, medical, and veterinary degrees where applicants with good upper second-class degrees will also be considered.

Carnegie Scholarships are open only to those holding a degree with first-class honours from a Scottish university and nominated by a member of staff, although final year students who are expected to get first-class honours may also apply.

Applications: Regulations and application forms can be obtained from the secretary. Preliminary telephone enquiries are welcome. Applicants should be under 31, but older applicants may be considered for first degrees. The trustees meet in February, June, and November.

The Carnegie United Kingdom Trust

£857,000 (1994)

Community service, amateur arts, restoration

Comely Park House, 80 New Row, Dunfermline, Fife KY12 7EJ
01383-721445

Correspondent: John Naylor, Secretary

Trustees: The trust is run by members of the executive committee: Dame G Wagner; G Adamson; G Atkinson; Mrs L Brown; T Colman; Sherriff J S Forbes; W Hutchinson; Prof D Ingram; Mrs J Kinna; Dr A Lawson; A Mould; Lord Murray; D T Quilter; Mrs J Spittal; Sir K Stowe; W Thomson.

Beneficial area: UK and Eire.

Information available: Since its inception in 1913, the trust has produced detailed and exemplary annual reports which it makes a major effort to distribute widely, and which can be found in all main public libraries. A guidelines booklet for 1991-95, most of which is reproduced below, is also available on receipt of an A5 SAE. The trust is producing a new set of guidelines which should be available by April 1996.

General: This famous foundation invests substantial resources in research into areas in which the trust feels there may be scope for effective future action. A recent example has been the Carnegie Inquiry into the Third Age in which the trust's initial funding was supplemented by large grants from companies, government and other foundations. This has now been followed by a three-year Carnegie Third Age Programme aiming to ensure implementation of the key inquiry recommendations.

Policy
The trust decided that between 1991 and 1995, it would work in the following areas.

Community service
Grants to organisations concerned with parenting, particularly where projects work for the improvement of parental care through practical support services and informal educational projects. Schemes providing primarily counselling services and conciliation are excluded. Both national and regional agencies supporting local activity are considered.

Projects concerned with young people are also supported, in particular those working with people over the age of 16 who are at risk, aiming to develop responsibility and leadership potential. Particular consideration is given to schemes working with those who have not benefited from higher education and to ventures organised jointly by the voluntary and statutory sectors.

As a result of the Carnegie Inquiry into the Third Age, applications are invited from organisations focusing on the needs of people between the ages of 50 and 75 working on cross-generational initiatives, particularly involving young people. Grants are not awarded to organisations involved in caring for elderly people nor for residential or day-care facilities or for study.

Additionally, grants are awarded for training courses which develop the potential of voluntary organisations, particularly where working with volunteers is concerned and improving committee management. Viable courses focusing on areas such as "training the trainer" are also considered.

Courses on specific aspects of care in the community, especially those concerned with voluntary work with young people, parenting and family care and issues around the third age are looked on favourably. Both national and regional agencies are considered, although local groups are not. In 1994, grants to Scottish organisations in this category included Sense Scotland (£25,000), SPP Pensioner Welfare Services (£4,000), Scottish Council of YMCAs (£20,000), Scottish Council for Voluntary Organisations (£15,000) and Victim Support Scotland (£19,500). Small grants are also awarded, such as £150 to the Chain and Sprocket Youth Motorcycle Club at the Fisherrow Community Centre in Edinburgh.

Arts

Grants to amateur arts projects involving young people. Subjects include arts and crafts, drama, music, sculpture and computer design. Projects should provide courses designed to integrate young people into arts activity so that they continue arts and crafts post school. Particular emphasis is placed on choirs, brass and wind bands, computer graphics with synthesizer accompaniment for animation.

National, regional and local arts and crafts societies are supported.

The trust also supports organisations linking arts with the environment, eg. parish maps and sculpture trails. Regional and local arts agencies which involve volunteers in arts and environmental work are considered.

The trust has set up the ADAPT Fund to encourage arts venues to improve access for disabled and elderly people and to provide models of good practice. Arts venues should apply directly to the ADAPT Fund (see applications below).

National organisations working with disabled or elderly people may be supported

where there is an agenda for the arts. Regional or national initiatives involving arts in hospitals and hospices are also supported.

Training with an arts bias is supported on a similar basis as for community service above. Amateur agencies are considered where volunteers and paid staff work together to improve amateur practice.

In 1994, grants to Scottish organisations included £5,000 to Pamis (the Profound and Multiple Impairment Service) at Dundee University to produce a creative arts resource for those working with people with profound learning and physical disabilities.

Restoration

The trust considers grants for historic artefacts in small independent museums, registered with the Museums and Galleries Commission. Artefacts include ceramics, costume, embroidery and tapestry, furniture, glass, paper, sculpture and machinery. Paintings and transport are not included. Grants to a maximum of £5,000 are awarded to museums which can account for the historic significance, either locally or nationally, of a particular artefact. Priority is given to projects involving volunteers and where a report on the conservation of the museum's collection has been obtained.

Independent museums with charitable status are considered. Grants are not awarded to military, commercial or local authority museums.

Grants are also given to restore historic gardens where they are linked to a museum and open to the public. The garden should have a historic feature and should involve volunteers in the restoration work. Grants can cover the costs of restoration, as well as of plants, equipment, fees for advisers and volunteers' expenses. Staff salaries are not considered. Again military and commercial schemes are excluded, but in certain circumstances local authority museums may be considered. Museums should involve volunteers and be registered as charitable.

Grants are awarded to village hall committees to provide activities and services to benefit the local community, especially young people, young mothers, retired people and unemployed people. Grants are limited and up to £5,000 can be paid for refurbishment and equipment for a new activity. General building repairs are not funded.

The scheme is open to village halls covering a local area with a population of less than 3,000.

Training with a restoration bias follows the basic guidelines for training outlined in the community service section.

Within this category, grants to Scottish organisations in 1994 included £15,000 to Scottish Conservation Projects Trust, £5,000 to the Scottish Field Studies Association and Scottish Maritime Museum, £3,000 to Fife Museums Forum, £2,000 to the Dundee Heritage Trust and Fife Folk Museum. Village halls funded in Scotland included Kincraig in Inverness-shire (£2,500), Ardrishaig in Argyll (£1,750), Bridgehouse in West Lothian (£3,000) and Spittal in Caithness (£600).

The Carnegie Awards

The Carnegie European Award for amateur arts agencies is given to amateur choirs, bands, orchestra or theatre particularly where young people are selected to perform at a venue or festival in a European country. A grant of up to £5,000 is awarded for essential travel and the provision of music for the event and consideration of a grant of up to £5,000 for future education and training during the following year. Funding is not available for tours. Up to six awards are made annually.

The Carnegie Training Award

These are for individuals working as volunteers and staff of voluntary organisations. Contact the trust for further details.

Exclusions: Grants are not awarded for general appeals, general funds or to clear debts, for personal memorials, endowment funds or for campaigns, for closed societies or to relieve statutory bodies of mandatory responsibility. No grants to individuals. Applications are also not considered for the following:

- Restoration, conversion, repair and purchase of buildings
- Formal education
- Schools, colleges and universities
- Sports
- Community businesses
- Medical/healthcare work
- Animal welfare
- Films, media work and equipment
- Research or publications except in certain circumstances
- Students or organisations for personal study, travel or for exhibitions.

Additionally, applications for general work in the following areas are not funded:

- Holidays, adventure centres and youth hostels
- Youth and community centres
- Residential care, day-care centres and housing
- Conciliation and counselling services
- Pre-school groups and play schemes
- Arts centres, professional arts companies and festivals
- Heritage and environmental tasks, including displays and trails, libraries and museums (except for projects falling within the trust's restoration category).

Organisations should have a charitable title as approved by the Inland Revenue.

Applications: Application forms are available for the Carnegie European Awards, training awards, new activities in village halls, historic gardens and historic artefacts.

Projects falling within the remit of the ADAPT Fund can obtain an application form and guidelines from Geoffrey Lord, Honorary Director, The ADAPT Fund, Cameron House, Abbey Park Place, Dunfermline, Fife KY12 7PZ.

Projects falling within other categories should apply in writing to the correspondent at the above address after studying the trust's policy guidelines (available free on receipt of an A5 SAE).

Applications should include concise details of the organisation, its aims, achievements, a description of the project and costs. Applications should not exceed two to three typed pages with relevant supplementary information such as a budget, recent audited accounts, the main part of the constitution and committee membership. Applications can be submitted at any time.

The Cattanach Charitable Trust

£66,000 (1993/94)

General

The Royal Bank of Scotland plc, Private Trust & Taxation, 2 Festival Square, Edinburgh EH3 9SU
0131-523 2648

Correspondent: The Trust Officer

Trustees: The Royal Bank of Scotland plc; R M Barge; C H K Corsar; The Lord MacLay; F W Fletcher.

Beneficial area: UK.

Information available: This entry is based on information supplied by the trust and its latest annual report and accounts.

General: Established in 1992, this trust invested to achieve long-term growth of both capital and income. In 1992/93, the trust had an income of £73,000 and in this initial year

made no grants. In 1993/94, grants of £66,000 were awarded.

In its first year of grant-making, the trust's beneficiaries were the Royal Society for the Prevention of Cruelty to Children (£26,340), Royal National Lifeboat Institution (£14,000), Ex-Services Mental Welfare Society (£7,000) and the Scottish Society for the Prevention of Cruelty to Animals (£19,000).

Applications: In writing to the correspondent.

The Cephas Trust

£6,000 (1994/95)

Christian projects

Mhor Lodge, Portencross Road, Seamill, West Kilbride KA23 9PZ
01294-823808

Correspondent: Andrew Mackie

Trustees: A Mackie; Mrs E M Mackie.

Beneficial area: Scotland.

Information available: Information is available from the trust.

General: In 1994/95, the trust gave a total of £6,400 in grants. The trustees focus support on organisations which promote Christian education and Christian travel either from or to Scotland. In 1994/95, grants included £300 towards the costs of a Christian expedition abroad.

The trust's funds are currently fully committed.

Applications: The trust seeks out organisations. Applications are therefore not invited. This entry has not been confirmed by the trust. The address details are correct at time of going to press.

The Challenge Trust

£17,000 (1992/93)

Relief of poverty, education, Christian projects

Orchardlea, Craigerne Lane,
Peebles EH45 9HQ
0131-661 9963

Correspondent: A Naismith, Trustee and Honorary Treasurer

Trustees: J L MacLellan; Ms R A MacLellan; A Naismith.

Beneficial area: Worldwide.

Information available: The annual report for 1992/93 was provided by the trust.

General: In 1992/93, the trust had assets of £1.1 million and an income of £226,000. The trust states that "gifts" are given at the discretion of the trustees and a total of £17,000 was awarded in 1992/93 to organisations involved mainly in Christian work.

Beneficiaries included the National Bible Society of Scotland for the distribution of Bibles in Mozambique (£6,440) and Scripture Union (£1,140). Missionary work in developing countries is also supported.

Applications: Applications are not invited.

Chest Heart & Stroke Scotland

£480,000 (1994/95)

Medical research and related areas

65 North Castle Street, Edinburgh EH2 3LT
0131-225 6963

Correspondent: Mrs Fiona Swann-Skimming

Beneficial area: Scotland.

Information available: The annual report for 1994/95 was provided by the trust.

General: In 1994/95, a total of £480,000 was awarded to organisations in Scotland undertaking research, rehabilitation, welfare, health promotion and prevention in areas relating to cardiac and pulmonary illnesses. Grants are awarded to cover project costs, travel, equipment, biomedical technology, research into nursing and specific therapy, and for postgraduate studentships. Grants may also be made to individuals with a chest, heart or stroke illness.

Applications: Contact the correspondent for further details. Those with a chest, heart or stroke illness should apply through social work departments which have copies of welfare grant forms.

The Claremont Trust

£9,000 (1993/94)

Christian work, social welfare

9 Kilbryde Crescent, Dunblane,
Perthshire FK15 9BA
01786-823147

Correspondent: Mrs Janet Craig, Secretary

Trustees: Ms J R Baxter; Mrs J Craig; Ms C Davis; Ms A Gammack; D McHenry; Ms H Mein; I Moir; P Robinson.

Beneficial area: Scotland and overseas.

Information available: The trust produces a set of guidelines for applicants and a leaflet about its work, as well as an annual report.

General: The trust was set up in 1948 to help small innovative projects involved in Christian witness and social action.

The trust's assets in 1993/94 were valued at £103,000, which generated an income of £8,000. Grants totalled £9,000.

Grants usually range between £200 and £500, although larger grants are occasionally made. In 1993/94, grants were awarded to establish a family house for orphaned children in Bulgaria (£500), to set up a Christian-Jewish dialogue to prepare a common liturgy (£400), for the Scottish Churches' Housing Agency's work with homeless people (£500) and as a contribution to the Likhubula Youth Centre in Malawi (£750).

Exclusions: Large building appeals, general appeals from well-established charities and applications from individuals for study or travel, whether in Scotland or abroad are not considered.

Applications: Application forms are available from the correspondent.

The Coila Charitable Trust

£5,000 (1993/94)

Evangelical Christianity

40 Switchback Road, Glasgow G61 1AD

Correspondent: Anne Sinclair, Chair

Trustees: G A Sinclair; Ms A Cochrane; Ms A Sinclair; J Cochrane.

Beneficial area: UK, with a preference for Scotland.

Information available: The following information was supplied by the trust.

General: The trust's funds in 1993/94 amounted to £400. Grants totalled £5,260 (£4,210 in 1992/93).

Grants of £100 to £1,600 were mainly to religious organisations, such as Living Stones Christian Fellowship (£100), British Youth for Christ (£250), Evangelical Alliance (£150), Gospel Radio Fellowship (£100), Mark

Ministries (£680), Youth with a Mission (£250). Larger grants were awarded to the Christian Centre in Bishopbriggs (£1,430) and Latin Link (£1,660).

Applications: In writing to the correspondent. This entry has not been confirmed by the trust, and we were unable to confirm the address details.

The Combe Trust

£2,000 (1994)

Social welfare, education

31–32 Moray Place, Edinburgh EH3 6BZ
0131-226 5151

Correspondent: Miss E A Couper

Trustees: Hon. Lord Clyde; H Morrison; J K Burleigh.

Beneficial area: Unrestricted.

Information available: The following information was supplied by the trust.

General: The trust was set up by George Combe in the mid 19th century. Trustees award grants to "promote the well-being of society".

The trust's gross income in the year ending 1994 totalled £2,500 and grants were given to various youth groups promoting the "improvement of mankind in the natural order".

Applications: In writing to the correspondent.

The Martin Connell Charitable Trust

Not known

General

Messrs Ernst & Young, George House, 50 George Square, Glasgow G2 1RR
0141-552 3456

Correspondent: c/o The Trustees

Beneficial area: UK with a preference for Scotland.

Information available: No financial information was available.

General: Grants are only given to registered charities. No further information was available from the trust.

Applications: In writing to the correspondent.

The Craignish Trust

Not known

Social welfare

Messrs Geoghegan & Co, 6 St Colme Street, Edinburgh EH3 6AD
0131-225 4681

Correspondent: The Secretaries

Trustees: Mrs Caroline Hobhouse; Mrs Margaret Matheson; Clifford Hastings

Beneficial area: UK.

Information available: No financial information was available.

General: Grants are awarded to charities running projects which promote the welfare of the local community. No further information was available.

Exclusions: No grants to individuals.

Applications: There is no formal application form; applicants should write to the correspondent. Details of the project should be included together with a copy of the most recent annual report and accounts.

The Cray Trust

£10,000 (1993/94)

Young people, animals, deprived areas, general

Dundas House, Westfield Park, Eskbank, Midlothian EH22 3FB
0131-663 9701

Correspondent: Mrs Murray, Administrator

Trustees: J G S Gammell; Mrs S P B Gammell; P R Gammell.

Beneficial area: Scotland.

General: The trust's income available for distribution in 1993/94 totalled £19,000 after expenses. Grants totalling £10,200 were awarded to 37 organisations whose work was of concern to the trustees.

Grants ranged between £100 and £1,200 with the vast majority of grants being in the £100 to £500 range. These included £500 each to Compass School, Marie Curie Cancer Scotland and Scottish Grouse Research Trust, £400 to Duke of Edinburgh Awards, £300 to Sunshine Home for the Blind, £250 to Oxfam, £200 each to Cancer Research East Lothian, Child Concern, Montrose YMCA and Paintings in Hospitals, and £100 each to Highland Handicapped Child, Lochend Neighbourhood Centre, Verdant Works and Tusk Force.

Organisations receiving the largest grants were West Lothian NHS Trust (£1,000), Rutland Historic Churches (£1,000) and the Priory Church of St Mary (£1,200).

Exclusions: The trust only supports charitable organisations.

Applications: Note: Unsolicited correspondence is not welcome. The trustees meet twice yearly.

Mrs Doris M Crichton's Charitable Trust

£2,500 (1992/93)

Animal welfare, conservation

W & J Burness, Solicitors, 16 Hope Street, Charlotte Square, Edinburgh EH2 4DD
0131-226 2561

Correspondent: The Secretary

Trustees: G M Menzies; H Ross.

Beneficial area: Scotland with a preference for East Lothian and Berwickshire.

Information available: Accounts for 1992/93 were provided by the trust.

General: The trust's investments were valued at £156,000 in 1992/93 (£145,000 in 1991/92). Grants are given for general charitable purposes and in 1992/93, a single grant of £2,500 was given to the Scottish Wildlife Fund.

Applications: In writing to the correspondent.

Hamish Crichton's Charitable Trust

£1,500 (1992/93)

Animal welfare, conservation

W & J Burness, Solicitors, 16 Hope Street, Charlotte Square, Edinburgh EH2 4DD
0131-226 2561

Correspondent: The Secretary

Trustees: G M Menzies; H Ross.

Beneficial area: Scotland with a preference for Berwickshire.

Information available: Accounts for 1992/93 were provided by the trust.

General: The trust had funds totalling £112,000 in 1992/93 (£81,000 in 1991/92).

In 1992/93, one grant of £1,500 was awarded to the Scottish Wildlife Fund. The trust also has commitments to the Scottish Wildlife Trust and the National Trust for Scotland in South East Scotland.

Applications: In writing to the correspondent.

The Cross Trust

£183,000 (1993/94)

Young people between 16 and 35, music, drama and knowledge of Scotland

PO Box 17, 25 South Methven Street, Perth PH1 5ES
01738-620451

Correspondent: Mrs Barbara Anderson, Assistant Secretary

Beneficial area: Unrestricted.

Information available: Guidance notes are available from the correspondent.

General: The trust's assets in 1993/94 were valued at £3.26 million, generating an income of £148,000. Grants totalled £183,000 including the distribution of unspent income from the previous year.

Although the main focus of the trust is on individuals "to extend their boundaries of knowledge of human life", a limited number of grants are available for charities concerned with music, drama and knowledge of Scotland. Individuals must be between 16 and 35 of Scottish birth or parentage. Grants for individuals typically range between £280 and £4,600.

The trustees consider applications for study, research or special training or travel abroad which will help a career or support a special interest. An award for all or part of the total cost is only made after the trustees have considered an applicant's qualities and abilities as well as their financial circumstances. There should also be clear evidence of how the proposal will help to broaden the applicant's experience. "Grants are awarded on a competitive basis based on merit as demonstrated on record. The trustees are bound to take into account the financial circumstances of applicants and have complete discretion as to whether or not to make an award in any individual case."

Exclusions: Grants are not given to anyone who is not of Scottish birth or parentage and anyone over 35 years of age. Support for postgraduate study is given only in very limited circumstances.

Applications: Contact the correspondent for details of the application procedure for charities.

The Cunningham Trust

£180,000 a year

Medical research

Inchcape House, St Mary's Place, St Andrews,
Fife KY16 9QP
01334-472291

Correspondent: Cantley & Caithness, Solicitors

Trustees: Mrs M O Anderson; Professor C Blake; A C Caithness.

Beneficial area: Scotland.

Information available: 1992/93 accounts were provided by the trust.

General: In 1994/95, the trust's assets totalled £5.1 million, generating an income of £219,000. Grants total £180,000 a year and are mainly to departments of the Scottish University medical faculties.

In 1992/93, beneficiaries included Dundee University, Department of Pathology (£28,723) and Department of Surgery (£21,500); Edinburgh University, Department of Anatomy (£13,747), and Department of Medicine (two grants totalling £78,390); Glasgow University, Department of Biochemistry & Microbiology (£23,198), Department of Dermatology (£11,887) and Department of Oral Medicine (24,766).

A number of the beneficiaries had received grants previously, and the trust had made further commitments to three departments for the following year. It is unlikely that applications from non-regular beneficiaries will be supported.

Applications: In writing to the correspondent. Current information about dates and procedures for submitting applications is supplied to the Deans of Faculty.

The Dickson Minto Charitable Trust

£4,000 (1992/93)

Legal education, general

Dickson Minto, 11 Walker Street,
Edinburgh EH3 7NE
0131-225 4455

Correspondent: Neil S Russell

Trustees: B W Minto; R L Bruce.

Beneficial area: UK, worldwide.

Information available: Accounts are available for 1992/93.

General: The trust's assets amounted to £11,000 in 1992/93 with an income of £7,700.

The trust was established to promote the advancement of legal education. It also contributes towards the relief of poverty, the advancement of religion, the arts and other areas of public benefit both in the UK and overseas.

Applications: In writing to the correspondent. This entry has not been confirmed by the trust. The address details are correct at time of going to press.

The Douglas Charitable Trust

£33,000 (1994/95)

General

Messrs Dundas & Wilson, Saltire Court, 20 Castle Terrace, Edinburgh EH1 2EN

Correspondent: The Secretary

Trustees: Rev Prof D Shaw; D Connell; E Cameron.

Beneficial area: Scotland.

Information available: Accounts for 1994/95 were available from the trust.

General: In 1994/95, the trust's funds amounted to £264,000. Grants totalled £33,000. Preference is given to the universities of Edinburgh and St Andrews and church restoration projects in Edinburgh and St Andrews.

Grants ranging between £1,000 and £2,000 were awarded to organisations such as Law for All, Shelter and Oxfam. More substantial grants were given to the Oxfam Rwanda Emergency Appeal (£4,000), the Parish Church of the Holy Trinity in St Andrews (£7,000) and the University of St Andrews (£11,000).

Applications: In writing to the correspondent.

The Jack Drake Charitable Trust

£6,000 (1992/93)

General

Bank of Scotland, Trustees Department, PO Box 41, 101 George Street, Edinburgh EH2 3JH
0131-442 7777

Correspondent: The Secretary

Trustees: The Governor and Company of the Bank of Scotland; John Raffles Flint Drake.

Beneficial area: Scotland.

Information available: Accounts for 1992/93 were supplied by the trust.

General: In 1992/93, the trust had funds totalling £82,000 and grants totalled £6,000. Funds are only distributed to those organisations which have received grants over the last three years.

Grants typically range between £50 and £1,000, and in 1992/93 included £200 to Shelter, £300 to LEPRA, £500 to the Samaritans and an exceptional grant of £1,000 was awarded to Action Aid.

£100 each went to Age Concern Scotland, Crisis at Christmas, Ex-services Mental Welfare Society, National Trust for Scotland, Oxfam, Scottish National Orchestra, St John's Episcopal Church, Rothiemurchus.

Applications: In writing to the correspondent. The trust stated that it did not want to appear in the Guide.

The Drummond Trust

£15,000 (1993)

Christian publications

3 Pitt Terrace, Stirling FK8 2EY
01786-450985

Correspondent: Douglas S Whyte

Trustees: J F Sinclair; Rev B W Dunsmore;
Rev A Sheila Blount; D B Cannon; Miss M J S
Henderson; Rev G Richards; J K Sinclair,
A J Skilling; Rev A A S Reid.

Beneficial area: UK, worldwide.

Information available: 1993 accounts
were available from the trust.

General: In 1993, the trust's assets totalled
£200,000 and generated an income of £20,000.
Grants totalled £14,500 and ranged between
£100 and £2,000. Beneficiaries included the St
Andrew Press and British Church Growth
Association.

Applications: Application forms are
available from the correspondent. Completed
forms must be returned by 31st January or
31st July of each year.

Mrs J C Dunn's Trust

£5,000 (1993)

General

16 Walker Street, Edinburgh EH3 7NN
0131-225 4001

Correspondent: J H MacFie

Trustees: J H MacFie; J S F MacGregor; E M
Paget.

Beneficial area: UK with a preference for
Scotland.

Information available: 1993 accounts
were available from the trust.

General: The trust has an annual income of
about £4,600. Grants, which are awarded for
general charitable purposes, totalled nearly
£5,000 in 1993. Beneficiaries, each of which
received £1,185, were Barnardo's, Salvation
Army, Royal Society for the Relief of Indigent
Gentlewomen of Scotland and the RNLI.

The trustees are also interested in
organisations such as the Royal Edinburgh
Hospital for Incurables, Orphan Homes of
Scotland, Church of Scotland Deaconess
Hospital and City of Edinburgh & Leith
County Scout Council for Poor Scouts at
Spylaw House.

Applications: In writing to the
correspondent.

The Earl of Perth Charitable Trust

£15,000 (1986)

General

Stobhall, By Perth PH2 6DR

Correspondent: The Countess of Perth

Trustees: Rt Hon J David, the Earl of Perth;
Rt Hon N Seymour, Countess of Perth.

Beneficial area: UK with a preference for
Scotland.

Information available: 1986 was the most
recent year for which information was
available.

General: In 1986, the trust's assets were
£36,000 with income amounting to £4,700.
Grants totalled £14,800 and were mainly
given to Scottish organisations, those
promoting Catholicism and organisations
concerned with disability issues.

Exclusions: No grants to individuals.

Applications: In writing to the
correspondent. Applications are not
acknowledged unless a grant is to be given.

The Christina Mary Eckford Estate

Not known

Not known

48 Castle Street, Edinburgh EH2
0131-220 2345

Correspondent: George R Russell

Beneficial area: Not known.

Information available: No financial information was available.

General: No information available.

Applications: In writing to the correspondent. This entry has not been confirmed by the trust, although the address details are correct at time of going to press.

The Edinvar Trust

£2,000 (1993/94)

Community welfare, housing issues

Wellgate House, 200 Cowgate,
Edinburgh EH1 1NQ
0131-225 2299

Correspondent: Robin Burley, Trustee

Trustees: Ms M Marshall; R Hellewell; D Herd; R Burley.

Beneficial area: Scotland, with a preference for Edinburgh and the Lothians.

Information available: Accounts for 1993/94 were available from the trust.

General: The trust was founded by Edinvar Housing Association to support its charitable activities. In 1993/94, the trust had assets of £104,000 (£98,000 in 1992/93), generating an income of £6,000 (£14,000 in 1992/93). Grants totalled £2,000 (£4,000 in 1992/93) for the

year and included £1,000 to the Peffer Environmental Group and £300 to a volunteer advocacy service in South Edinburgh. Grants typically range between £100 and £5,000.

Applications: In writing to the correspondent.

The Erskine Cunningham Hill Trust

£41,000 (1994)

Church of Scotland, general

121 George Street, Edinburgh EH2 4YN
0131-225 5722

Correspondent: D F Ross, Secretary

Trustees: G W Burnett; H Cole; W G P Colledge; A C E Hill; Very Rev. Dr W B Johnston; D D McKinnon; R K Will.

Beneficial area: UK.

Information available: Annual report and accounts for 1994 were available from the trust.

General: In 1994, the trust had assets of £804,000 (£930,000 in 1993) and grants totalled £41,200. The trust makes grants in about equal proportions to Church of Scotland schemes and recognised charities.

Half of the total grants figure, £20,550, was awarded to the Church of Scotland. Other charities benefiting included the Aberlour Child Care Trust, Broomhill Day Centre Association (Penicuik), Council for Music in Hospitals, Edinburgh & Leith Old People's Welfare, Edinburgh Association for Mental Health, Glasgow & West of Scotland Outward Bound Association, Leonard Cheshire Foundation in Edinburgh, Lothian Association of Youth Clubs, National Trust for Scotland, Royal Caledonian Schools, Scotland Yard Adventure Centre, Scottish Churches Architectural Heritage Trust,

Strathcarron Hospice, The Samaritans (Edinburgh) and Thornhill & District Age Concern. Each organisation received £750.

Exclusions: No grants to individuals.

Applications: In writing to the correspondent.

The Falkland Community Trust

£11,000 (1994/95)

Poverty, disadvantaged groups

130 Constitution Street, Leith, Edinburgh EH6 6AJ
0131-555 0474

Correspondent: John Norman

Trustees: Ms M Stuart; Ms M Bremner; Ms H Steven; F McGachy; Ms S Kerr; J Norman.

Beneficial area: Scotland.

Information available: Annual accounts for 1994/95 and guidelines for applicants are available from the correspondent.

General: The fund is managed by trustees who are active in their own communities. They offer support for:

- Projects that benefit the poor or marginalised, with special consideration given to projects in deprived areas.
- Projects taking a community approach to issues and encouraging shared responsibilities. Grass roots initiatives that significantly involve project users are given particular consideration.
- Projects promoting peace and working for social justice and equality in areas such as race and sex.

In 1994/95, a total of £11,000 was awarded to charitable projects. Grants typically range between £100 and £1,000 although larger amounts are occasionally considered.

Requests for revenue funding for more than one year may be considered if it can be demonstrated that such funding would be vital to the success of the project, all other potential sources of funding have been explored and the project falls within the priority areas outlined above.

Exclusions: No grants for national organisations, publications, research, capital building projects or projects that come within the normal range of statutory responsibility, or that are supported by major charities. Grants are only given to charities accorded charitable status by the Inland Revenue or for purposes considered charitable.

Applications: Application forms are available from the correspondent. The trustees meet every three or four months to consider applications. However, smaller grants of up to £300 can be awarded between meetings where the success or survival of a project is at stake.

The J & C Fleming Trust

Not known

Religion, medical research, refugees, elderly people

1 Doune Crescent, Newton Mearns, Glasgow G77 5NR
0141-639 6694

Correspondent: Mrs E Goodbrand, Chairman of Trustees

Trustees: Mrs E Goodbrand, Chairman; Mr and Mrs J A C Balir; N A C Blair.

Beneficial area: Scotland.

Information available: No financial information available.

General: Donations are given in Scotland for religious causes, medical research and "special appeals for the relief of refugees etc. and elderly in real need etc.". No further information was given about the grant total, size of donations, or the beneficiaries.

Applications: In writing to the correspondent.

The Russell & Mary Foreman 1980 Charitable Trust

Not known

Children, animals, ecological projects

Royal Bank of Scotland plc, Trustee Division, Regent's House, PO Box 348, 49 Islington High Street, London N1 8XL

Correspondent: The Secretary

Beneficial area: Scotland.

Information available: No financial information was available.

General: The trust supports charities concerned with children, animals and ecological projects. Grants are given to registered charities only.

Applications: In writing to the correspondent by February of each year. The trust stated that it did not wish to appear in the Guide.

The Emily Fraser Trust

£73,000 (1993/94)

Relief of poverty, elderly, illness

W & J Burness, 16 Hope Street, Charlotte Square, Edinburgh EH2 4DD
0131-226 2561

Correspondent: W & J Burness WS

Trustees: Lady Fraser of Allander; Hon. A L Fraser; Ms P L Fraser; Dr K Chrystie; B Smith.

Beneficial area: Scotland.

Information available: Accounts were available for 1993/94.

General: In 1993/94, the trust's assets totalled £982,000 and its income amounted to £118,000 (after expenses).

The trust's main focus is on individuals working in the drapery and allied trades, in printing, publishing, bookselling, stationery and newspaper and allied trades and their dependants.

However, the organisation does give grants to small charitable organisations, concerned with the relief of poverty, elderly people and people who are ill.

In 1993/94, the largest grants were awarded to Bethesda Nursing Home Trust (£10,000) and the Scottish Bobath Association (£30,000). Smaller grants were also given.

Applications: In writing to the correspondent. The trustees meet on a quarterly basis.

The Gordon Fraser Charitable Trust

£87,000 (1994)

General

Holmhurst, Westerton Drive, Bridge of Allan FK9 4QL

Correspondent: Mrs M A Moss

Trustees: Mrs M A Moss; W F T Anderson.

Beneficial area: UK with a preference for Scotland.

Information available: Full accounts are on file at the Charity Commission.

General: In 1993/94, the trust had assets of £2 million generating an income of £89,000. Grants totalled £87,000 in the same year.

The trustees have absolute discretion as to the charities to be supported. Currently the trustees are particularly interested in help for children/young people in need, the environment and the visual arts. The trust states that "applications from or for Scotland will receive favourable consideration, but not to the exclusion of applications from elsewhere".

In 1993/94, a total of 174 grants were given. The largest were to the Aberlour Child Care Trust (£10,000, and £13,500 in 1992), Braedam Family House (£8,000), Hunterian Art Gallery (£4,000) and Royal Botanic Garden, Edinburgh (£5,000, and £10,000 in 1992).

There were 17 grants of between £1,000 and £3,750 to a wide range of organisations such as British Red Cross, Buildings of Scotland Trust, Crisis, Girl Guides Association (Scotland), and the Scottish Youth Theatre, many of which had received grants over recent years. The remaining grants were for less than £1,000.

Exclusions: No grants to individuals. Organisations must be registered as charities either with the Charity Commission in England or Wales or with the Inland Revenue in Scotland.

Applications: In writing to the correspondent. Applications are considered in January, April, July and October. (Grants for national or international emergencies can be considered at any time.) The trust does not have an application form. All applications are acknowledged; an SAE enclosed with the application would therefore be appreciated.

The Hugh Fraser Foundation

£487,000 (1993/94)

General

W & J Burness WS, 16 Hope Street, Edinburgh EH2 4DD
0131-226 2561

Correspondent: W & J Burness

Trustees: Lady Fraser of Allander; Hon. Ms A L Fraser; Ms P L Fraser; Dr K Chrystie; B Smith.

Beneficial area: West of Scotland and deprived areas of Scotland.

Information available: Accounts for 1993/94 were available from the trust.

General: The trust had funds totalling £19 million in 1993/94 and grants to organisations totalled £487,000.

Grants are made towards medical facilities and research, the relief of poverty, ill health and elderly people, as well as towards the education, development and training of young people and music and the arts. In 1993/94, 86 organisations received grants.

The largest were awarded to the University of Stirling (£50,000), Greater Glasgow Health Board, Scanning Programme (£31,000), Sense in Scotland (£28,000), Laurelbank School (£27,000), the Cancer Relief Macmillan Fund and Glasgow & West of Scotland Society for the Deaf (£25,000 each).

Exclusions: Grants are not awarded to individuals. Major highly publicised appeals are rarely supported.

Applications: In writing to the correspondent. The trustees meet on a quarterly basis to consider applications.

The J G Fyfe Charitable Trust

£8,000 (1993)

General

Bank of Scotland, Trustee Department,
PO Box 41, 101 George Street,
Edinburgh EH2 3JH
0131-442 7777

Trustees: J G Fyfe; Governor and Company of the Bank of Scotland.

Beneficial area: Scotland and Devon.

Information available: Accounts for 1992/93 are available from the trust.

General: The trust's funds totalled £124,000 in 1992/93. Five grants of £1,600 were given totalling £8,000.

Recipients were the Princess Louise Scottish Hospital, National Trust for Scotland, Guide Dogs for the Blind Association, Multiple Sclerosis Society in Scotland and St Margaret's Somerset Hospice Appeal; all organisations favoured by the trustees.

Applications: In writing to the correspondent. The trust stated that it did not want to appear in the Guide.

The Gamma Trust

£45,000 (1994)

General

Clydesdale Bank, Trust & Executry Unit,
PO Box 102, 150 Buchanan Street,
Glasgow G1 2HN
0141-223 2507

Correspondent: The Manager

Beneficial area: Scotland.

Information available: Accounts are available from the trust.

General: In 1994, grants totalled £45,000 and ranged from £100 to the Highland Fund up to £5,000 to a children's hospice. The trust supports general charitable purposes and the following examples of grants provide a flavour of its interests:

Fairmile Maire Centre (£5000); British Heart Foundation, Cancer Research and Erskine Hospital (£3,000 each); Institute of Neurological Sciences Research, Glasgow Leukaemia Trust, Scottish Churches Architectural Heritage, Scottish Kidney Research, Yorkhill Children's Trust (£2,000 each); Scottish Motor Neurone Disease Association, Alzheimer's Scotland, Oban RNLI (£1,000 each); Hansel Village (£200).

Applications: In writing to the correspondent.

The Gannochy Trust

£1,407,000 (1993/94)

Youth, recreation, general

Kincarrathie House Drive, Pitcullen Crescent,
Perth PH2 7HX
01738-620653

Correspondent: Mrs Jean Gandhi, Secretary

Trustees: Russell A Leather (Chairman); James Ross; Mark Webster; James A McCowan; Stewart Montgomery

Beneficial area: Scotland, with a preference for Perth and its environs.

Information available: The information for this entry was supplied by the trust.

General: Grants are given for the capital costs of a wide range of charitable organisations with a preference for youth and recreation projects. Projects must be in Scotland, there being an obligation to show a preference for Perth and its environs. Grants normally cover a single project and may amount to £1 million.

"The Gannochy Trust was founded in 1937 by Arthur Kinmond Bell, whisky distiller and philanthropist. A K Bell built the Gannochy Housing Estate in Perth consisting of 150 houses and completed in 1932. This model scheme was a significant element in the foundation of the trust. The trustees maintain the Gannochy Housing estate and their other properties. In recent years they have enlarged the housing estate by providing 48 sheltered houses for the elderly, and a further 21 are in the course of construction.

"A reserve fund is administered by the trustees from which donations are made to charitable organisations. Prime objects are the charitable needs of youth and recreation, but the trustees are not confined to these objects."

In 1993/94, the trust had assets of over £80 million, and an income of £4.3 million, an increase of 19% from the previous year. The trust had commendable administrative expenses of less than 2% of gross income, and it must also be applauded for joining the rare few which support openness in an area where trusts are often shrouded by secrecy.

Grants totalled £1,407,000, and the trust also made commitments of over £2.5 million to specific charitable projects. The previous year the proportions were reversed: just over £2 million in charitable donations with a further £1.4 million set aside for specific charitable projects. The trust categorised its donations as shown and states that "in all sectors, the interests of youth were amply served".

Category	1993/94	1992/93
Education	11%	29%
Social welfare	36%	19%
Health	15%	19%
Arts	17%	16%
Recreation	15%	13%
Environment	6%	4%

The trust lists its three main donations which exceed £70,000, in its 1993/94 report.

£312,800 was given to Perth & Kinross Recreational Facilities Ltd (£314,300 was given the previous year). Of this grant, £100,000 was to help with small village halls and similar community needs in the Perth and Kinross district; £20,000 was given to the AK Bell Library, and £12,000 for a flood protection study at the Gannochy Trust Sports Complex, built with the help of the trust in previous years.

The Perth and Kinross Heritage Trust was given £100,000, matching the £100,000 in 1992/93, for its general purposes.

£257,000 was given to the Kincarrathie Trust (£167,000 the previous year) for major roof repairs and dining room improvements. This trust operates the Kincarrathie Residential Home for the Elderly. The trustees take a special interest in this project which is adjacent to the offices of the Gannochy Trust, itself based in what was once the home of A K Bell. Three of Gannochy's trustees are also trustees of the Kincarrathie Trust, and "the home depends on donations from the Gannochy trust to provide in particular the capital expenditure necessary to meet rising expectations, for example en suite facilities, and the inexorable requirements of the Social Work Department".

£736,600 was also distributed in "other donations not exceeding £70,000", but since the trust prefers not to disclose its smaller beneficiaries, it is not possible to present an overall view of the trust's main areas of work. However, the trust has informed us that around 180 grants a year are given under this heading, ranging from £200 to £10,000. Some of them recurrent, and they are distributed throughout Scotland.

The trust has also earmarked £2,750,000 for specific charitable projects. £900,000 was committed to extend sheltered housing on the Gannochy Housing Estate, in keeping with the Settlor's wish that the number of houses on the estate should be increased as needed. £1.5 million was set aside for the Perth College Library; £200,000 was committed to the National Museum of Scotland, and further provision of £150,000 was made for the A K Bell Library. The trust has maintained its support for large-scale projects. This attitude is exemplified by its connection with the Perth Library which has been helped by the trust with funding of £2 million in previous years. In its 1992/93 report the trust stated: "The total contribution represents about 30% of the total cost of the project, and it has been a significant factor in getting the project off the ground. It is almost a century since a single benefactor provided the funds for the construction of the existing public library, now obsolete and inadequate. Few charities have the resources to fund entirely, projects of this magnitude today". The trust sounds almost apologetic for having to fund projects that should be wholly financed by central or local government in this enlightened age.

Exclusions: No grants to individuals. Donations are confined to organisations recognised by the Inland Revenue as charitable, and the trustees have absolute discretion in the choice of recipient.

Applications: In writing to the correspondent, including where possible a copy of the latest accounts. "It is the practice of the trustees to scrutinise accounts before making donations." The trustees meet when necessary to consider applications.

The Gateway Exchange Trust

Not known

Young people, self-help groups, drugs, ex-prisoners, disadvantaged groups

13 Inverleith Place Lane, Edinburgh EH3 5QJ
0131-552 4262

Correspondent: Anna Robb, Administrator

Trustees: J Boyle; Ms S Boyle; Ms B Orton; R Stares;

Beneficial area: Scotland and northern England.

Information available: A leaflet outlining the trust's criteria is available from the trust.

General: The trust states that it supports organisations such as "self-help groups or networks further establishing themselves against the odds. In the majority of cases those supported have come from areas or sections of the community that have been severely disadvantaged." It is particularly keen to foster creative abilities in young people.

The trust provides small grants for training, hands-on technical help or to help an organisation establish itself.

Most grants are awarded on a one-off basis, although the trust is occasionally able to make a larger and sustained commitment where the trust considers that a model of good practice could emerge.

The trust gives priority to organisations where local authority funding is not available.

Applications: In writing to the correspondent including full details of the project and the organisation's financial situation.

The Helen & Horace Gillman Trusts

£20,000 a year

Bird protection

31-32 Moray Place, Edinburgh EH3 6BZ
0131-226 5151

Correspondent: J K Burleigh

Trustees: J K Burleigh; R G Ritchie; F Hamilton.

Beneficial area: Great Britain and Ireland, with a special interest in Scotland.

Information available: Information was available from the trust.

General: The trusts, which were set up in 1982, are valued at about £450,000. Their joint income before tax and expenditure amounted to £24,000 in 1994.

The trustees work with various bird charities, in particular the Royal Society for the Protection of Birds. Grants range between £500 and £10,000 and other organisations supported include the Islay Natural Heritage Trust, Port Charlotte and the Isle of May Bird Observatory.

Applications: In writing to the correspondent.

The Goodacre Benevolent Fund

£800 (1990)

Religion and education

34 Stonehaugh Way, Darras Hall, Ponteland, Newcastle-upon-Tyne NE20 9LX

Correspondent: M Hutt

Trustees: W Whatmore; Mrs P Whatmore; G E Stone; D C Skey; E D Walker.

Beneficial area: UK.

Information available: Accounts were on file at the Charity Commission.

General: In 1993/94, the trust had assets totalling £71,000, generating an income of £3,000. Grants totalled £750. No grants were given in the previous year.

The trust gives grants for general charitable purposes, including religious organisations, and organisations concerned with education.

Applications: Contact the correspondent for further information.

The Gough Charitable Trust

£4,000 (1993/94)

Youth, preservation of the countryside, general

Lloyds Private Banking Ltd, Thames Valley Area Office, The Clock House, 22–26 Ock Street, Abingdon, Oxon OX14 5SW
01235-554000

Correspondent: Mrs E Ostorn-King (Ref: TT/98625/EOK)

Trustees: Lloyds Bank plc; N de L Harvie.

Beneficial area: Preference for Scotland.

Information available: Full accounts were on file at the Charity Commission for 1992.

General: In 1993/94, the trust had an income of only £33,000. This was made up of: £20,000 generated by £333,000 invested in a Guernsey Fixed Term Deposit Account; £8,500 from shares, £4,000 from an Income Tax repayment and just over £400 in other income. A balance of £67,000 was carried over from the previous year.

Only 12 grants were given totalling less than £4,000. Three grants of £1,000 were given to: Downside Settlement; Scottish Scenic Trust and Childline. ISCA received £500, Trinity Hospice £100 and the other grants ranged from £10 to £50. In each month between £1,200 and £1,600 was deposited in the Guernsey Deposit Account and the trust still carried forward £79,000 to the next year. It is not known why the trust is accumulating its income in this way.

In 1992, the trust had assets of about £140,000 and an income of £64,000. Grants totalled £51,000 and were given to 22 organisations working in a wide variety of fields. Beneficiaries included the National Trust for Scotland (£10,000); National Army Museum (£7,000) and £5,000 each to Trinity Hospice, Calcutta Tercentenary Trust and the International Scientific Support Trust. The Highland Hospice received £3,000. Seven grants were paid to regular beneficiaries, mainly service and insurance benevolent funds.

Exclusions: No support for non-registered charities and individuals including students.

Applications: In writing to the correspondent at any time. No application forms are available, no acknowledgements are sent. Applications are considered quarterly.

The Very Reverend Dr John R Gray's Trust

£3,000 (1992/93)

Religious purposes connected with the Church of Scotland

J M & J Mailer, Solicitors, 2a King Street, Stirling FK8 1BA
01786-450555

Correspondent: Brian C Herbertson, Solicitor, Clerk to the Trust

Trustees: Mrs L G Quattlebaum; A M Quattlebaum; Dr S M Gray; J C R Gray; C McLay.

Beneficial area: Scotland.

Information available: Accounts for 1992/93 were supplied by the trust.

General: The trust's total income for 1992/93 amounted to £1,400 with a surplus income of £5,200 carried forward from the previous year. The trust's deed specifies grants toward the work and welfare of the Church of Scotland and in 1992/93 a total of £3,400 was awarded. The sole beneficiaries

were Dunblane Cathedral (£2,930) and St Columba's Church, Stirling (£500).

Applications: Contact the correspondent for further details.

The Elizabeth Green Trust

£4,000 (1993/94)

General

KPMG, 24 Blythswood Square, Glasgow G2 4QS
0141-226 5511

Correspondent: The Secretary

Trustees: P L Stewart; C A Johnston; Ms B J Baker.

Beneficial area: Scotland and UK.

Information available: Accounts for 1993/94 were supplied by the trust.

General: In 1994, the trust's assets amounted to £59,000 (£51,000 in 1992/93). Grants ranged between £10 and £525 and totalled £4,000.

49 awards were made, with well over half of these for amounts under £100. Recipients of small grants included Care of the Wild (£75), Ex-Services Mental Welfare Society (£50), Mayfield Radio Unit (£50) and the Abbeyfield Society (£50).

The largest grants were given to the United Reformed Church, Dalkeith Road, Edinburgh (£250) and St Michael's Church, Malton (£525). Organisations receiving £100 to £200 included the Cancer Research Campaign, Christian Aid, Royal National Lifeboat Institution, St Leonard's Hospice and the United Reformed Church in London.

Exclusions: No grants to individuals.

Applications: In writing to the correspondent.

The Ann Jane Green Trust

£37,000 (1992)

Relief of need or sickness, children

8 Queen Anne's Grove, Bedford Park, London W4 1HN

Correspondent: Jacqueline Barchan, Secretary

Trustees: Jacqueline Barchan; George Green; Douglas Harvey.

Beneficial area: UK, with an interest in Scotland.

Information available: Accounts are available from the trust.

General: The trust supports hospitals and other organisations which are helping children, those who are sick or who are in need.

In 1992, the trust had assets of £836,000, and an income of £127,000. The trust distributed £37,000 in grants, leaving a surplus for the year of £82,000. 95 grants ranging between £25 and £3,000 were given. The trust lists the two grants over £1,000, which were Concern Worldwide Somalia Appeal (£1,500) and the Davidson Clinic (£3,000).

Exclusions: The trust does not respond to applications for grants from individuals.

Applications: In writing to the correspondent.

The Susan H Guy Charitable Trust

£11,000 (1993/94)

General

24 Blythswood Square, Glasgow G2 4QS
0141-226 5511

Correspondent: KPMG, Factors to the Trustees

Trustees: G D Caldwell; R W Speirs.

Beneficial area: UK.

Information available: Accounts for 1993/94 were available.

General: In 1993/94, the trust had assets totalling £301,000 (£242,000 in 1992/93). Grants for that year amounted to £11,000 (£12,000 in the previous year).

The trust's objects are widely drawn and grants range between £1,000 and £2,500. In 1993/94, six of the eight grants were for £1,000, received by Christian Aid Scotland, Glasgow & Renfrewshire Branch of the Red Cross, National Trust for Scotland, Prince & Princess of Wales Hospice, Royal Society for the Prevention of Cruelty of Children and Scout Association.

The two larger awards of £2,500 were to the Royal Society for the Protection of Birds and the Royal Lifeboat Institution. A number of the grants were recurrent from the previous year.

Exclusions: No grants to individuals.

Applications: In writing to the correspondent.

The Guy-Lockhart Charitable Trust

Not known

General

Thom Matthew & Co, 180 Main Street, Kilwinning KA13 6EE
01294-552545

Correspondent: Thom Matthew & Co

Beneficial area: Scotland.

Information available: No financial information was available.

General: The trust supports the following named charities: Orphan Homes of Scotland, Salvation Army, Aged Christian Friend Society of Scotland and Princess Louise Scottish Hospital.

It is not known if other charities are supported.

Applications: In writing to the correspondent.

J M Haldane's Charitable Trust

£6,000 (1993/94)

Arts, particularly music, third world

Chiene & Tait, 3 Albyn Place,
Edinburgh EH2 4NQ
0131-225 7515

Correspondent: J M Haldane

Trustees: J M Haldane; Mrs Haldane.

Beneficial area: UK, with a preference for Scotland and developing countries.

Information available: The information for this entry is based on the annual report and accounts available from the correspondent.

General: This trust generally makes grants ranging from £50 to £250 to development agencies and music groups and schools.

In 1993/94, grants totalled £6,400 and beneficiaries included: Project Trust and Scottish Opera (£100 each), Music in Blair Atholl (£75), Water of Life (£35) and the Edinburgh Appeal for Sarajevo (£50). An exceptional grant of £5,000 was made to the Edinburgh Festival Theatre Trust.

Applications: In writing to the correspondent.

The Roderick Harbinson Charitable Trust

£7,000 (1993/94)

General

Grant Thornton, Chartered Accountants,
112 West George Street, Glasgow G2 1QF
0141-332 7484

Correspondent: The Secretaries to the Trust

Trustees: D R Harbinson; Mrs M E Harbinson; T F O'Connell; W G Cochrane.

Beneficial area: UK, with a preference for Scotland.

Information available: Accounts for 1993/94 are available from the trust.

General: The trust's total assets in 1993/94 were £176,000 and its income amounted to £10,000 before expenditure (£16,000 in 1992/93). Grants in 1993/94 totalled £7,000.

All grants were for under £1,000 and given to organisations for general charitable purposes.

Applications: In writing to the correspondent.

Miss K M Harbinson's Charitable Trust

£171,000 (1994)

General

190 St Vincent Street, Glasgow G2 5SP
0141-204 2833

Correspondent: Sir James B Highgate

Trustees: Sir James Highgate; G A Maguire; G C Harbinson; R Harbinson.

Beneficial area: Unrestricted, but with a preference for Scotland.

Information available: Accounts for 1993/94 are available from the trust.

General: The trust had a capital sum of £4.2 million in 1993/94 and an income of £180,000. Grants totalled £171,000 and ranged between £1,000 and £9,000. They were awarded to 49 organisations, often in two instalments in the year.

The smallest amounts of £1,000 each were awarded to organisations such as the Princess Royal Trust for Carers, Womankind, Scottish International Piano Competition and Scottish Medical Research Fund.

Organisations benefiting from larger grants included the John Muir Trust, Scottish Wildlife Trust, Cystic Fibrosis Research Trust and Artists General Benevolent Fund (£2,000 each), Care Britain and Ethiopiaid (£4,000), Cancer Research Campaign (£5,000) and the Chest Heart and Stroke Association (£8,000).

The largest grant of £9,000 was awarded to each of the Intermediate Technology Development Group, UNICEF, Action Aid and Marie Stopes International.

Applications: Contact the correspondent for further details.

The Harbour Trust

£5,000 (1994/95)

Evangelical Christian work

5 East Harbour Road, Charlestown, Fife KY11 3EA
01383-872604

Correspondent: Hugh McCormick, Trustee

Trustees: H McCormick; Mrs H McCormick; Dr A H I McCormick; Mrs R McCormick.

Beneficial area: Unrestricted.

Information available: Information is supplied by the trust.

General: Grants totalled £5,000 in 1994/95 and ranged between £10 and £600. Recipients included Organisation Mobilisation (£600), New Tribes Mission (£300) and the Scottish Christian Counselling Trust (£200).

The trust states that its funds are currently fully committed and that grants are only made to organisations known to the trustees personally or recommended to them.

Applications: Applications are not invited and unsolicited appeals do not receive a response.

Mrs D L Harryhausen's 1969 Trust

£51,000 (1992/93)

Animal welfare, general

W & J Burness, 16 Hope Street, Edinburgh EH2 4DD
0131-226 2561

Trustees: Simon Mackintosh; George Menzies; Alistair Sutherland.

Beneficial area: UK, with an interest in Scotland.

Information available: Accounts are available from the trust.

General: In 1992/93, the trust's assets were £179,000 generating an income of £22,000. Grants totalled £51,000 for the year. The accounts list those grants over £1,000 up to the highest grant for the year, £18,500 to the Ray & Diana Harryhausen Foundation.

A large number of the larger grants were to animal welfare charities. Scottish beneficiaries included SSPCA Shetland Appeal (£2,000) and the David Livingstone Centre (£12,000).

Applications: In writing to the correspondent.

The Douglas Hay Trust

£23,000 (1993/94)

Physically disabled children under 18

Tigh Na H'ath, Dulnain Bridge,
Morayshire PH26 3NU
0147985-1266

Correspondent: The Secretary

Beneficial area: Scotland.

Information available: Information was supplied by the trust.

General: Grants are usually only given for individuals and are awarded through local authority social work departments. However, the trust occasionally gives grants to organisations concerned with disability when funds allow. In 1994/95, Learning for the Disabled received a grant of £500.

Applications: Applications are not invited.

The Hayward Foundation

£188,000 (1993)

Social welfare, medicine

45 Harrington Gardens, London SW7 4JU
0171-370 7063

Correspondent: Mark T Schnebli, Administrator

Trustees: E G Sykes; I F Donald; J Hayward; Dr J C Houston; Mrs S J Heath; G J Hearne; C W Taylor; J N van Leuvan.

Beneficial area: UK.

Information available: Full report and accounts are available from the foundation for £5.

General: In 1993, a total of £1,037,000 was given to 71 organisations. Of this, grants totalling £188,000 were awarded to 11 organisations based in Scotland.

Grants usually range between £10,000 and £50,000 for capital or project funding. Very few grants are recurrent.

The foundation's report states: "Priority is given to the needs of the frail and elderly, with emphasis on care in the community and on those schemes which seek to support and encourage the elderly to stay in their homes through care and outreach schemes.

"The second largest area of concern ... is the special needs group of the population and this includes education and schools for children with special learning needs, sheltered employment and training schemes for people who are unable to make their way in the everyday world as well as organisations who address the problems of mental illness in it widest context.

"Medical research continues to be an important aspect of the foundation's work but the funds are targeted to those peripheral areas of research where they can make an impact and where few other foundations or trusts would give financial support.

"Besides these three main headings the foundation has applications from, and has supported organisations which are concerned with, general welfare for the needy and deprived and from community and youth organisations which either address themselves to the needs of those young people at risk, those who have come out of prison and generally those who need guidance in their younger years to help them find their way in life.

"Art and education forms a small part of the foundation's budget but where both headings of art and education and possibly access for the disabled can be combined then the trustees will occasionally support a well-put case.

"In all cases the trustees are looking for projects with a strong voluntary element and will not support organisations simply because they are not-for-profit. The foundation is also unable to make up or replace grants or financial support which has been withdrawn by government departments or local authorities. They feel it is not up to charitable foundations to make good that which the state has abandoned.

"Trustees are conscious of the fact that the needs of organisations outside London and the Home Counties must be addressed and therefore grants have been spread geographically over a wide area of the UK."

In 1993, organisations funded in Scotland included the Scottish Association for Autistic Children which received £27,000.

Exclusions: Grants are not awarded to individuals, nor for revenue costs, holidays, travel, churches, expeditions, vehicles, or general appeals. The foundation will also not cover deficit costs, nor what is properly the responsibility of a statutory body.

Applications: Applications should contain a brief outline of the benefits a grant would make, how many people will benefit or what savings would be achieved. A full set of the latest audited accounts must be included and the application must be signed by a trustee.

The A Sinclair Henderson Trust

£14,000 (1994/95)

General, religion, medical, education, historic building maintenance

Messrs Thorntons WS, Whitehall Chambers, 11 Whitehall Street, Dundee DD1 4AE
01382-229111

Correspondent: Mrs S A Stewart

Trustees: J S Fair; Mrs A Thoms; Mrs V Oyama; C Thoms.

Beneficial area: UK.

Information available: Information was supplied by the trust.

General: The trust has an income of about £19,000 a year. Grants range between £250 and £2,500 and totalled £14,000 in 1994/95. Grants are made throughout the year to a range of charities, including medical, youth and historic buildings preservation.

Exclusions: No grants to individuals.

Applications: In writing to the correspondent.

The Christina Mary Hendrie Trust for Scottish & Canadian Charities

£105,000 (1994)

Young and elderly people

48 Castle Street, Edinburgh EH2 3LX
0131-220 2345

Correspondent: G R Russell/Anderson Strathern WS

Trustees: G A S Cox; Mrs A D H Irwin; C R B Cox; J K Scott Moncrieff; Miss C Irwin; Brig A S H Irwin; R N Cox.

Beneficial area: Scotland and Canada.

Information available: Information was supplied by the trust.

General: The trust was established in 1975 following the death in Scotland of Christina Mary Hendrie. The funds constituting the trust originated in Canada and grants are now distributed mainly to charities throughout Scotland and Canada, especially charities connected with either young or elderly people. Grants range between £1,000 and £20,000 and in 1994 included £5,000 to Highland Hospice to assist a new project.

Applications: In writing to the correspondent.

The Herd Charitable Trust

£11,000 (1993/94)

Religion, education, general

Messrs Bowman Gray Robertson & Wilkie
Solicitors, 27 Bank Street, Dundee DD1 1RP
01382-322267

Correspondent: B N Bowman

Trustees: B N Bowman; Mrs P M M
Bowman; Mrs E N McGillivray.

Beneficial area: UK.

Information available: Accounts for
1993/94 were available from the trust.

General: The trust was established in 1982
to made grants to religious, educational and
other charitable organisations. In April 1994,
it had assets of £142,000.

In 1993/94, grants totalled £11,000 and
ranged between £930 and £2,000, with the
majority of grants for £1,000.

Organisations supported included
Barnardo's, British Red Cross Society
(Dundee branch), Dundee Invalid and
Crippled Children's Aid Association, Royal
Dundee Blindcraft Products, Royal National
Lifeboat Institute (Dundee branch), Royal
Scottish Society for the Prevention of Cruelty
to Children, Strathmartine Parish Church
New Hall Project and Youth Support Group.

Applications: Contact the correspondent
for further details. This entry has not been
confirmed by the trust. The address details
are correct at time of going to press.

The Highgate Charitable Trust

£12,000 (1994)

General

190 St Vincent Street, Glasgow G2 5SP
0141-204 2833

Correspondent: Sir James B Highgate

Trustees: G A Maguire; N A Fyfe;
Mrs E A Thomson.

Beneficial area: Scotland, with a
preference for the West of Scotland.

Information available: Accounts for
1993/94 are available from the trust.

General: The trust had a capital value of
£120,000 in 1993/94 and an income of about
£9,000. Grants totalled £12,000.

One exceptional grant of £8,000 was awarded
to the High School of Glasgow Educational
Trust towards a new organ. The remaining
grants ranged between £25 and £500, and
beneficiaries included Cruse (£500), Salvation
Army (£275), National Bible Society of
Scotland (£250), Scottish Law Agents Society
(£100) and Earl Haig Fund (£50).

Applications: In writing to the
correspondent.

The Hilden Charitable Fund

£25,000 (1993/94)

Minorities and race relations, social welfare, penal affairs, homelessness (especially young people) third world

c/o Scottish Council for Voluntary
Organisations (SCVO), 18–19 Claremont
Crescent, Edinburgh EH7 4QD
0131-556 3882

Correspondent: Martin Sime, Director, SCVO

Trustees: Mrs G J S Rampton; Dr M B H Rampton; Mrs A M A Rampton; J R A Rampton; Dr D S Rampton; Mrs H M C Rampton; Prof C H Rodeck; Mrs E K Rodeck; I C Caplan; Mrs M G Duncan; C H Younger.

Beneficial area: Scotland.

Information available: The information for this entry is taken from the trust's annual report and accounts which are on file at the Charity Commission in London, and from a report prepared by the Scottish Council for Voluntary Organisations (SCVO).

General: The Fund supports organisations within the categories: minorities and race relations, penal affairs, homelessness (especially young people) and third world. Within these categories of interest support is mainly to community level activities.

The Fund allocates £25,000 of its income each year to SCVO for distribution in Scotland. SCVO's grant-making is very much in keeping with the Hilden Charitable Fund's traditional interests although it is perhaps more focused on social welfare.

Grants range from £200 to £750 and recent recipients include: Age Concern Orkney (£200), Scottish Society for Autistic Children (£500), Edinburgh Council for Single Homeless (£750), Books Abroad (£250) and Scottish Chamber Orchestra (£300).

Exclusions: No grants to individuals.

Applications: There is no application form. Write with full details of the project, financial budget and funds raised to date.

The L E Hill Memorial Trust

£17,000 (1994/95)

General

Messrs Dundas & Wilson, Saltire Court, 20 Castle Terrace, Edinburgh EH1 2EN

Correspondent: The Secretary

Trustees: Dundas & Wilson Trustees Ltd; J Ivory; M H H Hill.

Beneficial area: UK.

Information available: Accounts for 1994/95 are available from the trust.

General: The trust's assets in 1994/95 amounted to £324,000. Grants totalled £16,700 (£32,000 in the previous year).

Grants ranged between £200 and £4,000 with the largest to St John's Episcopal Church in Forfar. £2,000 was given to the Doon School English Charitable Trust Foundation, Magdalene College and the Rwanda Emergency Appeal.

Awards of under £1,000 were given to organisations such as the British Red Cross, Salvation Army in Tayside, Gordonstoun Schools Ltd, Reswalke Hall Trust and Dundee Heritage Trust.

Exclusions: The trust does not support non-registered charities.

Applications: Contact the correspondent for further details.

L S Hill's Charitable Trust

Not known

General

4 Lynton Avenue, Giffnock, Glasgow

Correspondent: L S Hill

Trustees: L S Hill.

Beneficial area: UK.

Information available: No financial information available.

General: Grants are at the discretion of the trustees and usually range between £5 and £250. No further information available.

Applications: Applications are not invited. This entry has not been confirmed by the trust, and we were unable to confirm the address and correspondent details.

The M V Hillhouse Trust

£21,000 (1994)

General

Hillhouse Estates Ltd, Hillhouse Quarry, Troon, Ayrshire KA10 7HX
01292-313311

Correspondent: The Secretary

Trustees: G E M Vernon; H R M Vernon.

Beneficial area: Scotland.

Information available: No financial information was available, other than a grant total.

General: Grants are only awarded to organisations known to the trustees and totalled £21,000 in 1994. There is no further information about the organisations the trust supports.

Exclusions: Registered charities only.

Applications: Contact the correspondent for further details, but note the above.

The Hope Trust

£96,000 (1994)

Temperance, Reformed Protestant churches

31–32 Moray Place, Edinburgh EH3 6BZ
0131-226 5151

Correspondent: John Karl Burleigh, Secretary

Trustees: Rev Prof D W D Shaw; Rev Prof A C Cheyne; Very Rev Dr W J G McDonald; J K Burleigh; Prof G M Newlands; Prof D A S Ferguson; Rev G R Barr.

Beneficial area: Worldwide, with a preference for Scotland.

Information available: Accounts for 1994 were available from the trust.

General: The Hope Trust was established over 100 years ago to provide education and distribute literature in the fields of its operation. It also supports individuals and organisations where they are involved in the "promotion of the ideals of Temperance to combat evils of drink and drugs" and "promotion of the principles of the Reformation as practised by Reformed Churches throughout the world".

The trust's assets totalled £2.5 million in 1994, generating a net income of £96,000 after staff and management costs. This amount was given in grants to individuals and organisations. Grants range between £200 and £10,000 and are given to organisations such as the World Alliance of Reformed Churches in Geneva, National Bible Society, Scottish Reformation Society and Waldensian Mission Aid Society (Scottish branch).

Applications: In writing to the correspondent.

The Housing Associations Charitable Trust (HACT)

£52,000 grants and loans in Scotland (1994)

Housing

Yeoman House, 168–172 Old Street,
London EC1V 9BP
0171-336 7877

Correspondent: Ms V Knibbs, Director

Trustees: Sir H Cubitt; Ms G Johnson; Ms R Crawley; Ms A Forte; R Hilken; Ms A O'Hara; A Robertson; D Wolverson; Rt Hon Viscount Gage; Ms A Gohil; Ms H Llewelyn-Davies; Ms B Dennis; Ms L Meikle; P Tennant; J Harris; Ms E Panahi; Ms M Bennett; Ms C Forrester; A Dalvi; P Richardson.

Beneficial area: UK.

Information available: The trust produces information sheets outlining the organisation's funding criteria, an annual report as well as a newsletter which is produced twice a year.

General: In 1994, the trust had net assets of £2.9 million and an income of £1.5 million. Grants and loans totalled £1.3 million with Scottish organisations receiving £52,200.

The trust gives grants for projects whose work falls within the following categories:

• Housing for people with special needs – this includes disabled people, people with learning difficulties, people with mental health problems, people with drug or alcohol problems, people who have been in prison or who are at risk of offending, people who have HIV or AIDS, women at risk of domestic violence, single homeless people, including young homeless people with support needs. In addition, applicants must target or promote one of the following: user participation; rural areas; people with additional mental health problems; black, minority ethnic or refugee communities; women with additional support needs.

• Housing for elderly people – in particular elderly people from ethnic minority groups and elderly people with mental health problems and older homeless people.

• Housing for black, ethnic minority and refugee groups.

HACT states that in all cases it aims to promote good practice, innovation, user involvement, quality of life for users, provision for unmet needs and a strong voluntary housing sector.

Requests for funds for the following purposes are considered:

• Towards the costs of establishing a new voluntary organisation aiming to cater for a previously unmet need (eg. registration costs, information leaflets, basic training).

• For training or consultancies for small organisations.

• Towards the cost of research to provide evidence of need in order to secure statutory funding.

• For the salary and other costs of a worker to develop a new service.

• For the costs of work to promote good practice.

• As contributions towards capital costs of small scale projects in London.

• Loans for the capital costs of housing related services in some circumstances.

A total of 237 grants were awarded across the UK, with nine grants to Scottish groups. Whilst this may seem a small proportion of the total number of grants, the trust is committed to supporting Scottish organisations and works closely with the Scottish Housing Associations Charitable Trust (SHACT) – *see separate entry.*

In 1994, grants ranged between £100 and £20,000. Organisations funded in Scotland included SHACT which received £20,000 to fund grants for elderly people, people with special needs and people from black, ethnic minority and refugee groups; and INASS which was awarded £15,000 to establish an independent needs assessment and advocacy service for people with mental health problems. Additionally, SFHA in Edinburgh received £8,000 towards the salary costs of a race and housing worker; West Gerinish Amenity Trust in the Western Isles was supported with two grants totalling £6,500 as a contribution towards the cost of a centre providing social support for the community and facilities for elderly people; Care and Repair Project in Buchan was awarded £2,900 to fund a handyperson service. All the above support came in the form of grants rather than loans.

Exclusions: No grants to individual applicants. HACT will not generally fund projects eligible for statutory housing finance via housing association funding mechanisms. Nor are requests for on-going revenue funding considered.

Applications: For further information and details of how to apply contact:
Reena Mukherji, Adviser, Black, Minority Ethnic and Refugee Housing;
Jane Minter, Senior Adviser, Housing for Elderly People; or
Ginny Castle, Special Needs Housing Adviser.

The James Thom Howat Charitable Trust

£212,000 to organisations (1994/95)

General

Biggart, Baillie & Gifford, Dalmore House, 310 St Vincent Street, Glasgow G2 5QR
0141-228 8000

Correspondent: Mrs Lane

Trustees: Leslie Duncan; Christine Howat; James Howat; Russell Howat; Gordon Wyllie.

Beneficial area: Scotland, in particular Glasgow.

Information available: Accounts are available from the trust.

General: In 1992/93, the trust's assets were £2.1 million, generating an income of £229,000. Administration amounted to £15,000. Grants totalled £222,000 including £9,750 in 16 grants to individuals.

In 1994/95, £198,000 was given to organisations and £14,000 to individuals.

The accounts for 1992/93 list those grants which were in excess of 2% of the gross income. The following beneficiaries each received £7,500: Crossroads (Scotland) Care Attendants Scheme; Eastpark Home for Infirm Children; Glasgow Royal Infirmary, Renal Unit; Scottish Opera; University of Glasgow; University of Strathclyde and the University of Stirling, Scottish Centre for Japanese Studies. The Heatherbank Museum of Social Work received a grant of £5,000. There are no further details on the remaining smaller grants which totalled £154,625.

Applications: In writing to the correspondent, including details of the project and a copy of the most recent report and accounts. Appeals are considered quarterly.

The Howman Charitable Trust

£8,000 (1993/94)

Conservation, medical, education

22 Meadowside, Dundee DD1 1LN
01382-201534

Correspondent: The Secretary

Trustees: Mrs M J B Howman; K C R Howman; A McDougall.

Beneficial area: Scotland and overseas.

Information available: The information for this entry is based on the trust's latest annual report and accounts.

General: Mrs M J B Howman set up this trust in 1977 and is still one of the trustees. The trust mainly supports organisations working in nature conservation.

In 1993/94, grant recipients included the World Pheasant Association, Salmon & Trout Association Charitable Trust and St Mary's Church of Scotland, Kirriemuir. Grants ranged between £500 and £16,000.

Exclusions: No grants to individuals.

Applications: The trust states that no applications will be considered or acknowledged.

Miss Agnes H Hunter's Trust

£192,000 (1993)

General (see below)

Robson McLean WS, 28 Abercromby Place, Edinburgh EH3 6QF

Correspondent: Mrs Jane Paterson, Grants Administrator

Trustees: The board is comprised of three trustees.

Beneficial area: UK, with a preference for Scotland.

Information available: Information was supplied by the trust. An explanatory leaflet is also available from the above address.

General: The trust was established in 1954 under testamentary deed. In 1993, assets in property and investments were valued at

£3.16 million. 50 grants totalling £191,500 were approved.

The main aims of the trust are to help charities for blind people in Scotland, disabled people, providing training and education for disadvantaged people and working towards establishing the cause, relief or cure of those with cancer, tuberculosis or rheumatism. These aims are currently being pursued in the following areas: children and family support, youth development, the elderly, homelessness, mental illness and the environment.

The trustees are highly selective and priority is given to Scottish projects. The trustees review their policies periodically and areas of interest may change.

In 1993, grants ranged between £500 and £10,000, although grants above £5,000 are exceptional and given to only a few specialist organisations.

Exclusions: No grants to individuals nor to organisations under the control of the UK government.

Applications: In writing to the correspondent.

The Mrs E Y Imries Trust

£6,000 (1993/94)

Visual impairment, elderly

Archibald Campbell & Harley, 37 Queen Street, Edinburgh EH2 1JX 0131-220 3000

Correspondent: Mrs M Auld

Trustees: D W Cockburn; K W Dunbar.

Beneficial area: Scotland.

Information available: The information for this entry was supplied by the trust.

General: In 1994, the trusts had assets amounting to £103,000. Typical grants range between £1,000 and £2,000 and beneficiaries included the Fife Society for the Blind (£2,400), Royal Blind Asylum and School (£1,600) and Society for Welfare and Teaching of the Blind (£1,600).

Applications: In writing to the correspondent.

The Inchrye Trust

£16,000 (1993/94)

Health, elderly people, medical research

Messrs Dundas & Wilson, Saltire Court, 20 Castle Terrace, Edinburgh EH1 2EN
0131-228 8000

Correspondent: The Trustees

Trustees: P W Turcan; Miss R Finlay; Mrs J David.

Beneficial area: UK, with a preference for Scotland.

Information available: Accounts are available for 1993/94.

General: The trust had assets of £419,000 in 1993/94. Grants totalled £16,000. The objects of the trust are wide but it is particularly concerned with relieving ill-health, care of the elderly, training and research.

Grants ranged from £100 to £5,000 and beneficiaries included Humanitarian Aid, Monmouth (£2,000), Scottish Opera (£700), Dunsyre Holiday Park (£500), Family Mediation Service (£200) and Agincourt School (£100). £5,000 was given to medical research and to Rugby School.

Applications: In writing to the correspondent.

The Gilbert Innes Trust

£2,000 (1994/95)

Education

City of Glasgow Society of Social Service, 30 George Square, Glasgow G2 1EG
0141-248 3535

Correspondent: James Smillie, General Secretary

Beneficial area: Scotland.

Information available: Information was provided by the trust.

General: In 1994/95, the trust had assets totalling £35,000, generating an income of £2,000, all of which was given in grants.

No information was available as to the range of grants distributed or the beneficiaries

Applications: Contact the correspondent for further information.

The Inverclyde Bequest Fund

£45,000 (1994)

Merchant seamen's charities

Merchants House of Glasgow, 7 West George Street, Glasgow G2 1BA
0141-221 8272

Correspondent: The Collector

Trustees: The Directors of the Merchants House of Glasgow.

Beneficial area: UK and USA.

Information available: This entry is based on information supplied by the trust.

General: In 1994, the trust had assets totalling £870,000, generating an income of £44,000. Grants to seafarers' charities totalled £45,000 in the same year.

Two-fifths of this fund's income is given to Scottish seamen's charities, with remaining income distributed to similar organisations in Northern Ireland and the US.

Exclusions: The fund does not give grants to individuals.

Applications: Contact the correspondent for further details.

P M Ireland's Charitable Trust

£7,000 (1994/95)

General

c/o Messrs Lawson, Coull & Duncan, Solicitors, 136 Nethergate, Dundee DD1 4PA
01382-227555

Trustees: D G Lawson; H D McKay.

Beneficial area: Scotland.

Information available: The entry for this trust is based on its annual reports and accounts.

General: The trust's assets were valued at £200,000 in 1994/95, generating an income of £8,800. Grants totalled £7,400.

All grants were of £275 and recognised charities were funded. Beneficiaries have included the Church of Scotland, National Trust for Scotland, Dundee Old People's Welfare Association, Oxfam and Pestalozzi Children's Village Trust.

Exclusions: Grants are not made to individuals.

Applications: In writing to the correspondent enclosing background information about the charity.

The Lady Eda Jardine Charitable Trust

Not known

General

Messrs Anderson Strathern, 12 South Charlotte Street, Edinburgh EH2 4AY
0131-225 5764

Correspondent: Mrs Pennell, Secretary

Beneficial area: Scotland.

Information available: No financial information was available.

General: There is a distribution of income made once a year following the trustees' meeting in July. Grants are awarded for general charitable purposes, although a category of beneficiaries is chosen each year.

Applications: Contact the correspondent for further details. This entry has not been confirmed by the trust. The address details are correct.

The Jeffrey Charitable Trust

£32,000 (1994)

Medical research, disability

29 Comrie Street, Crieff, Perthshire PH7 4BD
01764 652224

Correspondent: R B A Bolton

Trustees: R B A Bolton; R S Waddell; Mrs M E Bolton.

Beneficial area: Scotland.

Information available: Provided as necessary following initial requests.

General: In 1994, the trust had an income of £35,000 and made grants to organisations and individuals totalling £32,000.

16 grants were given mainly to organisations. Grants ranged between £175 and £10,000. The trust gives substantial support to research carried out at the Diabetic Centre at Glasgow Royal Infirmary and is also committed to long-term support of the Princess Royal Trust for Carers.

Exclusions: Animal-related charities and projects eligible for statutory support are not considered.

Applications: In writing to the correspondent. However, continuing support to long-term projects and anticipated repeat grants to other organisations previously helped mean it is unlikely that new requests for assistance can beconsidered in the short to medium term.

The K C Charitable Trust

£3,000 (1991)

Drug use, medical research, children and young people, elderly people

PO Box 191, 10 Fenchurch Street, London EC3M 3LB
0171-956 6600

Correspondent: The Trustees

Trustees: Kleinwort Benson Trustees Ltd.

Beneficial area: Scotland, with a preference for Edinburgh.

Information available: The entry is based on information supplied by the trust.

General: In 1991, the trust's assets totalled £146,000 with the organisation's income amounting to £21,000. Grants totalled £3,000 and small local charities in Scotland and particularly Edinburgh are supported. The trust focuses on drugs projects, medical research organisations, organisations working with young people (particularly where unemployed young people are offered training), as well as projects working with older people.

Exclusions: No grants to individuals.

Applications: In writing to the correspondent. Applications are considered twice a year, and are not acknowledged unless they are successful.

Robert Kaye's Trust

£4,900 (1993/94)

Church of Scotland

c/o Maclay Murray & Spens, 151 St Vincent Street, Glasgow G2 5NJ
0141-248 5011

Correspondent: The Secretary.

Trustees: I M Stubbs; Rev G M Newlands.

Beneficial area: Scotland.

Information available: No financial information other than a grant total.

General: The trust gave grants totalling £4,900 solely for the benefit of the Church of Scotland. No further information available.

Applications: In writing to the correspondent.

The Ronald & Mary Keymer Trust

£15,000 (1994/95)

Churches, medical, aid work overseas, war service charities

16a Greyfriars Garden, St Andrews, Fife KY16 9HG
01334-472424

Correspondent: Ronald C Keymer

Trustees: Mary Keymer; Ronald Keymer; Derek Warren.

Beneficial area: Worldwide.

Information available: Information was provided by the trust.

General: In 1994/95, the trust had assets totalling £100,000, generating an income of £13,000. Grants totalled £14,800.

Grants range between £100 and £400 and are given for the work of the Anglican and Presbyterian churches, for medical missionary work and to charities involved in overseas aid. Grants are also awarded to organisations for general charitable purposes and medical work.

Beneficiaries included the Church of Scotland (£1,200); Sudan Church Association and Egypt Diocesan Association (£400 each), and the Salvation Army, CMS and USPG (£300 each).

The trust mainly gives to charities which are known to the trustees rather than responding to applications.

Exclusions: No grants to individuals.

Applications: Contact the correspondent for further details.

The Kinpurnie Charitable Trust

Not known

General

Kinpurnie Estate, Smiddy Road, Newtyle PH12 8TB
01828-650500

Correspondent: R S C Shanks, Estate Manager

Beneficial area: Scotland.

Information available: No financial information available.

General: Grants made by the trust are small. There is no further information available as to the size of grant, or who the likely beneficiaries might be.

Exclusions: Only registered charities are supported.

Applications: Contact the correspondent for further details.

The Kintore Charitable Trust

£48,000 (1994/95)

Environment, young people, general

Messrs Dundas & Wilson, Saltire Crescent, 20 Castle Terrace, Edinburgh EH1 2EN

Correspondent: The Trustees

Trustees: The Countess of Kintore; Dundas & Wilson.

Beneficial area: Scotland, with a preference for Grampian.

Information available: Accounts for 1994/95 are available from the trust.

General: The trust's total assets at the end of March 1995 were £438,000 (£469,000 the previous year) with an income before expenses of £53,000 (£89,000 in 1993/94).

The trust awards grants to projects involving young people, environmental groups and local projects in the Grampian area.

The total amount paid in grants was £48,000 in 1994/95 (£24,000 in 1993/94). Grants ranged between £160 and £15,000 and were made to 34 organisations. This included the Crail Museum, Frigate Unicorn and Thirlestone Castle Trust which each received a Kintore Trust Conservation Award of £1,000.

The largest grants were to the Museum of Scotland Project (£15,000), Mackie Academy for the Earl of Kintore Awards (£3,000), Council for Music in Hospitals (£2,000) and Edinburgh Book Festival (£5,000). The Royal Incorporation of Architects in Scotland and the Duke of Edinburgh's Award both received £1,000.

Applications: In writing to the correspondent.

The Lord & Lady Laing of Dunphail Charitable Trust

£61,000 (1992/93)

General

W & J Burness, Solicitors, 16 Hope Street, Edinburgh EH2 4DD
0131-226 2561

Correspondent: The Secretary

Trustees: J Mann; G Menzies; J Rudd.

Beneficial area: UK, with an interest in Scotland.

Information available: Accounts were available from the trust.

General: This trust will distribute its annual income until 31st December 2000, when it will be wound up. In 1992/93, it had assets of £418,000 and an income of £78,000. Grants to organisations totalled £61,000 with a further £16,000 given to three individuals.

The accounts list grants over £2,000 up to the largest grant £12,500 given to the Forres Academy. Other Scottish beneficiaries included the Treloar Society (£2,500) and Edinkillie Parish Church (£3,000). A further 26 grants were for less than £2,000 and totalled £18,250.

Applications: In writing to the correspondent.

The Hon Mark Laing Charitable Trust

£4,400 (1993/94)

General

W & J Burness, Solicitors, 16 Hope Street, Edinburgh EH2 4DD
0131-226 2561

Correspondent: The Secretary

Trustees: George Menzies; Mark Laing; Mrs Susanna Laing.

Beneficial area: Scotland.

Information available: Accounts for 1993/94 were available from the trust.

General: In 1993/94, the trust had assets of £19,000, generating an income of £3,300. Donations to seven organisations totalled £4,400.

The beneficiaries were the Edinburgh Festival Theatre Trust (£2,500); Edinkillie Church and Cliftonhall School (£500 each); Treloar Trust (£300); Dingwall Hydrotherapy Pool and Highland Handicapped Child Centre (£250 each), and East Lothian Handicapped Children (£100).

Applications: In writing to the correspondent.

The Robert Laing Charitable Trust

£900 (1991/92)

Religious groups, general

W & J Burness, Solicitors, 16 Hope Street, Edinburgh EH2 4DD
0131-226 2561

Correspondent: The Secretary

Trustees: R J Laing; G MacBeth Menzies.

Beneficial area: Scotland.

Information available: Accounts were available for 1991/92.

General: The trust had assets of £18,000 in 1991/92. Grants totalled £900 and were given to Ark Housing Association (£100), Trelour Trust (£500) and Scotland Yard Appeal (£250).

Applications: In writing to the correspondent. This entry has not been confirmed by the trust. The address details are correct.

The Timothy & Charlotte Laing Charitable Trust

£9,000 (1990)

General

W & J Burness, Solicitors, 16 Hope Street, Edinburgh EH2 4DD
0131-226 2561

Correspondent: The Secretary

Trustees: W & J Burness (Trustees) Ltd; Charlotte Laing; Timothy Laing.

Beneficial area: UK, with an interest in Scotland.

Information available: Accounts for 1990 were obtained from the trust.

General: In 1990, the trust had assets of £60,000, and an income of £18,000. Grants to 23 organisations ranged between £50 and £1,000 and totalled £9,000.

Beneficiaries reflected a wide range of interests and included Edinburgh University, Dermatological Appeal (£500); Royal Scottish Agricultural Benevolent Institute (£100); Scottish Dyslexia Appeal (£1,000), and Queen Victoria School, Dunblane (£250).

Applications: In writing to the correspondent.

The Landale Charitable Trust (formerly the D & G Charitable Trust)

£25,000 (1992/93)

General

Coopers & Lybrand, Trust Accountants, PO Box 90, Erskine House, 68–73 Queen Street, Edinburgh EH2 4NH
0131-226 4488

Correspondent: The Secretary

Trustees: Sir D W N Landale; Ms N M Landale; P Landale; W Landale; J Landale.

Beneficial area: UK, with a preference for Scotland.

General: This trust was originally endowed with £10,000, but now has assets worth over £250,000, following a major injection of money in 1990/91.

In 1992/93, the trust had an income of £31,000, and grants totalled £25,000. Grants ranged between £50 and £11,000 and organisations benefiting included Comedia (£11,000), Campaign for Oxford (£5,000), Kirmahoe Parish Church and Kirkmahoe–Dalswinton Barony Kirk (£2,000 each) and Brogdale Horticultural Trust (£1,000).

Applications: Contact the correspondent for further details. This entry has not been confirmed by the trust.

The Allen Lane Foundation

£352,000 (1992/93) – total for the UK

Social welfare, mental health, less popular causes

32 Chestnut Road, London SE27 9LF
0181-761 4835

Correspondent: Gillian Davies, Secretary

Trustees: Ms C Morpurgo; S Morpurgo; Ms C Teale; Ms Z Teale; B Whitaker; C Medawar.

Beneficial area: UK, and a limited and specific programme in Ireland.

Information available: An information sheet is available from the foundation.

General: The foundation gives grants to organisations working in areas of social disadvantage and is particularly concerned to support groups which the trustees consider undeservedly unpopular, such as groups working with disadvantaged children, refugees, victims of violence, ex-offenders, young people at risk, women's groups, minority groups, community projects, travellers and others.

In 1992/93, a total of £352,000 was awarded to organisations across the UK and the Republic of Ireland. Grants to over a dozen organisations based in Scotland totalled £30,000 and included £2,500 to the Scottish Child Law Centre and £1,000 to Mothers of Sexually Abused Children, in Edinburgh.

Exclusions: Grants are not given to large general appeals or for work which the trustees consider to be the responsibility of the state. Grants are currently also not available for projects concerned with addiction, animal welfare, the arts, building costs, holidays, holiday playschemes, overseas travel, personal need, private education, the purchase costs of property, publications, the restoration of historic buildings, sectarian religion, academic or similar research, nor for the cost of purchasing vehicles. Loans are not offered.

Applications: In writing to the correspondent, enclosing full information about the aims and structure of the organisation applying and details of the funding required. Other sources of funding should also be identified and plans for the future outlined. The trustees meet three times a year in February, June and October to consider grant applications.

The Lankelly Foundation

£157,000 (1993/94)

Social welfare, disability, heritage and conservation

2 The Court, High Street, Harwell, Didcot, Oxfordshire OX11 0EY
01235-820044

Correspondent: Peter Kilgarriff

Trustees: A Ramsay Hack; C Heather; W J Mackenzie; Shirley Turner; Lady Merlyn Rees, Georgina Linton.

Beneficial area: UK.

Information available: An information leaflet is available from the foundation.

General: The foundation had assets totalling £26.8 million in 1993/94. Grants awarded across the UK totalled £2.38 million with grants to Scottish based organisations totalling £157,000.

Grants are given to organisations concerned with social welfare, people with disabilities, heritage and conservation.

1993/94 Grant Distribution	
Alcohol and drugs	£24,000
Arts/community arts	£170,000
Arts and disability	£41,000
Community work	£250,000
Elderly	£155,000
Ethnic minorities	£127,000
General social welfare	£400,000
Heritage and conservation	£121,000
Homelessness	£258,000
People with disabilities and special needs	£593,000
Penal affairs	£89,000
Youth	£153,000

Grants awarded to Scottish based charities included £48,500 to Family Action in

Rogerfield and Easterhouse (Glasgow) to underpin a coordinator's salary for three years and £10,000 to Flysheet Camps, Lockerbie towards building a workshop.

Exclusions: Grants are not awarded to advance religion, for general appeals, conferences or seminars, festivals or theatre productions, research or feasibility studies, publications or films, sport, the under-fives, youth groups, travel or expeditions, medical research, hospital trusts, formal education, individual needs, endowment funds, holidays, community business initiatives, animal welfare and other grant-making bodies.

Applications: In writing to the correspondent enclosing brief information about the origins and present company/ charitable status; a recent annual report where available; a description of the project, development plans to meet that need; information about timescale; detailed financial information including accounts and estimates, covering the organisation's general work and particular need described in the application.

The R J Larg Family Trust

£68,000 (1994/95)

Religion, education, general

Messrs Thorntons WS, Whitehall Chambers, 11 Whitehall Street, Dundee DD1 4AE
01382-229111

Correspondent: Mrs S A Stewart

Trustees: R W Gibson; A S Brand; D A Brand.

Beneficial area: UK.

Information available: Information was supplied by the trust.

General: The trust has an annual income of about £72,000. Grants, which totalled £68,000 in 1994/95, range between £500 and £7,500 and are made throughout the year.

A range of organisations were supported including organisations concerned with cancer research and other medical charities, youth organisations, university students' associations and amateur musical groups.

Exclusions: No grants to individuals.

Applications: In writing to the correspondent.

Duncan Campbell Leggat's Charitable Trust

£17,000 (1994)

General

190 St Vincent Street, Glasgow G2 5SP
0141-204 2833

Correspondent: Sir James B Highgate

Trustees: Sir James Highgate; G A Maguire; Mrs J M L Leggat.

Beneficial area: The West of Scotland.

Information available: Accounts are available for 1993/94.

General: The trust had assets of £210,000 in 1993/94, and has a total income of £15,000 a year. Grants in 1994 totalled £17,100 and ranged between £100 and £1,000.

Organisations benefiting included the Freedland Church of Scotland (£1,250), Shelter Scotland (£1,000), Prince & Princess of Wales Hospice, St Vincents Hospice Society, Scottish Society for Indigent Women, Princess Louise Scottish Hospital, Scottish Garden Scheme and Glasgow Zoo (£500 each), Salvation Army (£250) and Bridge of Weir Boy Scouts (£100).

Applications: In writing to the correspondent.

The Lethendy Trust

£39,400 (1994/95)

General

Henderson & Logie, Chartered Accountants, 11 Panmure Street, Dundee DD1 2BQ
01382-200055

Correspondent: George Hay

Trustees: W R Alexander; D L Laird; I H K Rae; N M Sharp, Chairman; D B Thomson.

Beneficial area: Scotland, with a preference for Tayside.

Information available: Accounts are available from the trust.

General: The trust was established in 1979 to support general charitable purposes in Dundee. It has since widened its geographical area to include Angus, Perthshire and Fife. The trustees have a preference for education and the development of young people.

In 1994/95, the trust had assets of £1 million generating an income of £42,000. Grants totalled £39,400. £35,000 was given to 11 organisations in grants ranging between £500 and £10,000. In addition, 11 individuals received grants between £200 and £1,000 and totalling £4,400.

Organisations receiving grants the previous year included the University Chair of Accountancy (£10,000); Duncan of Jordanstone College of Art (£3,000); Dundee Spastics Association and Childlink Scotland (£2,000 each); Scottish Veterans Residences, Scottish Veterans Garden City Association and Tenovus Scotland (£1,000 each) and Dundee Society for the Welfare of the Blind (£500).

Applications: In writing to the correspondent.

Lindsay's Charitable Trust

£3,000 (1994)

Conservation, the environment, arts, medical research

11 Atholl Crescent, Edinburgh EH3 8HE
0131-229 1212

Correspondent: W B Roberston

Trustees: Lindsays Trustees Ltd.

Beneficial area: Scotland.

Information available: Accounts for 1994 were available.

General: The trust's capital totalled £110,000 in 1994 (£77,000 in 1992/93) with an income of £3,800 (£18,800 in 1992/93).

The trust funds organisations working in the fields of conservation, the environment, wildlife, the arts and medical research. Charities based in Scotland which are generally smaller, less well known and work in specialist areas tend to receive support.

Grants totalled £2,900 in 1994, ranging between £50 and £1,000. Organisations funded included the Queensberry House Hospital, Royal Blind Asylum and School, Artlink and Paintings in Hospitals, Scotland.

Applications: In writing to the correspondent.

John Liston's Scottish Charitable Trust

Not known

General

Macmillan & Co Chartered Accountants, 98 West George Street, Glasgow G2 1PJ
0141-332 5906

Correspondent: J H Dover

Beneficial area: Scotland.

Information available: No financial information available.

General: No information available.

Applications: Contact the correspondent at the above address for further details. The trust stated that it did not want to appear in the Guide.

The Andrew & Mary Elizabeth Little Charitable Trust

£70,000 (1992) including grants to individuals

Relief in need

Wilson Chalmers & Hendry, Solicitors, 33a Gordon Street, Glasgow G1 3PH
0141-248 7761

Correspondent: Mrs Joan Wright

Trustees: Dr Robin Green; Dr Maud Menzies; R Munton Andrew Abbot; Col A Lawrie.

Beneficial area: Scotland, with a preference for Glasgow.

General: The trust was established to care for sick, elderly, poor, blind or otherwise distressed people. Grants are mainly given to individuals.

In 1992, the trust's assets were £914,000, and whilst the large majority of the beneficiaries were individuals, four organisations also received small grants: Age Concern Scotland (£150); Ayrshire Hospice (£300); Glasgow Old People's Welfare Committee (£150) and Shelter (£200).

The trust states that as the demands on the trust are now so great (and income is falling), grants will be restricted to those in need in

Glasgow, unless there are exceptional circumstances.

Exclusions: Grants are currently restricted to those in need living in the City of Glasgow.

Applications: In writing to the correspondent. Applications for individuals should be made through an appropriate third party.

The Logie Charitable Trust

£18,000 (1991/92)

General

W & J Burness, Solicitors, 16 Hope Street, Edinburgh EH2 4DD
0131-226 2561

Correspondent: The Secretary

Trustees: W & J Burness (Trustees) Ltd; Colin Baxter; Mrs Graeme Laing; Rt Hon The Earl of Leven & Melville.

Beneficial area: UK, with an interest in Scotland.

Information available: Accounts are available from the trust.

General: In 1991/92, the trust's assets were £62,000, and income totalled £37,000. Grants to 18 organisations ranged between £20 and £5,000 and totalled £18,000.

Beneficiaries included the Croftinloan School Appeal (£5,000); Edinkillie Church and Queen Victoria School, Dunblane (£2,000 each); Moray & Banff SSAFA (£50); the Erskine Hospital (£25) and Scotland's Garden Scheme (£20).

Applications: In writing to the correspondent.

The Marquess of Lothian's Charitable Trust

£1,000 (1993/94)

Christian

15 Atholl Crescent, Edinburgh EH3 8HA
0131-228 3777

Correspondent: Brodies Solicitors

Trustees: Dr M White; Dr V E Hartley Booth; Lady M von Westenholz.

Beneficial area: UK.

Information available: Accounts for 1993/94 were available from the trust.

General: The trust's assets totalled £161,000 in 1993/94 (with a market value of £281,000). Total income was £14,000; administration expenses were £2,075, and one grant of £1,000 was made.

The remit of the trust is primarily to assist Christian charities and individuals. The trustees now meet annually in the autumn to distribute grants. Under this new arrangement in 1993/94, one grant of £1,000 was given to the Scottish Branch of the Order of Christian Unity.

In 1992/93, grants ranging between £500 and £1,500 were awarded to organisations such as the Order of Christian Unity which received six grants throughout the year totalling £7,000, one of which was to its Scottish Branch; Elizabeth Fitzroy Homes (£500), SPUC Educational Research Trust, Life and St Elizabeth's School and Home (£1,000 each).

Exclusions: Organisations should be registered charities.

Applications: Contact the correspondent for further information.

The Low & Bonar Charitable Fund

£41,000 (1994/95)

Social welfare, medical

Bonar House, Faraday Street,
Dundee DD1 9JA

Correspondent: M G T Long

Trustees: G C Bonar; R D Clegg; J W Leng; H W Laughland; N D McLeod; J L Heilig; P A Bartlett; J B Marx.

Beneficial area: Worldwide, UK, Scotland (with an emphasis on Dundee and Tayside).

Information available: Accounts for 1994/95 were available from the trust.

General: The fund's assets in 1994/95 amounted to £218,000 and grants totalled £41,300.

The main focus of the fund's activities is on organisations working in the medical field, including research and the treatment and welfare of patients, as well as the elderly, the protection of children and young people, and the relief of human suffering.

Grants typically range between £100 and £2,000 and beneficiaries included the British Heart Foundation (£1,000), Scottish Opera (£500), World Wide Fund for Nature (£500) and Royal Scottish Society for the Prevention of Cruelty to Children (£1,000).

Applications: In writing to the correspondent.

Mrs M A Lumsden's Charitable Trust

£3,400 (1994/95)

General

Messrs Dundas & Wilson, Saltire Court, 20 Castle Terrace, Edinburgh EH1 2EN 0131-228 8000

Correspondent: N A MacLeod

Trustees: J R Andrews; N A MacLeod.

Beneficial area: Scotland.

Information available: Accounts for 1994/95 were provided by the trust.

General: The trust was set up in 1969 to provide funding for recognised charities and other organisations in which the trustees have an interest. The trust's total funds stood at £100,000 in 1994/95, and grants totalled £3,400.

Grants range between £250 and £1,000 and in 1994/95 were awarded to Yester Parish Church (£1,000), Arthritis & Rheumatism Council (£800), Coeliac Society of the UK (£500), and Scottish Council for the Care of Spastics and Marie Curie Memorial Foundation (£250 each). A number of these grants were recurrent from the previous year.

Applications: In writing to the correspondent.

The Anne Lynch Memorial Fund

£1,000 (1994/95)

General

Ernst & Young, Chartered Accountants, George House, 50 George Square, Glasgow G2 1RR 0141-552 3456

Correspondent: Ernst & Young

Trustees: Thomas Lynch; William McLellan.

Beneficial area: UK, with an interest in Scotland.

Information available: Accounts for 1994/95 were available from the trust.

General: In 1994/95, the trust had assets of £65,600 and an income of £1,700. £1,000 was distributed in grants. In 1993/94, income had been £22,000, and grants £6,500 with an undistributed surplus of £16,000. As no list of grants was attached to the accounts, there is no further information about the type of beneficiary or the donations given.

Applications: In writing to the correspondent.

The McCrone Charitable Trust

£16,000 (1993/94)

General

c/o Hardie Caldwell, Savoy Tower, 3rd Floor, 77 Renfrew Street, Glasgow G2 3BY 0141-333 9770

Correspondent: The Secretary

Trustees: Sir J B Highgate; G A Maguire; D P MacLean; R G S Mackay.

Beneficial area: Unrestricted.

General: In 1993/94, the trust had assets of £214,000 and an income of £15,000. Grants totalled £16,000, a slight decrease compared to the previous year's total of £18,800.

The trust was established in 1977 by the McCrone family and an annual award of £3,500 is given to Strathclyde University in memory of the late R W McCrone. Other grants are smaller, between £50 and £1,000. Grants were given to 35 organisations in 1993/94 (excluding Strathclyde University).

Six organisations received less than £100; 13 received £100; 10 received between £100 and £1,000 and five organisations received £1,000. The five organisations to receive £1,000 were Emmanuel Church, the Bow Club, Newnham College, Royal National Lifeboat Institute and St Anne's Church Organ Fund.

Other beneficiaries included Glasgow High School and the Prince's Trust (£500 each), Breadline Africa (£250), St Dionis Church, Freedom Association, Help the Aged, Christian Responsibilities in Public Affairs and British Red Cross (£100 each), and the Queen Elizabeth Foundation for the Disabled and Animal Welfare Trust (£50 each).

Applications: In writing to the correspondent at the above address. This entry has not been confirmed by the trust which did not wish to be included in the Guide. The address details are correct at time of going to press.

The R S MacDonald Charitable Trust

£23,000 (1994)

Visual impairment, cerebral palsy, children and animals

6 Alva Street, Edinburgh EH2 4QQ
0131-226 3781

Correspondent: Steedman Ramage, Agents for the Trustees

Trustees: E D Buchanan; D W A MacDonald; P B Cullen.

Beneficial area: Scotland.

Information available: Information is available from the trust.

General: The trust was set up in 1978 and assets at April 1994 were valued at £868,000, generating an income of £22,450 after expenses. Donations to charities in 1994 totalled £22,800.

Grants are awarded to charities carrying out work relating to:

- The care and welfare of people with visual impairments and/or those with cerebral palsy.
- Research into the causes, prevention or treatment of visual impairment and/or conditions resulting from cerebral palsy.
- The prevention of cruelty to children.
- The prevention of cruelty to animals.

Applications: In writing to the correspondent. This entry has not been confirmed by the trust. The address details are correct at time of going to press.

The N S MacFarlane Charitable Trust

Not known

Not known

Wright Johnston Mackenzie Solicitors, 12 St Vincent Street, Glasgow G1 2EQ
0141-248 3434

Correspondent: A M Simpson

Beneficial area: Not known.

Information available: No financial information available.

General: No information available.

Applications: In writing to the correspondent. This entry was not confirmed by the trust which did not want to appear in the Guide. The address details are correct at time of going to press.

The Elspeth McKenzie Memorial Fund

£5,000 (1993/94)

Cancer research, RNLI, scouts

Macdonalds Solicitors, 1 Claremont Terrace, Glasgow G3 7UG
0141-248 6221

Correspondent: T C McNeil

Trustees: G G Morris; W C Frame; T A Smith.

Beneficial area: Scotland.

General: The trust gives grants for three purposes:

- The RNLI
- Cancer research
- Scouts.

The trust has assets of about £66,000 generating an income of about £4,400. Grants range from £100 to £4,000.

In 1993/94, the RNLI received £4,000 towards a new boathouse at Stranraer, Glasgow University Department of Oncology received a grant for equipment for research into human cancer genes, and small grants were given to individual scout groups (usually groups in deprived areas in greater Glasgow) for camping equipment etc.

Applications: RNLI and cancer research applications should be made in writing in the first quarter of each year, for consideration at the annual meeting usually held in April or May.

Individual scout groups should apply through the Great Glasgow Scout Council.

The Maclay Charitable Trust

£2,000

International causes, third world, general

Duchal, Kilmacolm, Renfrewshire PA13 4RS

Correspondent: Lord Maclay

Beneficial area: Worldwide, but with a preference for Scotland.

Information available: The entry was compiled from the trust's annual report.

General: Grants range between £25 and £1,000 and total £2,000. Organisations funded recently included the Scottish Conservation Projects Trust and Ardgowan Hospice (£50 each), Salvation Army (£100), Save the Children Fund (£200) and Glasgow City Mission (£1,000).

Applications: In writing to the correspondent.

The Maclay Murray & Spens Charitable Trust

£5,400 (1994)

General

c/o Maclay Murray & Spen, 151 St Vincent Street, Glasgow G2 5NJ
0141-248 5011

Correspondent: The Trustees

Trustees: Ms J D Johnson; D M White.

Beneficial area: Scotland.

Information available: The entry was compiled from the trust's annual report.

General: The trust's annual income is about £7,000 from deeds of covenant.

Grants totalled £5,400 in 1994 and are made for general charitable purposes, including cultural, educational, religious or welfare work and schemes to relieve poverty.

Grants range between £100 and £650 and organisations that have received funding include the Cancer Research Campaign, Salvation Army, Childline and St Columba's Hospice.

Applications: In writing to the correspondent.

The MacLennan Trust

£9,000 (1993/94)

Young people, general

Royal Bank of Scotland plc, Private Trust & Taxation Office, 2 Festival Square, Edinburgh EH3 9SU
0131-556 8555

Correspondent: The Trust Manager

Trustees: D Birrell; Royal Bank of Scotland plc.

Beneficial area: UK.

Information available: The annual report for 1993/94 was available.

General: The trust's assets in 1993/94 amounted to £187,000. Grants ranged between £500 and £1,500 and totalled £9,000. Beneficiaries included Barnardo's, Carberry Tower for the Religious Instruction of Youth and Royal Scottish Society for the Prevention of Cruelty to Children (£700 each); Girl Guides Scotland and Boys Brigade (£600); Childline, Royal Blind Asylum and School and Trefoil Centre (£500 each); Royal Caledonian Schools (£300) and Scottish Adventure Playground Association (£200).

The largest grants were awarded to the Church of Scotland Board of Social Responsibility (£1,500) and St Columbus Hospice (£1,000).

Exclusions: No grants to individuals.

Applications: In writing to the correspondent.

The George MacLeod Charitable Trust

£7,000 (1993/94)

Advancement of peace

15 & 19 York Place, Edinburgh EH1 3EL
0131-556 8444

Correspondent: Morton Fraser Milligan

Trustees: J M N MacLeod; E M E MacLeod; N D MacLeod.

Beneficial area: UK.

Information available: Accounts are available for 1993/94.

General: The trust's assets totalled £72,000 in 1993/94, generating an income of £3,800. Grants totalled £6,600 and were given to organisations advancing peace. No further information available.

Applications: Contact the correspondent for further details.

The MacRobert Trusts

£687,000 (1994/95)

See below

Balmuir, Tarland, Aboyne, Aberdeenshire AB34 4UA
013398-81444; Fax: 013398-81676

Correspondent: Major General J A J P Barr, Administrator

Trustees: I G Booth; Air Vice-Marshal G A Chesworth; D M Heughan; A S Macdonald; Dr June Paterson-Brown; A M Scrimgeour; R M Sherriff; A M Summers

Beneficial area: UK, with a preference for Scotland.

Information available: Annual reports and accounts are available from the trusts.

General: The MacRobert Trusts are comprised of four trusts: the Sir Alexander MacRobert Memorial Trust; the MacRobert Trust; the Douneside Trust, and the Lady MacRobert Special Trust Fund all set up by Lady Rachel Workman MacRobert of Douneside and Cromar in the 1940s. In the mid-60s, the trusts were administered as one. Each trust has its own trustees, but they share one administrator.

The trusts are keen to support service charities, in particular the Royal Air Force Benevolent Fund, although the trustees have been given discretionary powers to respond to applications. Four trustees are nominated by the King George's Fund for Sailors, the Earl Haig Fund (Scotland), the Royal Air Force Benevolent Fund and the Royal Highland and Agricultural Society of Scotland respectively.

Grants are awarded under the "major" categories: science and technology, sea and services, ex-servicemen's hospitals and homes, disability, youth, education and social welfare. However, the trust also awards funds to charities working in the "minor" categories described as agriculture/ horticulture, arts and music and operating in the areas of Tarland and Deeside. The trustees also state that they "recognise the need to assist voluntary organisations which need funds to complement those already received from central government and local authority sources" and that "at present, experiment and innovation are much more difficult to fund and the trust's role in funding them the more significant".

Grants usually vary but most range between £100 and £5,000. Recurring grants for up to three years are occasionally made. Although project funding is preferred, core/revenue grants are also made. Grants are awarded to recognised charities only.

The trust's accounts for 1994/95 show combined assets of around £35 million, mostly held in the MacRobert Charitable Investment Trust. The lion's share of the grants are awarded by the MacRobert Trust. (Smaller amounts totalling £36,000 and £10,500 were given by the Douneside Trust and the Lady MacRobert Special Trust Fund respectively.)

The MacRobert Trust gave grants totalling £640,200 in 1994/95 categorised as shown below.

Category	£	No.
Medical Care	228,253	8
Education	113,984	15
Ex-Servicemens' Hospitals	80,000	5
Armed Services & Merchant Marine	47,325	12
Community Welfare	44,700	20
Youth	39,000	20
Disabled & Handicapped	36,440	13
Music & the Arts	24,875	10
Science & Technology	22,000	4
Tarland & Deeside	3,625	7

The largest grants in each of the above categories respectively were to the Children's Hospice Association Scotland (£214,803 as the first part of a £2 million donation being made during 1994-1996 as a special project to build and equip Scotland's first Children's Hospice to mark the 50th Anniversary of the Trust); University of Aberdeen (£50,000); Royal Air Forces Association, Sussexdown Convalescent Home (£25,000); Sailors' Families Society, Hull and Bomber Command Association (£10,000 each); PARC Glasgow and Voluntary Service Belfast (£7,500 each); Abernethy Trust and Co-operation North, Belfast (£10,000); Penumbra (Respite Care) Ltd, the Adapt Trust, the Seagull Trust and the Trefoil Centre (£5,000);

Haddo House Arts Trust (£5,000); Edinburgh International Science Festival (£8,000); and the Tarland Welfare Trust (£1,600).

The MacRobert Trust gave 102 grants having received 750 donations, more than 40% up on the previous year. In 1993/94, the success rate had been 1:4; in 1994/95 the ratio was around 1:7.

The scale of grants is varied ranging from £50 to the exceptional grant of £214,803 for the children's hospice detailed above. Most grants fell between £1,000 and £5,000. In 1993/94 five grants were between £10,000 and £50,000; 25 were less than £1,000.

The lion's share of the grants are given in Scotland, although there are a smaller number of beneficiaries in England and Northern Ireland.

The trusts are largely reactive, so, with a very few exceptions, only applications made to the trusts will be considered. The need to help voluntary organisations and complement those funds already received from central government and local authority sources is recognised. But where statutory bodies fail to continue their support the trusts may not necessarily make a grant. Project support is favoured but core/revenue grants may also be given.

Exclusions: Grants are not normally given for: religious organisations (but not including youth/community services provided by them, or projects of general benefit to the whole community, or local churches); organisations based outside the UK; individuals, endowment or memorial funds; general appeals or "mailshots"; political organisations; student bodies (as opposed to universities); fee-paying schools (apart from an Educational Grants scheme for children attending, or wishing to attend, a Scottish independent secondary school); expeditions; retrospective grants for university departments (unless the appeal gains the support of, and is channelled through, the principal).

Applications: In writing to the correspondent at the above address. There is no application form. Applications should include the charity title or a description of the charity's activities, or evidence of tax-exempt status; a list of the charity's key people; details of the project for which the grant is sought including costings, funds raised in relation to the target and funds promised (if any), and the latest full audited accounts and annual report.

The trustees look for clear, realistic and attainable aims. Unsuccessful organisations should wait at least one year from the date of applying before re-applying. Successful organisations should wait at least two years from receipt of a donation before reapplying.

All applications are acknowledged. In most cases the application undergoes scrutiny which may include a visit from the administrator.

The trustees meet in March and October each year. Applications for the March meeting need to reach the trusts by late October, and for the October meeting by early June. Applicants are informed of the trustees' decision within one week of the meeting.

The Ian MacTaggart Trust

Not known

Not known

Breeze Paterson and Chapman, 257 West Campbell Street, Glasgow G2 4TU
0141-248 5432

Correspondent: R R Pender, Administrator

Beneficial area: Not known.

Information available: No financial information available.

General: No information available. This trust offered to provide a copy of the accounts on payment of a fee. As the number of trusts in this book would have made payment on each set of accounts prohibitive, the offer was declined, and no further information is available on the activities of this trust.

Applications: In writing to the correspondent.

The MEB Charitable Trust

Not known

Not known

McGrigor Donald Solicitors, Pacific House, 70 Wellington Street, Glasgow G2 6SB
0141-248 6677

Correspondent: Jacqueline Kane

Information available: No financial information was available.

Beneficial area: Not known.

General: No information available.

Applications: In writing to the correspondent. This entry has not been confirmed by the trust which did not wish to be included in the guide. The address details are correct at time of going to press.

The Melville Trust for Care & Cure of Cancer

Probably about £60,000

Research into the alleviation and cure of cancer

Tods Murray WS, 66 Queen Street, Edinburgh EH2 4NE
0131-226 4771

Correspondent: The Trustees

Trustees: Melville Estate Trustees.

Beneficial area: Lothian, Borders and Fife.

Information available: Information was provided by the trust.

General: The trust's assets were £1.2 million in 1990, generating an income of £69,000. Grants are awarded to universities, medical schools and scientific bodies for research into the causes, cure and alleviation of cancer.

Exclusions: Grants are not awarded to charities generally.

Applications: Application forms are available from the correspondent.

Mrs Henni Mester Will Trust

£24,000 (1992/93)

Medical research in the field of rheumatism and arthritis

Bank of Scotland, Trustee Department, PO Box 41, 101 George Street, Edinburgh EH2 3JH
0131-442 7777

Correspondent: The Secretary

Trustees: The Governor and Company of the Bank of Scotland.

Beneficial area: Scotland.

Information available: Accounts are available for 1993 from the trust.

General: The trust's assets totalled £257,000 in 1993, generating an income of £46,000. Grants amounted to £24,000 and in 1992/93. All funds were awarded to the Arthritis & Rheumatism Council.

Applications: Contact the correspondent for further details. The trust stated that it did not want to appear in the Guide.

The Mickel Fund

£33,000 (1993/94)

General

126 West Regent Street, Glasgow G2 2BH
0141-332 0001

Correspondent: J R C Wark

Trustees: D W Mickel; Lord Goold;
J R C Wark.

Beneficial area: UK, with a preference for
Scotland.

Information available: Accounts for
1993/94 are available from the fund.

General: In 1993/94, assets totalled £748,000
(£715,000 in 1992/93). The trust's income
before expenditure totalled £59,000 (£43,000
in 1992/93) and grants to charities were
£33,000 (£39,000 in 1992/93).

Beneficiaries of larger grants in 1993/94 were
the Ewan Marwick Memorial Trust and
Reserve Forces Ulysses Trust (£1,000 each),
and Edinburgh and Leith Old People's
Welfare Committee and East Park Home
(£2,000 each).

The fund awards grants for general
charitable purposes typically ranging
between £100 and £500, although larger
amounts up to a maximum of £10,000 are
also considered.

Smaller grants in 1993/94 included £345 to
the British Red Cross, £115 to the Edinburgh
Youth Orchestra and £420 to the Salvation
Army.

Exclusions: Unsolicited applications from
individuals will not be acknowledged.

Applications: In writing to the
correspondent.

The Andrew Millar Charitable Trust

Not known

General

Thorntons, 11 Whitehall Street,
Dundee DD1 4AE
01382-229111

Correspondent: The Secretary

Beneficial area: England and Scotland.

Information available: No financial
information was available.

General: The trust gives grants to a group of
listed charities only. Unsolicited applications
will not be supported.

Applications: Applicants should note the
above.

The Miller Foundation

£50,000 a year

Animal welfare, social welfare, disability, education

c/o Maclay Murray & Spens, 151 St Vincent
Street, Glasgow G2 5NJ
0141-248 5019

Correspondent: G R G Graham

Trustees: A R Miller; C Fleming Brown;
C C Wright; G R G Graham.

Beneficial area: Mainly Scotland.

Information available: Limited
information was provided by the trust.

General: The trust gives about £50,000,
mainly to organisations based in Scotland. Its
focus is on human and animal welfare as
well as projects working with disabled
people. Educational projects are also

supported, with an emphasis on tertiary education.

Applications: In writing to the correspondent.

The Hugh & Mary Miller Bequest Trust

Not known

Disability

Maclay, Murray & Spens, 151 St Vincent Street, Glasgow G2 5NJ
0141-248 5011

Correspondent: The Secretary

Beneficial area: Scotland.

Information available: No financial information was available.

General: The trust only supports registered charities concerned with disability. No further information is available.

Applications: In writing to the correspondent. This entry has not been confirmed by the trust, although the address details are correct at time of going to press.

The Roy Miller Charitable Trust

£1,000 (1993/94)

Christian

8 Carfrae Park, Edinburgh EH4 3SP
0131-336 1480

Correspondent: Robert M M Miller

Trustees: Mrs M B Miller; R G Miller; Ms C M Miller.

Beneficial area: Unrestricted but with a preference for Scotland.

Information available: Information has been supplied by the trust. Audited accounts for the year ending 1993/94 are available.

General: The trust was formed in 1988 and for the past six years grants have been given to organisations involved in Christian work. Grants range between £40 and £500.

Beneficiaries have included Covington Parish Church of Scotland (£500) and the National Bible Society of Scotland (£40).

Exclusions: Grants are only given to organisations engaged in Christian work.

Applications: In writing to the correspondent.

The Agnes C Mongomerie Charitable Trust

Not known

Health, disability, elderly people

Charities Section, Pacific House, 70 Wellington Street, Glasgow G2 6UA
0141-248 6677

Correspondent: The Secretary

Beneficial area: Scotland.

Information available: No financial information was available.

General: The trust gives grants to charities in Scotland concerned with medical and health issues, the welfare of disabled people and of those who are elderly.

Exclusions: Grants are given to registered charities only.

Applications: In writing to the correspondent. This entry has not been confirmed by the trust, which did not wish to appear in the Guide.

The Moray & Nairn Educational Trust Scheme

£8,500 a year

Education in Moray and Nairn

Grampian Regional Council, Department of Education, Woodhill House, Westburn Road, Aberdeen AB9 2LU
01224-664664

Correspondent: Assistant Director of Education (Finance)

Beneficial area: Moray and Nairn.

Information available: Guidelines for applicants are available from the Grants Section of Grampian Regional Council.

General: Grants can normally be made only to:

- People living in the former combined county of Moray and Nairn;
- Pupils or young people attending schools or further education centres in Moray and Nairn;
- School pupils whose parents are living in Morayshire or Nairnshire;
- Moray and Nairn schools and further education centres;
- Clubs and organisations benefiting the people of Morayshire or Nairnshire.

Grants can be given for eligible applicants attending Scottish Universities, Scottish Central Institutions or Training Colleges; and for travel.

Help can be given towards special equipment for schools; adult education courses; sports facilities and school excursions. Grants total up to £8,500 a year.

Applications: Application forms are available from the correspondent. The closing date for applications is 30th September of each year.

The Stanley Morrison Charitable Trust

£66,000 (1993/94)

Sports for young people, education, general

Grant Thornton, Chartered Accountants, 112 West George Street, Glasgow G2 1QF
0141-332 7484

Correspondent: The Secretaries to the Trust

Trustees: S W Morrison; J H McKean; Mrs M E Morrison; T F O'Connell; G L Taylor; A S Dudgeon.

Beneficial area: The West Coast of Scotland, with a preference for Glasgow and Ayrshire.

Information available: Accounts for 1993/94 are available from the trust.

General: The trust's assets in 1993/94 amounted to £1.3 million generating an income of £145,000. Grants totalled £66,000, an increase of more than 100% on the previous year.

The trust states that grants are awarded to:

1. Sporting activities in Scotland, with particular emphasis on the encouragement of youth involvement.
2. Charities which have as their principal base of operation and benefit the West Coast of Scotland, and in particular the Glasgow and Ayrshire areas.
3. Those charities whose funds arise from, or whose assistance is provided to, persons having connection with the licensed trades and in particular the whisky industry.
4. Scottish educational establishments.

Grants typically range between £3,000 and £5,000 and in 1993/94 the trust funded five organisations – Ayr Rugby Football Club (£3,000), IFWLA World Cup Lacrosse 1993 (£3,000), Scottish Cricket Union (£4,650) and

Scottish Lacrosse Association (£5,000). An exceptional grant of £43,000 was awarded to Kirkoswald Parish Church.

Applications: In writing to the correspondent.

The Morriston Davies Trust

£18,000 (1993)

Research into the prevention and cure of tuberculosis

Bank of Scotland, Trustees Department, PO Box 41, 101 George Street, Edinburgh EH2 3JH
0131-442 7777

Correspondent: The Trustees

Trustees: A R Somner; I A Campbell; R D H Monie.

Beneficial area: Scotland.

Information available: Accounts for 1993 were available from the trust.

General: The trust's funds in 1993 amounted to £463,000 and £18,000 was awarded to establish the Morriston Davies Scholarship. Funds are also awarded for research and education on prevention, treatment and the cure of tuberculosis and other respiratory diseases.

Applications: In writing to the correspondent. The trust stated that it did not wish to appear in the Guide.

The James & Elizabeth Murray Charitable Trust

£4,000 (1993/94)

General

1 East Craibstone Street, Bon-Accord Square, Aberdeen AB9 1YH
01224-581581

Correspondent: James & George Collie, Solicitors

Trustees: Mrs G Murray; D G Morgan.

Beneficial area: Scotland, with a preference for Aberdeenshire.

Information available: Accounts for 1993/94 were available from the trust.

General: In 1993/94, the trust had assets of £75,000 with a net income of £3,400 after expenses.

Grants range between £500 and £2,000 and in 1993/94, beneficiaries included Grampian Tape Services for the Blind, Salvation Army, Voluntary Services Aberdeen Fuel Fund and Aberdeen Hospitals Relay Association.

Applications: In writing to the correspondent. The trustees meet annually.

Sir George Nairn's Charitable Trust

£1,000 (1992/93)

General

Ernst & Young Financial Management Ltd, George House, 50 George Square, Glasgow G2 1RR
0141-552 3456

Correspondent: Ernst & Young

Trustees: Sir M Nairn; C B Nairn; H J M Blakeney; J S Robertson.

Beneficial area: Scotland.

Information available: Accounts were available for 1992/93.

General: The trust's assets in 1992/93 totalled £11,000 and the trust's income totalled £364 after expenses. Grants totalled £1,250 (£2,000 the year before) and are awarded for general charitable purposes.

In 1992/93, grants of £250 each were given to the Cystic Fibrosis Trust, Royal National Lifeboat Institution, St Columba's Hospice, Edinburgh, St Michael's Church, Ballintium and Scottish National Institute for the Blind.

Applications: In writing to the correspondent.

The Nairne Trust

Not known

General

Thom Matthew & Co, 180 Main Street, Kilwinning KA13 6EE
01294-552545

Correspondent: The Secretary

Beneficial area: Scotland.

Information available: No financial information was available.

General: The trust supports the following named charities: Princess Louise Scottish Hospital, Scottish National Institution for the War Blinded, Orphan Homes of Scotland, Church of Scotland and British Empire Cancer Campaign.

No further information was available.

Applications: In writing to the correspondent.

The Stanley Nairne Memorial Trust

Nil (1993)

Youth

10 Mertoun Place, Edinburgh EH11 1JZ
0131-229 6049

Correspondent: Alexander Gemmill, Trustee

Trustees: D C Sinclair; I Ash; D Blaikie; Dr H Boyd; A Gemmill; A McKean; K Sinclair; Mrs P Tait; J Taylor; D Williamson; D Young.

Beneficial area: Scotland.

Information available: The information for this entry was supplied by the trust. Annual reports and accounts are available from the SSC (a Club for the Youth of Scotland) at 20 South Frederick Street, Glasgow G1 1HJ

General: Grants are rarely made but when given can be up to £1,000. In the last few years recipients have included the North Merchison Club which received a grant for equipment and the SSC which received funding for leadership training.

Applications: In writing to the correspondent. The trustees meet twice a year.

The Netherdale Trust

Not known

Not known

Pearsons WS Solicitors, 23 Alva Street, Edinburgh EH2 4PU
0131-225 4133

Correspondent: R G W Weir

Beneficial area: Not known.

Information available: No financial information available.

General: No information was available.

Applications: In writing to the correspondent. This entry has not been confirmed by the trust. The address details are correct at time of going to press.

The Network Foundation

£435,000 (1994)

Environment, human rights, peace, arts, health

BM Box 2063, London WC1 3XX

Correspondent: Vanessa Adams, Administrator

Trustees: P Boase; J S Broad; I Broad; S P Clark; C Gillett; O Gillie; M Goodwin; H MacPherson; S Robin.

Beneficial area: UK and worldwide.

Information available: Accounts are on file at the Charity Commission, but without a list of grants.

General: The income of this foundation, which does not seek applications, comes from donations by members of the associated company, the Network for Social Change Ltd, "a community of wealthy individuals seeking to realise their visions in ways that enable others". In 1994, £435,000 was awarded in grants to approximately 80 projects.

The foundation's bulletin states, "The Network as a whole has no expressed policy on the types of organisation or projects it will back. The responsibility for bringing forward applications lies with the members. Because they are a diverse group, so are the applications. However, ... Network members' interests tend to lie in smaller projects and organisations, in backing the inspired project or individual who is in a good position to create wide ripples".

There are four headings under which grants are awarded:

Peace and Preservation of the Earth
Human Rights and Solidarity
Health and Wholeness
Arts and Media.

Applications: The foundation chooses the projects it wishes to support and does not solicit applications. Unsolicited applications will not even be considered.

The New Horizons Trust

£42,000 (1994)

Projects set up by retired people

Paramount House, 290–292 Brighton Road, Croydon, Surrey CR2 6AG
0181-666 0201

Correspondent: Tony Neale, Administrator

Trustees: M Pilch; Mrs C Pilch; P Miles; T Neale; Ms K Dibley.

Beneficial area: UK.

Information available: The trust's annual report for 1993/94 was available.

General: The trust's assets amounted to £66,000 in 1993/94 (£60,000 in 1992/93), with an income of £18,000 (£8,000 in 1992/93).

Grants totalled £42,000 (£38,000 in 1992/93).

The main focus of the trust is on providing "seeding" money of up to £5,000 to projects to assist the community, initiated by retired people. Funds are available for equipment, restoration of buildings or objects, publishing reminiscences and work on environmental projects.

Typical grants range between £100 and £500 and Scottish projects supported include Pictures of Leith (£2,500), Woodside Community Laundry Aberdeen (£1,760), Aberdeen New Horizons Day Centre (£1,080), Stirling Senior Citizens' Sports (£360) and Edinburgh First Aid Course for Chinese Elderly (£355).

Exclusions: No grants for tutoring fees or travel costs. Applicants must have the signatures of 10 people, five of whom should be retired.

Applications: Application forms, leaflets and full information are available from the correspondent at the above address or from the Scottish Field Officers:

Peter Anderson, 2 Craigmount Gardens, Edinburgh EH12 8EA *(Southern Scotland)*

Graeme T G Crum, Kiscadale, Station Road, Errol, Perth PH2 7SN *(Northern Scotland)*.

The Bill & Margaret Nicol Charitable Trust

Not known

General

Messrs MacRoberts, 152 Bath Street, Glasgow G2 4TB
0141-332 9988

Correspondent: D J C MacRobert

Beneficial area: Scotland.

Information available: No financial information was available.

General: No information available.

Applications: In writing to the correspondent. The trustees do not welcome unsolicited applications, which are unlikely to receive a reply.

The 1970 Trust

£20,300 (1992/93)

General

12 St Catherine Street, Cupar, Fife KY15 4HN

Correspondent: David Rennie

Trustees: David Rennie.

Beneficial area: UK, with an interest in Scotland.

Information available: The 1992/93 accounts were provided by the trust.

General: In 1992/93, the trust had assets of £206,000, generating an income of £25,000. The trust gave grants to 33 organisations totalling £20,000. Grants ranged between £200 and £1,500.

Beneficiaries included Central Scotland Adopted Children's Support Group (£300); Paisley & District Women's Aid (£200); Scottish Women's Aid (£500); University of Glasgow (£500).

Applications: In writing to the correspondent.

The North British Hotel Trust

£196,000 (1994/95)

Disability, elderly, medical aids and equipment

1 Queen Charlotte Lane, Edinburgh EH6 6BL
0131-554 7173

Correspondent: The Secretary to the Council

Trustees: N D Beith; W G Crerar.

Beneficial area: UK with a preference for Scotland.

Information available: Information was provided by the trust.

General: The trust made grants totalling £196,000 in 1994/95. The trust focuses mainly on organisations concerned with disability and elderly people. Grants may occasionally be given for medical equipment. Grants are usually one-off and are not normally given for salaries or running costs.

Beneficiaries included Marriage Counselling Scotland (£10,000), RUKBA (£8,000) and the Salvation Army (£11,500). A total of £4,830 was awarded to various youth societies.

Exclusions: No grants to individuals.

Applications: In writing to the correspondent.

The Oil Industry Community Fund

£15,000 a year

Community groups

PO Box 185, Aberdeen AB9 8XD

Correspondent: Alex Mair, Chairman

Trustees: Representatives from the North Sea Oil industry.

Beneficial area: The Sheriffdom of Grampian, Highlands and Islands.

Information available: Information was provided by the fund.

General: Grants totalling £15,000 are awarded annually to community related groups and charitable organisations operating within the beneficial area above. Grants range between £50 and £500.

Exclusions: No grants to national charities, religious organisations or for overseas trips.

Applications: In writing to the correspondent. This entry has not been confirmed by the trust.

The Harold Oppenheim Charitable Trust

£15,000 (1993/94)

General

32 Dunbar Street, Edinburgh EH3 9BR
0131-229 8751

Correspondent: James Kearney, Trustee

Trustees: Mrs E M Oppenheim Sandelson; Mrs J P Prevezer; Mrs R S Bello; Mrs F L Arghebant; J Kearney.

Beneficial area: Unrestricted.

Information available: Accounts are available from the trust.

General: The trust had assets in 1993/94 totalling £220,000, with an income of £12,000 and administration costs of £999.

Grants totalling £15,000 were awarded to nine charitable organisations. Typical grants ranged between £250 and £4,500, with larger sums awarded to cancer organisations and the University of Edinburgh.

Applications: In writing to the correspondent.

The Meyer Oppenheim Trust

£8,700 (1992/93)

Jewish, general

KPMG, 24 Blythswood Square,
Glasgow G2 4QS
0141-226 5511

Trustees: John Craig; Philip Oppenheim; David Young.

Beneficial area: Scotland.

Information available: Accounts are available from the trust.

General: The trust has wide-ranging interests which include support for the arts, Jewish organisations, education and social welfare, and the relief of need and suffering. In 1992/93, the trust's assets totalled £118,000, generating an income of £15,000. Grants between £150 and £800 were given to 36 organisations and totalled £8,700. All but five organisations had been beneficiaries in previous years.

Beneficiaries in Scotland included Royal Scottish Academy (£500), Scottish Chamber Orchestra and Scottish Baroque Ensemble (£300 each), Edinburgh Youth Orchestra Society (£250), Edinburgh Jewish Board of Guardians, Glasgow Jewish Welfare Board, Abbeyfield Edinburgh Society, Scottish National Institution for the War Blinded, Royal Edinburgh Hospital – Professor Walton's Research Fund (£150 each).

Exclusions: The trust responds to appeals from charitable organisations only, and does not give grants to individuals.

Applications: In writing to the correspondent.

The P F Charitable Trust

£731,000 (1993/94)

General

25 Copthall Avenue, London EC2R 7DR
0171-638 5858

Correspondent: The Secretary

Trustees: Robert Fleming; Gerald J A Jamieson; Valentine P Fleming; Philip Fleming.

Beneficial area: UK, with apparent special interests in Oxfordshire and Scotland.

Information available: Accounts for 1993/94 are on file at the Charity Commission.

General: The trust in 1993/94 had assets of £9.7 million (with a market value of £24.1 million), generating an income of £1 million. It gives around 500 grants a year, which are mostly recurrent, to an extremely wide range of beneficiaries.

The trust was established in 1951 by Philip Fleming, the P F of the title. In 1983, Robert (Robin) Fleming, the son of the settlor and chairman of Robert Fleming Holdings, made further gifts which considerably enhanced the value of the trust fund.

The settlor's personal list of charities to receive annual donations (51 organisations in all) is still followed but now only represents a small part of the trust's work.

In 1993/94, the donations were categorised as shown below.

Category	£	%
Medical research	166,000	22
Hospitals and associated organisations	165,000	21
Blind and deaf	33,750	5
Animals, birds, fish etc	9,480	1
Conservation, preservation, restoration etc	84,500	12
Youth clubs, youth associations etc	16,550	2
Welfare – old folks (including housing)	17,900	2
Welfare – youth	40,150	5
Welfare – rehabilitation including specialised housing	51,150	7
Welfare – miscellaneous	71,800	10
Welfare – settlements	2,250	0.3
Welfare – housing associations	3,750	0.5
Universities, schools	20,800	3
Music, theatre, art etc	27,700	4
Miscellaneous	20,200	3

The trust does support a large number of organisations in Scotland and these demonstrate the width of the trust's interests. Over a quarter of the grants for music, theatre and the arts for example were given in Scotland. Beneficiaries included the Edinburgh International Festival Endowment Fund (£4,000), and the Scottish Museums Council and Sculpture Workshop which received £2,500 each.

Other examples under some of the above headings were:

Medical research – Alzheimer's Disease Society of Scotland (£2,500), Chest, Heart and Stroke Association in Scotland (£1,000), the Royal Hospital for Sick Children Foundation (£5,000);

Conservation – Scottish Churches Architectural Heritage Trust (£15,000);

Welfare (elderly) – Scottish Veterans' Residences (£2,500);

Welfare (youth) – Scottish Craftsmanship Association (£2,000);

Welfare (rehabilitation) – Scotability Ltd (£2,000);

Welfare (Miscellaneous) – Crossroads (£1,000), the Scottish Council on Alcohol (£500)

Miscellaneous – SCVO (£250), Mountain Rescue Committee Scotland (£500).

Exclusions: No grants to individuals or non-registered charities. Individual churches are now excluded.

Applications: To the correspondent at any time, in writing with full information. Replies will be sent to unsuccessful applications if a stamped, addressed envelope is enclosed. Trustees meet monthly.

Miss M E S Paterson's Charitable Trust

£23,500 (1993/94)

Church of Scotland churches, youth, general

Lindsays Solicitors, 11 Atholl Crescent, Edinburgh EH3 8HE
0131-229 1212

Correspondent: C S Kennedy, Trustee

Trustees: C S Kennedy; M A Noble; J A W Somerville.

Beneficial area: Scotland.

Information available: Accounts are available from the trust.

General: In 1993/94, the trust's assets totalled £470,000, generating an income of £29,000. Grants to 17 charities totalled £23,500.

Donations ranged between £500 and £3,000. Five Church of Scotland churches received grants for building repairs (£3,000 each to Kyles Parish Church and Glenorchy Church, £2,000 to Newbattle Parish Church, £1,000 each to St Monance Parish Church and Creich Parish Church).

Other beneficiaries included Holywood Trust (£1,500), University of Edinburgh Development Trust, National Trust for Scotland, Holywood Church of Scotland, Camphill Village Trust, Trefoil Centre, Scripture Union and Carlton Youth Ministry (£1,000 each) and Montrose YMCA (£500).

Applications: In writing to the correspondent.

Andrew Paton's Charitable Trust

£32,000 (1993/94)

General

190 St Vincent Street, Glasgow G2 5SP
0141-204 2833

Correspondent: Sir James B Highgate

Trustees: Sir James B Highgate;
G A Maguire; N A Fyfe.

Beneficial area: Unrestricted but with a preference for the West of Scotland.

Information available: Accounts were available for the year 1993/94.

General: The capital value of the trust in 1993/94 was £650,000 and its total annual income is £40,000. Grants totalled £32,000.

The trust gives grants for general charitable purposes and 62 were made in 1993/94. Grants ranged between £50 and £3,000, with the vast majority under £1,000. The largest grants were to the Church of Scotland Mission (£3,000), Salvation Army Special Appeal and King George V Fund for Sailors (£2,000 each) and Abbeyfield Glasgow Society (£1,250). £1,000 went to each of CRUSE, TAK Tent, St Andrews Hospice, Scottish Conservative & Unionist Agents Benevolent Funds, Salvation Army Youth Appeal and Boys Brigade Glasgow Battalion.

Grants of under £1,000 were awarded to organisations such as the Action Research for the Crippled Child, Earl Haig Fund, Eastpark Home for Infirm Children, Glasgow & West of Scotland Society for the Prevention of Cruelty to Animals, Glasgow City Mission, Save the Children Fund, Wayside Club & Day Centre, Scottish AIDS Research Appeal, Scottish Council of Cystic Fibrosis, Scottish Motor Neurone Disease Association, Scottish Society for the Mentally Handicapped, Scripture Union Scotland and SENSE.

Applications: In writing to the correspondent.

The Hyman Phillips Trust for Charities

£1,000 (1992/93)

Jewish

MacLachlan & MacKenzie, Solicitors,
8 Walker Street, Edinburgh EH3 7LH
0131-220 2226

Correspondent: Mr Crocker

Trustees: I Shein; J Cosgrove; M L Cowan.

Beneficial area: Scotland.

Information available: Accounts for 1993/94 were available from the trust.

General: In 1992/93, the trust's income after expenses totalled £2,000 and grants totalled £1,250 in the same year. No grants were awarded in 1993/94.

This small trust awards grants to Jewish charities. In 1992/93, grants ranged between £250 and £750 and beneficiaries included World Jewish Relief (£250) and Edinburgh Hebrew Congregation (£750).

Applications: In writing to the correspondent.

A M Pilkington's Charitable Trust

Not known

Not known

Drummond Cook Macintosh, 18 Crossgate,
Cupar, Fife KY15 5HT
01334-652285

Correspondent: D Scringer

Beneficial area: Not known.

Information available: No financial information was available.

General: No information available.

Applications: In writing to the correspondent. This entry has not been confirmed by the trust. The address and correspondent details are correct.

The Prince's Scottish Youth Business Trust

£129,000 (1994)

Business enterprises set up by young people

Mercantile Chambers, 6th Floor, 53 Bothwell Street, Glasgow G2 6TS
0141-248 4999

Correspondent: Evelyn McDonald, Operations Manager

Trustees: B Thornton; Sir Douglas F Hardie; A K Denholm; M Fass; D Bradley; G Benedetti; A Proctor; W Brindle; Ms A Goldie.

Beneficial area: Scotland.

Information available: An annual report for 1994 was available from the trust.

General: The trust had assets in 1994 of £5.7 million, and an income of £996,000 before expenses.

The trust states: "The aim of the Prince's Youth Business Trust is to provide seedcorn finance and professional support to 18–25 year olds in Scotland, whoever they are and wherever they come from, so that they can set up their own businesses. The Trust has particular concern for the disadvantaged."

The trust is firmly established throughout Scotland in 18 regions. Regional managers are based at local enterprise trusts and are responsible for organising training and support for the trust. In 1994, grants totalling £129,000 were awarded to young people setting up businesses. Grants usually range between £250 and £3,000. Grants awarded include £1,000 to three young women to set up a children's day nursery in Glasgow.

Exclusions: Applicants must be unemployed and of limited means and aged between 18 and 25. They should have a potentially viable business idea and be unable to raise all or part of the funding from other sources. Some businesses will not be supported.

Applications: Contact the correspondent for details of the nearest regional manager who will help with the application.

The Reid Charitable Trust

£750 (1993/94)

Churches, medical organisations

Thornhill, Cults, Aberdeen AB1 9QJ
01224-867238

Correspondent: R C B Reid

Trustees: R C B Reid; W A H Reid.

Beneficial area: Scotland.

Information available: Accounts for 1993/94 are available from the trust.

General: The trust's assets in 1993/94 totalled £26,000, with income totalling £1,400 before expenditure. Grants totalled £745 (£900 in 1992/93) and seven organisations received grants ranging between £15 and £350.

Beneficiaries included Haddo House Hall Trust (£200), Lifeline (£50), Scottish Children's League of Pity (£75), Children in Need (£30), Ampleforth Abbey OSB (£25) and Medic Alert (£15). Additionally, the Catholic Chaplaincy at the University of

Aberdeen received a grant of £350, having also received £340 in the previous year.

Applications: In writing to the correspondent.

The Riddon Trust

£15,000 (1994/95)

General

Cooper Lancaster Brewers, 33–35 Bell Street, Reigate, Surrey RH2 7AW
01737-221311

Correspondent: A B Higgs

Trustees: James Campbell; Janet Campbell.

Beneficial area: UK, with a preference for Hertfordshire and Scotland.

General: In 1994/95, the trust's income was £22,000 (which was expected to increase in future years). 46 grants between £200 and £600 were given and totalled £15,000. The trust regularly gives to the same organisations. All but three beneficiaries in 1994/95 had received a grant in the previous year.

Around a quarter of the grants were given in Hertfordshire. Scottish organisations receiving a grant included the Scottish Council for Spastics and the Fet-Lor Youth Centre.

Exclusions: Grants to registered charities only. No grants to individuals.

Applications: In writing to the correspondent in October and November. The trust's funds are fully committed, and new applications are highly unlikely to succeed.

The Robertson Charitable Trust

£2,500 (1994/95)

General

15 Atholl Crescent, Edinburgh EH3 8HA
0131-228 3777

Correspondent: Brodies Solicitors

Trustees: J H Robertson; J C Robertson.

Beneficial area: UK.

Information available: Information is available from the trustees.

General: This is a small trust with limited resources. The trustees report that over the previous two years the average donation has been around £150 to £200. There were about 15 donations in 1994/95, although this number will be increased by at least a further six grants in 1995/96. No details are available about the beneficiaries.

Applications: In writing to the correspondent.

The Robertson Trust

£3,046,000 (1994/95)

General, mostly in Scotland

50 West Nile Street, Glasgow G1 2ND
0141-248 4296; Fax: 0141-242 5333

Correspondent: Sir Lachlan Maclean Bt, Secretary

Trustees: J A R Macphail, Chairman; J J G Good; K D M Cameron; B McNeil; T M Lawrie.

Beneficial area: UK.

Information available: An annual report is available from the trust.

General: This large trust was set up in 1961. Whilst the original benefactors, the three Misses Robertsons of Cawderstanes, Berwick Upon Tweed, were alive they preferred to keep their work as anonymous as possible. (A situation no longer legally possible for a public trust in Scotland.) Investments are held in Baillie Gifford Companies and in Edrington Holdings Limited, an unlisted private company. It is believed about 90% of its shares are held by the trust.

The trust supports a complete range of charitable activity as defined by the law of Scotland. The secretary has commented that whilst the bias of spending is towards charities in Scotland the trustees feel it is important not to "close the door to any applicant" and that they want to keep their perspectives as wide as possible and do not wish "to put a restraint on people". However the secretary has also said that "the bulk of money is disbursed against a plan", that some grants are made annually and reviewed, whilst a proportion of grants are reactive.

Some of the administrative arrangements are likely to alter, not least because of the greater exposure the trust is now getting. The sheer bulk of appeals may lead to greater public definition of their aims and priorities.

This entry is based on the trust's report and accounts for 1994/95, when assets were £10.6 million and income £3.6 million. Grants totalled £3.05 million. The report notes: "In the year under review the major areas benefiting included medical research, care of the elderly, the young and the infirm, education in universities and schools, the arts, public services and the national heritage."

Major grants: The trust itself has quoted in its report/accounts a list of those five organisations receiving grants in excess of 2% of its gross income. This shows the interesting range of UK, Scottish and local organisations and the trust's conviction in their choices by making such large single

grants, rather than staggered payments. (Recurrent grants are not known at this stage though it is understood that they are made.) These grants follow, listed according to their size:

Childcare Centre (Drumchapel Opportunities) £125,000

Medical Council on Alcoholism £100,000

University of Glasgow £248,000

University of Paisley £252,000

University of Strathclyde £757,000

No further information was available for this year; the following refers to 1992/93, when a full grants list was provided.

In all, the trust gave 220 grants in 1992/93. 12 were £50,000 and more, 34 grants were between £10,000 and £49,999. Only 10 grants were under £1,000. A broad analysis of these grants showed that over half the expenditure was to organisations in Scotland. Out of a total of £2.78 million, about £1.29 million was donated to UK–wide organisations or organisations based outside Scotland. It is not possible to tell if any of the grants disbursed to UK-wide organisations were earmarked for projects in Scotland.

Predominantly money is given to organisations working for the welfare of people in need – physically, mentally and socially – or those working to trace the causes of such need.

These included 25 to 30 membership associations relating to a wide range of health/disability problems such as the British Deaf Association (as well as the Scottish Association for the Deaf). Health research grants ranged from the Arthritis and Rheumatism Research Council to the Cystic Fibrosis Research Trust and the Dermatitis Research Unit. Organisations ranged from local Samaritans bases, hospices, and victim support schemes, to family conciliation.

The trust supported *Education in Universities and Schools.* This can be totalled as £720,000 in 1992/93 with the University grants totalling £684,000. Beneficiaries included some which could as appropriately be classed as Medical Research:

- Glasgow University – Physiology £70,000, Department of Immunology £50,000, Department of Virology £35,000, Stroke £12,000, Department of Statistics £20,000, Department of Physics & Astronomy £48,000;
- Strathclyde University – Bioprocessing Technology – Food Project £7,000;
- Napier University – £40,000.

The trust also runs, and gives donations to, the Robertson Scholarship Trust (£7,000 in 1992/93). Only a handful of schools (six) were supported directly, with funds totalling £29,000, which included the Dollar Academy as well as special needs schools.

Support of *the Arts* totalled about £168,000 and was absorbed mainly by the major grant to the Piping Trust (£150,000). Other grants, though small, seemed to show a particular response to music – Royal Scottish National Orchestra (£7,500), Glasgow Royal Concert Hall (£5,000), Council for Music in Hospital and Live Music Now (£1,000 each).

The trust had not noted its grants for *Environmental* organisations in its report. Some overlap with the *Heritage* grouping (conservation of buildings and churches). They included support for the National Trust for Scotland (£27,500), the Scottish Conservation Projects Trust (£15,000), Winchester Cathedral (£10,000), International Bird Preservation Council (£4,000), Wildfowl Trust, Scottish Churches Architectural Trust, Scottish Civic Trust (£2,000 each).

A total of £57,000 was also given also to *Animal Welfare and Pet Organisations*. Beneficiaries included the Animal Health Trust (£13,000), Fund for Replacement of Animals (£12,000), and International Horse Protection League (£11,000).

NB. The Robertson Trust has been noted in other guides as giving "mainly to Christian charities". The objectives of the trust are much broader than this. The trust receives innumerable requests from church restoration projects throughout the UK. This note is to disabuse parish church councils that a large source of funding exists to assist them with their plans (only about five churches in Scotland were grant-aided by the Robertson Trust totalling £14,500 in 1992/93).

Applications: The trust has no guidelines for applicants. Medical research requests are now required to complete a basic application form. All applicants are expected to be registered charities and to send a copy of their accounts. The trustees meet six times a year.

Miss Elizabeth T Robertson's Charitable Trust

£1,000 (1993/94)

General

c/o Maclay Murray & Spens, Solicitors, 151 St Vincent Street, Glasgow G2 5NJ
0141-248 5011

Correspondent: G R G Graham

Trustees: Miss E T Robertson; B P MacLellan.

Beneficial area: Scotland.

Information available: Information was supplied by the trust, but no accounts were available.

General: The trust awards grants to a range of organisations, including those which are charitable, cultural, educational, religious and concerned with welfare and the relief of poverty.

No further information was available other than that grants totalled £1,000 in 1993/94.

Applications: In writing to the correspondent.

The Rosemount Trust

About £3,500 a year

Conservation and wildlife

c/o Biggart Baillie & Gifford, 11 Glenfinlas Street, Edinburgh EH3 6YY
0131-226 5541

Correspondent: Mrs C A Mackenzie

Beneficial area: Worldwide but with a preference for the UK.

Information available: Information was supplied by the trust.

General: This trust has an income of about £3,500 a year.

Grants typically range between £100 and £400 and beneficiaries have included the Worldwide Wildlife Fund, Scottish Wildlife Trust and British Trust for Ornithology.

Applications: In writing to the correspondent.

The Hector Gordon Russell Trust

£20,000 (1993/94)

Air force charities, young people, general

Henderson & Co, Chartered Accountants, 73 Union Street, Greenock PA16 8BG
01475-720202

Correspondent: R T Henderson

Trustees: D Caldwell; D R Fairbairn; R T Henderson.

Beneficial area: Scotland.

Information available: Information is available from the correspondent.

General: The trust had assets totalling £123,000 in 1993/94, generating an income of £29,000.

The trust supports causes related to the Highlands of Scotland, the RAF and youth organisations and organisations in Inverness, Greenock and Campbeltown.

In 1993/94, the trust awarded £20,000 to charitable organisations including Erskine Hospital and Greenock Medical Aid Society (£1,000 each), and Campbeltown Sea Cadets and Polish Air Force Association in Great Britain (£500 each).

Applications: In writing to the correspondent.

The Andrew Salvesen Charitable Trust

£30,000 (1994)

General

c/o Meston Reid & Co, 40 Carden Place, Aberdeen AB1 1UP
01224-625554

Correspondent: Mark Brown

Trustees: A C Salvesen; Ms K Turner; V Lall.

Beneficial area: UK, especially Scotland.

Information available: Accounts for 1994 were supplied by the trust.

General: In 1994, the trust had assets of £613,000, and a net income of £150,000.

The trust makes grants to a range of charitable organisations and in 1994, £30,000 was awarded. Organisations receiving over £1,000 were Royal Zoological Society of Scotland (£7,500), Sick Kids Appeal (£5,000), Bield Housing Trust and Scottish Down's Syndrome Association (£3,500 each), Sail Training Association (£3,000), Multiple Sclerosis Society in Scotland (£2,400) and

William Higgins Marathon Account (£1,500). A number of miscellaneous distributions were also made, totalling £4,000.

Applications: Applications are not invited.

Mr & Mrs John Salvesen's Charitable Trust

£9,000 (1994/95)

General

Messrs Dundas & Wilson, Saltire Court, 20 Castle Terrace, Edinburgh EH1 2EN

Trustees: J I McC Salvesen; Mrs A M Salvesen; D A Connell.

Beneficial area: Unrestricted, but with a preference for Scotland.

Information available: Accounts for 1994/95 are available.

General: The trust's funds totalled £102,000 in 1994/95. Grants totalled £8,500 and ranged between £500 and £5,000.

Beneficiaries were the Royal Scottish Agricultural Benevolent Institution (£500), Scottish Children's Hospice (£2,000), Antony Nolan Bone Marrow Trust (£1,000) and Edinburgh Festival Theatre Trust (£5,000).

Applications: In writing to the correspondent.

Mrs M H Salvesen's Charitable Trust

Not known

Not known

Murray Beith & Murray WS, 39 Castle Street, Edinburgh EH2 3BH
0131-225 1200

Correspondent: William Murray

Beneficial area: Not known.

Information available: See below.

General: No information available. This trust offered to provide a copy of the accounts on payment of a fee. As the number of trusts in this book would have made payment on each set of accounts prohibitive, the offer was declined, and no further information is available on the activities of this trust.

Applications: In writing to the correspondent.

The John Scott Trust

£43,000 (1993/94)

General

63 Loudoun Road, Newmilns, Ayrshire KA16 9HG
01560-320092

Correspondent: John D Scott

Trustees: J D Scott.

Beneficial area: Scotland.

Information available: Accounts were provided by the trust.

General: The trust's assets were £374,000 in 1993/94 and grants totalled £43,000. The trust supports general charitable purposes.

Grants ranged between £500 and £10,000 and 15 organisations benefited, including Salvation Army, Barnardo's and Hansel Village (£5,000 each), Dumfries Area Scout Council (£2,000), Nith Inshore Rescue, WRCS and Tom Allan Centre (£1,000 each), and Ayrshire Fiddle Orchestra and Summerhill Youth Club (£500 each). The largest grant of £10,000 was awarded to the National Trust for Scotland.

Applications: Applications are not invited.

Mrs Elizabeth Scott's Charitable Trust

£10,000 (1993/94)

General

c/o Neill Clerk & Murray, Solicitors,
3 Ardgowan Square, Greenock PA16 8NG
01475-724522

Correspondent: D I Banner

Trustees: Miss J K Edgar; D I Banner;
D R Macdonald.

Beneficial area: Unrestricted but with a preference for the West of Scotland.

Information available: Accounts were provided by the trust.

General: The trust had assets of £135,000 in 1993/94. Grants, ranging between £250 and £1,000, totalled £10,000 and were awarded to 15 organisations. These included Alzheimer's Scotland, Intermediate Technology and Oxfam Indian Appeal (£1,000 each), Ark, Scottish Society for the Prevention of Cruelty to Animals, Borderline, Victim Support and Simon Community (£500 each) and Francis Gay Sunday Post Coal Fund (£250).

Applications: In writing to the correspondent. Distributions are made in June and December of each year and exceptionally at other times.

The Scottish Chartered Accountants' Trust for Education

£42,000 (1994)

Education and research into accountancy

27 Queen Street, Edinburgh EH2 1LA
0131-225 5673

Correspondent: A G Guest

Trustees: D A S Gellatly; M J Gilbert;
R A Johnson; T D Lynch; L L McAllister;
P C Millar; F F Kidd; J B Cowan;
J M Haldane; H M M Johnston; C H Ross;
I M Stubbs.

Beneficial area: UK.

Information available: Accounts for 1994 and an outline of the trust's policies are available from the trust.

General: The trust's assets were £927,000 in 1992/93, with an income of £84,000. The trust awards grants for:

- Research conferences organised by the Scottish Institute and for related publications.
- Research into teaching methods for the accountancy profession.
- Research on accounting and related subjects as well as other research projects relevant to the profession.
- Visits by academics to give addresses to members of the institute and students.
- Visits by practitioners from overseas to participate in the institute's educational programme.

In 1994, grants totalled £42,000 with a further £42,000 committed at the end of the year, and ranged between £550 and £23,000. They included £23,000 to the Institute of Chartered Accountants of Scotland as part of a commitment of £100,000 over two years to meet the costs of an international research adviser and a professorial research fellow, with further grants ranging between £550 and £2,000 towards the cost of various programmes of research, £1,500 to Edinburgh University towards the publishing costs of a booklet on the history of the Department of Accounting and Business Method, and £2,000 to provide scholarships for Scottish accountancy academics to attend conferences overseas.

Applications: Further information is available from the correspondent.

The Scottish Churches Architectural Heritage Trust

£80,000 (1994)

Scottish church buildings

15 North Bank Street, The Mound,
Edinburgh EH1 2LP
0131-225 8644

Correspondent: Mrs Florence Mackenzie, Director

Trustees: Lord Ross, Chairman; remaining trustees to be confirmed.

Beneficial area: Scotland.

Information available: Information was provided by the trust.

General: The trust was established "to care for Scottish church buildings in use for public worship, principally by raising funds for their repair and restoration and by acting as a source of technical advice and assistance on maintenance and repair".

In 1994, the trust had assets of £466,000 and an income of £113,000 including £75,000 in donations. Grants totalled £80,000.

Geographically, benefiting churches ranged from Scarista, Isle of Harris to Kirkcudbright in Galloway, and from Crimond in Aberdeenshire to Kilfinan in Argyll. Grants were made to 42 churches: 28 Church of Scotland, five Scottish Episcopal Churches, two Free Church of Scotland and seven to churches of other denominations including Methodist, Independent, Evangelical Union Congregational and one synagogue. Grants ranged from £500 to £5,000. The current average grant is £2,000 per church which "is usually a very small fraction of its expenditure on repairs". Specific projects included steeple and stonework repairs, rot and damp eradication, windows and stained glass repairs, and roof repairs.

Applications: In writing to the correspondent, after which an application form will be sent. The grants committee meets four times a year.

The Scottish Disability Foundation

Not known

Disability

Royal Bank of Scotland, 42 St Andrew Square, Edinburgh EH2 2YE
0131-556 8555

Correspondent: The Honorary Secretary and Treasurer

Beneficial area: Scotland.

Information available: No financial information was available.

General: The foundation supports the prevention of all forms of disability. Grants are given to organisations working in the field of disability to help improve services for disabled people in Scotland.

Applications: In writing to the correspondent. This entry has not been confirmed by the trust. The address details are correct at time of going to press.

The Scottish Homoeopathic Research & Education Trust

£27,000 (1991)

Homoeopathy and related sciences

Royal Bank of Scotland, 98 Buchanan Street, Glasgow G1 3BA
0141-942 1678

Correspondent: D McVicar

Trustees: W McL Cameron; Dr H MacNeill; M G Taylor; Dr R G Gibson; R G Hood; Dr R H Baxendale; Dr A D MacNeill; Dr D T Reilly; J McKechnie; C J Davison; B B Morrison; Miss M A Shields; Dr H W Boyd; W A Cuthbertson.

Beneficial area: UK, with a preference for Scotland.

Information available: Information was available for 1991.

General: In 1991, the trust had assets totalling £183,000, generating an income of £25,000. Grants totalled £27,000.

Grants are awarded to organisations undertaking research into homoeopathy, promoting homoeopathic education and producing publications relating to homoeopathy.

Applications: In writing to the correspondent. This entry has not been confirmed by the trust.

The Scottish Hospital Endowments Research Trust

£1,141,000 (1993/94)

Medical research

W & J Burness, 16 Hope Street, Charlotte Square,
Edinburgh EH2 4DD
0131-226 2561

Correspondent: W & J Burness, Secretaries to the Trust

Beneficial area: Scotland.

Information available: Information was available for 1993/94.

General: The Scottish Hospital Endowments Research Trust (SHERT) was set up by parliament in 1953 to distribute grants and bequests for medical research in Scotland. SHERT is an independent body and its members, appointed by the Secretary of State for Scotland, have the assistance of expert panels of advisers. Members exercise a large measure of autonomy in reaching their decisions about which Scottish biomedical researchers should receive support.

Grants are awarded from money held in the original trust fund augmented by later bequests and donations, together with money raised by SHERT's own fundraising arm, the Scottish Medical Research Fund.

The trust's assets in 1993/94 totalled £11.4 million generating an income of £1.1 million. Grants totalling £1.14 million were given to support Scottish biomedical research. Awards normally take the form of:

- Scholarships and fellowships
- Funds for individual or group research
- Capital grants
- Travel grants
- Grants for visitors.

Exclusions: Grants are only for projects carried out in Scotland.

Applications: Contact the correspondent for further information.

The Scottish Housing Associations Charitable Trust (SHACT)

£60,000 (1994/95)

Housing associations or housing related projects in Scotland

38 York Place, Edinburgh EH1 3HU
0131-556 5777

Correspondent: Alison Campbell, Trust Administrator

Trustees: Andrew Robertson; Ronald Ironside; David Harley; Harry Mulligan; Gavin McCrone; Anne Yanetta; Susan Torrance; Paul Farrell; Robert McDowall; Margaret Richards; David Chalmers.

Beneficial area: Scotland.

Information available: The charity produces an application form and guidance notes for applicants.

General: SHACT was set up in 1979. It exists to support the voluntary housing movement in Scotland. It gives grants and loans to housing associations and other voluntary organisations in the following general categories:

- Homelessness with emphasis on young homeless people.
- People with special needs including those with physical, mental health or learning difficulties.
- Older people.
- Care and repair charitable funds – for small repairs and to top up grant-aided work.
- Projects in rural areas.
- Projects to benefit people of ethnic minorities.
- Community regeneration projects run by housing associations or co-operatives.
- Research into Scotland's housing problems and solutions.
- Training for voluntary committee members.

In 1993/94 committed grants were broken down as follows:

Homelessness: £12,600 (26%) including support for Aberdeen Cyrenians, the Big Issue and the Scottish Youth Housing Network.

Elderly people: £9,600 (19%) including support for Lorne Social Centre (Leith), Partick Housing Association and Central Buchan Care & Repair.

Special needs: £3,700 (8%) including support for Moncrieff Terrace Neighbourhood Support Association and Special Needs Housing Conference.

Training: £800 (2%) to two housing associations.

Rural projects: £11,500 (24%) including support for Nithsdale Housing Advice Service, Orkney H A Low Energy Project and Western Isles Women's Aid.

Ethnic minorities: £2,000 (4%) to Dundee Asian Housing Forum.

Community regeneration: £8,300 (17%) including grants to Community Self-Build Scotland and Portree Self-Build Initiative.

Although SHACT is a separate trust with its own criteria, it can refer applications to the Housing Associations Charitable Trust (HACT), for which there is a separate entry.

Exclusions: Grants or loans will not be made to individuals, large national organisations except for specific projects or large general appeals.

Applications: The trustees meet four times a year and all applications will be acknowledged. Applicants are encouraged to telephone the Administrator beforehand for a general discussion about their proposal.

The Scottish International Education Trust

£74,000 (1994)

Education, the arts, economic and social welfare

22 Manor Place, Edinburgh EH3 7DS
0131-225 1113

Correspondent: John F McClellan

Trustees: J D Houston, Chairman; W Menzies Campbell; Sean Connery; Sir Samuel Curran; Sir Alastair Dunnett;

Alexander Goudie; Sir Norman Graham; Andy Irvine; Prof Alistair Macfarlane; Kenneth McKellar; Jackie Stewart.

Beneficial area: Scotland.

Information available: A brochure is available from the trust.

General: In 1994, the trust had assets totalling £1.2 million, generating an income of £84,000. Grants totalled £74,000.

The trust gives grants to organisations and individuals contributing to the cultural, economic and social development of Scotland. Grants range from £150 to £6,000 and beneficiaries have included the Royal Scottish Academy of Music and Drama.

Exclusions: No grants to commercial organisations.

Applications: In writing to the correspondent.

The Scottish Slimmers Charitable Trust

£25,000 (1994)

Poverty, education, health

11 Bon Accord Square, Aberdeen AB1 2DJ
01224-212070

Correspondent: Avis Lewis, Charitable Trust Manager & Trustee

Trustees: J L Reid; Ms C H Polson; Mrs A W Lewis.

Beneficial area: UK, with a preference for Scotland.

Information available: An information leaflet is available.

General: This trust's income is raised purely from fundraising events. In 1994, the trust raised over £50,000 (£25,000 in 1993). In recent years the trust's support has focused on large national healthcare charities such as the Cancer Relief Macmillan Fund, Breakthrough Breast Cancer and the British Heart Foundation. However, Crossroads Dundee and Scottish hospices such as Strathcarron Hospice in Denny, Ayrshire Hospice and Inverness Highland Hospice have also been supported.

Amounts vary but are usually to a maximum of £500.

Exclusions: Grants are not awarded to animal charities nor to overseas organisations.

Applications: In writing to the correspondent.

The Charles Neil Sharp Charity Trust

£2,000 (1993)

Poverty, young people

1–3 Wyvern Park, The Grange, Edinburgh EH9 2JY
0131-662 4145

Correspondent: William McDonald

Trustees: H McMichael; W McDonald; R D Fulton; C M Sharp.

Beneficial area: UK, with a preference for Scotland.

Information available: A copy of the trust's annual report and accounts is available from the correspondent.

General: The trust's assets amounted to £18,000 in 1993 with £1,600 given in grants.

Grants range between £50 and £100 and beneficiaries have included Barnardo's, Scout Association, RSPCC, Christian Aid, Royal National Lifeboat Institution and Marie Curie Foundation.

Applications: In writing to the correspondent.

The George Sinclair Charitable Trust

£2,000 (1994/95)

Christian

48 St Quivox Road, Prestwick KA9 1LU
01292-478625

Correspondent: Mrs Jean Sinclair

Trustees: Mrs J Sinclair; G Voysey; W Clark.

Beneficial area: UK, with a preference for Scotland.

Information available: Accounts were available from the trust.

General: The trust distributed £2,160 in 1994/95 amongst charitable organisations with a Christian bias. Grants ranged between £20 and £1,840 and the beneficiaries were Kyle Community Church (£1,840), WEC International (£130), Mark Ministries (£80), Navigators (£60), Latin Link (£30) and Care – Scotland (£20).

Applications: Applications are not invited.

The Society in Scotland for Propagating Christian Knowledge

£7,000 (1990)

Church of Scotland, missionary work

Tods Murray, 66 Queen Street, Edinburgh EH2 4NE
0131-226 4771

Correspondent: The Trustees

Beneficial area: UK with a preference for Scotland.

General: The organisation had assets of £65,000 and an income totalling £8,000 in 1990. Grants totalled £7,000 and support has been given to missions in the Highlands and Islands and work of the church of Scotland. Many grants are already committed.

Applications: In writing to the correspondent. This entry has not been confirmed by the trust. The address and correspondent details are correct.

The Souter Foundation

£316,000 (1993)

Christianity, third world, social welfare

21 Auld House Wynd, Perth PH1 1RG
01738-634745

Correspondent: Linda Scott, Secretary

Trustees: Brian Souter; Elizabeth Souter; Linda Scott.

Beneficial area: UK with a preference for Scotland; developing countries.

Information available: The latest annual report and accounts are available from the correspondent.

General: In 1992 and 1993 the trust's funds showed a large increase owing to receipt of donations of £658,000 worth of shares in Stagecoach Holdings plc from Brian Souter, one of the trustees. In 1993, the trust's income stood at £670,000, and a surplus of £352,000 was carried over after donations had been made.

Three major grants were made in 1993 to the Church of the Nazarene (£218,000), the SBAAT Awards (£20,000) and the Scottish Offenders Project (£15,000). Donations totalling £4,000 were also made for the benefit of individuals.

In the 1992, the trust's grant-making reflected a wide range of interests including the third world, Eastern Europe and social welfare in Scotland.

Applications: Applicants should apply in writing, setting out a brief outline of the project for which funding is sought. Trustees meet quarterly.

Miss D R Spalding's Charitable Trust

£4,000 (1993/94)

General

22 Meadowside, Dundee DD1 1LN
01382-201534

Correspondent: The Secretary

Trustees: Miss D R Spalding; T I Spalding; A McDougall.

Beneficial area: Unknown.

Information available: The information for this entry is based on the trust's latest annual report and accounts.

General: This trust was set up by Miss Daphne Rosemary Spalding in 1980. No details of grant-making are available.

Applications: The trust stated that no applications will be considered or acknowledged and that it did not wish to appear in the Guide.

The Sportsman's Charity

£40,000 (1992/93)

General

30 Murrayfield Road, Edinburgh EH12 6ER

Correspondent: John Frame

Trustees: J Frame; D McLean; A Cubie.

Beneficial area: UK.

Information available: Accounts for 1992/93 were available from the charity.

General: The charity was established in 1983 to raise money for distribution to charitable organisations throughout the UK. The charity's net assets only totalled £1,667 in 1992/93 (£2,658 in 1991/92), so the majority of its income seems to be from fundraising activities especially the annual dinner.

Support is given to:

- Organisations which are less well known, do not have a professional fundraising capacity and need assistance.
- Charities where members have successfully achieved their charity's purpose either in establishing the organisation or in completing a particular project.
- Organisations nominated by speakers at the Sportsman's Charity annual dinner.
- Charities which can provide suitable items for auction at the above dinner.
- Groups working for disadvantaged people, especially children.
- Organisations promoting sport for disabled people.

Grants totalling £40,000 in 1992/93 were made to a range of charities including Clyde Cruising Club, Craigroyston Community High School Field Trip programme, Drum Riding Centre for the Disabled, Endeavour Scotland, Myelin Project and Salvation Army Christmas Cheer programme.

Other Scottish organisations supported in the past include Edinburgh Walk in Numeracy Centre, Highland Hospice, Lothian Federation of Boys' Clubs, Scottish Adoption Association, Scottish Association for the Deaf, Scottish Council for Spastics, Scottish Disabled Sailors Association, Scottish Dyslexia Trust Appeal, Scottish Society for Autistic Children, Scottish Spina Bifida Fund.

Exclusions: Running costs are not funded.

Applications: In writing to the correspondent, with details of the organisation's aims and a breakdown of costs. This entry has not been confirmed by the trust.

The Springboard Charitable Trust

£3,400 (1993/94)

Young people, general

38 Suffolk Street, Helensburgh G84 9PD
01436-673326

Correspondent: Colin E Shannon

Trustees: C E Shannon; A M M Shannon.

Beneficial area: UK.

Information available: Information was provided by the trust.

General: Grants are awarded to organisations in the UK to further individual achievement by young people and to voluntary organisations undertaking general charitable work relating to individuals.

In 1994, a total of £3,400 was awarded to voluntary organisations for individuals. Grants range between £100 to £500.

Exclusions: The trust does not give grants to individuals for expeditions, the arts, second degree courses or to disabled people over 25 years of age or to overseas students. Exceptions are however sometimes made in certain circumstances. Expeditions are supported by a grant made to the Royal Scottish Geographical Society to whom applications should be made (Scottish groups only). Arts are supported by a grant to the Royal Scottish Academy of Music and Drama to whom applications should be made.

Applications: In writing to the correspondent.

The Spurgin Charitable Trust

£4,000 (1991)

Social welfare

Finlaystone, Langbank,
Renfrewshire PA14 6TJ

Correspondent: G G MacMillan

Trustees: G G MacMillan; Mrs L C Richardson.

Beneficial area: Scotland.

Information available: Accounts were on file at the Charity Commission up to 1988.

General: The trust had assets totalling £73,000 in 1991, generating an income of £7,600. Grants, which totalled £3,500, were awarded to social welfare organisations in Scotland. Both recurrent and one-off grants are awarded.

Applications: In writing to the correspondent.

The Hugh Stenhouse Foundation

£25,000

General

Lomynd, Knockbuckle Road,
Kilmalcolm PA13 4JT
01505-872716

Correspondent: P D Bowman, Secretary and Treasurer

Beneficial area: Preference for the West of Scotland.

Information available: No financial information other than the grant total.

General: The trust gives grants for general charitable purposes totalling £25,000. There is no further information about the size of grant or the type of beneficiary.

Applications: In writing to the correspondent, although applicants should note that most of the trust's funds are committed until at least the summer of 1996.

The Rennie Stenhouse Foundation

Not known

Not known

Lomynd, Knockbuckle Road, Kilmacolm PA13 4JT
01505-872716

Correspondent: P D Bowman, Secretary

Beneficial area: Not known.

Information available: No financial information available.

General: No information available.

Applications: In writing to the correspondent. This entry has not been confirmed by the trust.

Miss Margaret J Stephen's Charitable Trust

£6,000 (1993/94)

General

Maclay Murray & Spens, 151 St Vincent Street, Glasgow G2 5NJ
0141-248 3019

Correspondent: The Secretary

Trustees: P J R Miller; G R G Graham.

Beneficial area: UK and Scotland with a preference for Dundee.

Information available: Accounts for 1993/94 are available from the trust.

General: The trust's capital totalled £79,000 in 1993/94 and income amounted to £9,000. The total amount awarded to charitable organisations was £6,000.

The trust supports charitable, cultural, educational, religious or welfare organisations, organisations working to relieve poverty and those concerned with disadvantaged groups.

In 1993/94, grants of £1,000 were awarded to the Chest Heart & Stroke Association, Crossroads in Dundee and Red Cross in Dundee, and grants of £500 each went to City of Dundee Girl Guides Campsite Fund, Cue and Review, Dundee School Exchange for Muscular Dystrophy, Good Shepherd Sisters, Scottish Council on Alcohol and Tayside Mountain Rescue Association.

Applications: In writing to the correspondent.

The Govan Stewart Trust

£2,000 (1993/94)

Christian charities

58 Frederick Street, Edinburgh EH2 1LS
0131-225 8291

Correspondent: J M Hodge

Trustees: J M Hodge; K H Percival; A A Moynan; E Scott; Mrs I Monihan.

Beneficial area: Scotland.

Information available: Information was available from the trust.

General: The trust was set up by the late Mrs I Govan Stewart to provide a home for retired Christian workers. It has a small income which is used to maintain the house and make small grants.

Grants totalled £2,000 in 1993/94 and ranged from £200 to £2,000. Bethany Christian Trust, Japan Evangelistic Band and Faith Mission Workers each received £500.

Exclusions: Support is usually given to those organisations which are closely associated with the late Mrs Govan Stewart.

Applications: The trustees generally seek out organisations in which they have an interest. However, special applications should be made in writing to the correspondent.

The Sir Ian Stewart Foundation

Not known

Not known

Pearsons WS, 23 Alva Street, Edinburgh EH2 4PU
0131-225 4133

Correspondent: P C H Younie WS

Beneficial area: Not known.

Information available: No financial information available.

General: No information available.

Applications: In writing to the correspondent. This entry has not been confirmed by the trust. The address and correspondent details are correct.

The Alexander Stone Foundation

Not known

Not known

36 Renfield Street, Glasgow G2 1LU
0141-332 8611

Correspondent: Robert Black, Administrator

Beneficial area: Not known.

Information available: No financial information available.

General: No information available.

Applications: In writing to the correspondent. This entry has not been confirmed by the trust. The address and correspondent details are correct.

Mr & Mrs W G Strang's Charitable Trust

£2,000 (1994/95)

General

c/o Maclay Murray & Spens, 151 St Vincent Street, Glasgow G2 5NJ
0141-248 5011

Correspondent: The Trustees

Trustees: W G Strang; S M L Strang; M G Strang; G R G Graham.

Beneficial area: Unrestricted, with a preference for Scotland.

General: The trust's income totalled £3,000 in 1994/95 and the value of the trust's stocks and shares totalled £61,000.

Grants, which totalled £2,000, were given to a wide range of charitable causes and ranged from £50 to £100. Beneficiaries included Bearsden Company Boys Brigade, Bearsden North Church of Scotland, Christian Aid, Dumbarton Girl Guides, Earl Haig Fund, Erskine Hospital, Glasgow City Mission, Imperial Cancer Research, Multiple Sclerosis Society in Scotland, Royal Blind Asylum, Royal Commonwealth Society for the Blind, Salvation Army and Scripture Union.

Applications: In writing to the correspondent.

The Joan Strutt Charitable Trust

Not known

Not known

Bocker Robertson, 50 Albany Street,
Edinburgh EH1 3QR
0131-539 7720

Correspondent: A McDougall

Beneficial area: Not known.

Information available: No financial information available.

General: No information available.

Applications: In writing to the correspondent. This entry has not been confirmed by the trust. The address and correspondent details are correct.

The Sunflower Trust

£33,000 (1993/94)

Mental health

Messrs Dundas & Wilson, Saltire Court,
20 Castle Terrace, Edinburgh EH1 2EN

Correspondent: The Secretary

Trustees: Mrs S M Rankin; J Fenston;
I R Clark.

Beneficial area: Scotland.

Information available: Accounts for 1993/94 are available from the trust.

General: In 1993/94, grants totalled £33,000. Grants typically range between £200 and £300. Although most grants are awarded to individuals with mental health problems attending therapy sessions or clinics, one grant of £15,000 was made to the Discovery Foundation.

Applications: In writing to the correspondent.

The Verden Sykes Trust

£13,300 (1994)

See below

20 Forvie Circle, Bridge of Don,
Aberdeen AB22 8TA
01224-704907

Correspondent: Mrs Irene Merrilees, Administrator

Trustees: R Ellis; N Wilson; A J Winfield;
Rev J R McLaren; Mrs I Merrilees;
Mrs A McCallum; Mrs P G Robbie.

Beneficial area: UK with a preference for Scotland.

General: In 1994, the trust's assets totalled £185,000, generating an income of £16,000. Grants totalled £13,350. The trust has a wide brief and supports:

- Churches and Christian missions
- Religious education and music
- Education for children and adults
- Work with young people
- The welfare of the elderly and those who are infirm
- Scientific research into disease and physical and mental disability
- The relief of poverty and the effects of natural disaster in any part of the world
- Pensions to retired ministers.

In 1994, grants, ranging from £250 to £2,000, were given to charities such as Cornerstone Community Care (£2,500), Voluntary Service Association and Scottish Congregational College Bursary (£2,000 each), Scottish Down's Syndrome Association and Scottish Congregational Ministers' Central Pension Scheme (£1,500 each), Shelter and Aberlour Child Care Trust (£1,000 each), International

Voluntary Service – Aberdeen Workcamp (£500) and TEAR Fund (£200).

Exclusions: Normally to registered charities only.

Applications: On a form available from the correspondent.

The T C Charitable Trust

£10,000 (1993/94)

Education, general

KPMG, 24 Blythswood Square,
Glasgow G2 4QS
0141-226 5511

Correspondent: The Secretary

Trustees: D G Coughtrie; R J Thomson; W J M Kinnear.

Beneficial area: Scotland.

Information available: Accounts for 1993/94 are supplied by the trust.

General: In 1993/94, the trust had assets totalling £171,000. Grants totalled £10,000.

The trust gives priority to education as well as supporting general charitable purposes. In 1993/94, two organisations were supported: Northern Sinfonia (£2,000) and Laurel Bank School in Glasgow (£8,000).

Exclusions: No grants for individuals.

Applications: In writing to the correspondent.

Talteg Ltd

£92,000 (1992)

Jewish, welfare

90 Mitchell Street, Glasgow G1 3NQ
0141-221 3353

Correspondent: F S Berkeley

Trustees: F S Berkeley; M Berkeley; A Berkeley; A N Berkeley; M Berkeley; Miss D L Berkeley.

Beneficial area: UK, with a preference for Scotland.

Information available: Full accounts are on file at the Charity Commission.

General: In 1992, the trust had an income of £175,000 including £134,000 in covenants and Gift Aid payments. Grants totalled only £92,000. The trust is building up its assets which stood at £514,000.

48 grants were made, of which 34, including the larger grants, were to Jewish organisations. The British Friends of Laniado Hospital received £30,000, and £20,000 was given to both the Centre for Jewish Studies and the Society of Friends of the Torah. Other grants over £1,000 were to JPAIME (£6,000), Glasgow Jewish Community Trust (£5,000), National Trust for Scotland (£2,250) and the Friends of Hebrew University of Jerusalem (£1,000).

The remaining grants, all under £1,000, included several to Scottish charities such as Ayrshire Hospice (£530), Earl Haig Fund – Scotland (£200) and RSSPCC (£150). Others went to welfare charities, with an unusual grant of £775 to Golf Fanatics International.

Applications: In writing to the correspondent. This entry has not been confirmed by the trust, as the correspondent did not wish it to appear in the Guide.

The Tarnie Trust

£35,000

Social welfare, churches, general

45 Charlotte Square, Edinburgh EH2 4HW
0131-226 3271

Correspondent: James Ivory

Trustees: James Ivory; Bridget Thomson.

Beneficial area: UK, with a preference for Scotland.

Information available: The information for this entry was supplied by the trust.

General: This trust makes grants ranging from £100 to £5,000 and recently donations were made for a church minister's accommodation, parish functions, work with people with alcohol problems and organisations concerned with abuse.

Exclusions: Grants are not made to major appeals which are more appropriately funded by other sources.

Applications: In 1995, the trust's income was fully committed for the next five years. Applications for the year 2001 may be sent to the correspondent.

The Tay Charitable Trust

£49,000 (1993/94)

General

Holly Hill, 69 Dundee Road, Broughty Ferry, Dundee DD5 1NA
01382-779148

Correspondent: Ian C Low

Trustees: I C Low; Ms E A Mussen; G C Bonar.

Beneficial area: Great Britain, with a preference for Scotland and, within Scotland, a preference for Tayside.

Information available: The information for this entry was supplied by the trust.

General: In 1993/94, the trust's assets were £690,000 (£357,000 in 1992/93). The income was £48,000, the same as in 1992/93.

Grants totalled £49,000 and ranged from £100 to £3,000. The largest grants were to the

National Trust for Scotland (£2,000) and RNLI (£3,000).

Exclusions: Grants are only given to recognised charities.

Applications: In writing to the correspondent providing full financial information.

Tenovus–Scotland

£203,000 (1994/95)

Medical research

232 St Vincent Street, Glasgow G2 5RJ
0141-221 6268

Correspondent: E R Read, General Secretary

Trustees: The Committee.

Beneficial area: Scotland.

Information available: The information for this entry was supplied by the trust.

General: In 1994/95, the organisation had a gross income of £194,000. Administration costs were £25,600, and grants totalled £203,000. In addition, a further £156,000 had been approved for future projects.

Grants are given exclusively in Scotland for high quality projects in any area of medical and dental research. Applications from junior research workers and for innovative projects are particularly encouraged.

There are four regional committees; Aberdeen, Dundee, Edinburgh and Glasgow, with two district committees in Lanark and Paisley. The regional committees are responsible for raising their own funds which are allocated locally, subject only to each research project being approved by an Independent Scientific Advisory Committee.

Exclusions: Grants are only awarded to individuals who are members of approved research institutions.

Applications: Application forms are available from the correspondent.

The Len Thomson Charitable Trust

£30,000 (1993/94)

Young people, local projects, medical research

Messrs Dundas & Wilson, Saltire Court, 20 Castle Terrace, Edinburgh EH1 2EN
0131-228 8000

Correspondent: The Secretary

Trustees: D A Connell; Mrs E Thomson; S Leslie.

Beneficial area: Scotland.

Information available: Accounts for 1993/94 are available from the trust.

General: In 1993/94, the trust's funds totalled £493,000 (£240,000 in 1992/93). Grants totalled £30,000.

The trust is keen to support projects involving young people, local communities and organisations undertaking medical research. Grants, which ranged between £1,000 and £15,000, were given to Newtongrange Parish Church (£1,000), Girls' Brigade (£2,000), the Radiation Oncology Endowment Fund at Lothian Health Board (£5,000), Save the Children Fund (£7,000) and Youth Clubs, Scotland (£15,000).

Applications: In writing to the correspondent.

The Scott Thomson Charitable Trust

£16,000 (1993/94)

Relief of poverty, education, Christian religion

R Scott Thomson, Chartered Accountant, 36 Norwood Drive, Glasgow G46 7LS
0141-638 0960

Correspondent: R Scott Thomson

Trustees: R H Craig; R Scott Thomson; Ms M B Thomson.

Beneficial area: Scotland.

Information available: Accounts are available for 1993/94.

General: In 1993/94, grants totalled £16,000 and were awarded to organisations concerned with the relief of poverty, the advancement of education and the Christian religion. No further information is available.

Applications: In writing to the correspondent. This entry has not been confirmed by the trust.

The Tibbermore Charitable Trust

£12,000 (1993/94)

General

Methven Castle, Perth PH1 3SU
01738-840536

Correspondent: K L S Murdoch

Trustees: J Nwen; R Blake; D Noble.

Beneficial area: UK with a preference for Perth.

General: The trust has capital of £12,000. Funds are retained to restore the former

Church of Scotland, Tibbermore. However, concerts are held in Methven Castle, raising money for organisations such as Save the Children, Scottish Churches World Exchange, the Order of St John, Macmillan House Cancer Research, the Blind Asylum, Motor Neuron Research and Action Aid.

Applications: Contact the correspondent for further information.

The Tillyloss Trust

£3,000 (1993/94)

Youth, social welfare, Christian

KPMG, Royal Exchange, Dundee DD1 1DZ
01382-201234

Correspondent: The Secretary

Trustees: Mrs M Smith; Mrs P A O Sinclair; Mrs V M O Finlay; D H Tweedie.

Beneficial area: Scotland with a preference for Dundee.

Information available: Information was supplied by the trust and its latest annual report and accounts are available from the correspondent.

General: This trust makes grants ranging from £250 to £1,000 and in 1993/94, grants totalled £3,000. Beneficiaries included the Lochee Boys Club (£1,000), Dundee Battalion, Boys Brigade, (£650), Parent to Parent (£250) and Compass Christian Centre (£600).

Applications: In writing to the correspondent.

The Trinafour Trust

Not known

Not known

15 Sutherland Avenue, Glasgow G41 4JJ

Correspondent: P C M Roger

Beneficial area: Scotland.

Information available: No financial information available.

General: The trust is "very small". No further information is available.

Applications: In writing to the correspondent. The trust did not wish to be included in the Guide.

The TSB Foundation for Scotland

£242,000 (1993/94)

Education and training, scientific and medical research, social and community needs

Henry Duncan House, 120 George Street, Edinburgh EH2 4TS
0131-225 4555

Correspondent: Andrew Muirhead, Company Secretary

Trustees: A C L Bannerman; Hon. Dame M D Corsar; J W Cradock; A D Foulis; I R Guild; P C Paisley; J D M Robertson; R G E Peggie; C D Donald; Mrs E A Denholm.

Beneficial area: Scotland.

Information available: Annual report and accounts for 1993/94, which include a set of guidelines for applicants, are available from the correspondent.

General: The TSB Foundation allocates its funds to support the community in which it operates and to improve the quality of life of people in need. The 1993/94 annual report states that the foundation's overall policy is "to support underfunded voluntary organisations which enable disabled people and those who are disadvantaged through social or economic circumstances to make a contribution to the community."

The foundation's income in 1993/94 totalled £194,600, 4% higher than income for the previous year.

Three main objectives lie behind the foundation's grant-making: education and training, scientific and medical research, social and community needs. Below is an outline of the kinds of projects funded under each category.

Education and training

- Projects which motivate and train people to obtain employment with particular emphasis on young people.
- Projects providing employment training for disadvantaged and disabled people.
- Organisations promoting life skills for young people.
- Initiatives promoting life skills and independent living for disabled people.
- Educational opportunities for all age groups.

Scientific and medical research

- Underfunded research, related to illnesses preventing a significant percentage of the working population from remaining in employment.

Social and community needs

- Projects which help disadvantaged and disabled people to play a full part in the community, eg. community centres, crisis and advice centres, services for disabled people, health promotion services, organisations promoting civic responsibility and concerned with cultural enrichment.

The trustees are interested in directing support to local initiatives and projects undertaken by national organisations should be broken down into local or regional activities.

Most grants are made on a one-off basis – successful applicants should wait at least two years before applying for further funds. Grants range between £300 and £5,000 although the average grant for local or regional projects is about £2,500. Larger amounts are however considered.

Priorities for 1993/94, under the above categories were employment training, young people, rural areas, crime prevention, homelessness and carers.

For the year 1993/94, funds awarded and committed were regionally split as shown.

Region	£
Borders	4,000
Central	8,350
Dumfries & Galloway	9,136
Fife	12,400
Grampian	10,650
Highland	12,780
Lothian	84,659
Strathclyde	57,190
Tayside	13,800
Islands	10,000

The foundation also made a grant of £19,460 to the national pool, bringing the foundation's total grant expenditure to £242,425.

Exclusions: Grants are not awarded to organisations which are not recognised charities nor to individuals. Also no support for organisations concerned with animal welfare, the environment, overseas appeals, activities which are the state's responsibility, mainstream schools, colleges or universities, hospitals and medical centres requesting support for capital costs and running costs, marketing appeals, charities which collect funds for redistribution, endowment funds, fundraising activities, a charity's founder membership, loans or business finance, expeditions or overseas travel.

Applications: Application forms are available from the correspondent.

The John Tunnell Trust

£17,000 (1992/93)

Music

4 Royal Terrace, Edinburgh EH7 5AB
0131-556 4043

Correspondent: Kenneth M Robb, Secretary

Trustees: J C Tunnell; K Robb; J Hogel; Mrs W Tunnell; Mrs C C Hogel; T Green; C J Packard; D W S Todd.

Beneficial area: England, Scotland and Wales.

Information available: The following information is from the 1993 annual report.

General: The trust's assets totalled £152,000 in 1993, with an income of £32,000. Grants totalled £10,000.

The trust was set up in 1988 as a tribute to John Tunnell, leader of the Scottish Chamber Orchestra from its foundation in 1974 until his death in 1988.

The trust aims to encourage music clubs to promote the growth of chamber music in Scotland and offers grants to young professional British-based chamber musicians who have played together as an ensemble for a reasonable length of time with a postgraduate standard of excellence. Grants in 1993 typically ranged between £250 and £600 per concert and were awarded to London Cantilena (£7,645), Parnassus Ensemble (£3,600), Florilegium (£4,800) and the Chione Oboe Trio (£450).

Exclusions: Grants are not awarded to groups whose average age exceeds around 27 and whose members are not mainly British. Soloists and singers are also excluded.

Applications: On a form available from the correspondent. The completed form should be accompanied by a tape containing two or three contrasting pieces or movements and two written references from musicians of standing. Applications should be submitted by mid October. A selected number of groups will be invited to attend an audition in London in December.

The Turnberry Trust

Not known

Not known

Clydesdale Bank plc, PFS–Trust Unit, Brunswick House, Brunswick Street, Glasgow G1 2TB
0141-248 7070

Correspondent: P Hearn, Assistant Manager

Beneficial area: Scotland.

Information available: No financial information was available.

General: The trust can support organisations throughout Scotland, although there is some preference for Ayrshire.

Applications: In writing to the correspondent.

The Unemployed Voluntary Action Fund

£753,000 (1994/95)

Voluntary projects using unemployed people as volunteers (see below)

Comely Park House, 80 New Row, Dunfermline, Fife KY12 7EJ
01383-620780

Correspondent: Mrs Sandra Carter

Trustees: Dorothy Dalton (Convener); Patricia Carruthers; Rona Connolly; Helen

Guild; William Hawthorne; Donald McCalman; Elaine Ross.

Beneficial area: Scotland.

Information available: Detailed guidelines for applicants are available from the fund. The annual report and audited accounts are available on request.

General: The Unemployed Voluntary Action Fund (UVAF) gives grants to voluntary organisations to help projects which develop opportunities for volunteering, especially involving unemployed people as volunteers.

"Projects in the fields of social welfare, health, community education and community development must promote voluntary activity which develops a service which directly benefits individuals in the local community, for example:

Mutual help schemes, such as carers' support groups;

Pre-school and family centre developments;

Home-visiting and escort services for housebound and disabled people;

Recreational programmes to integrate people with learning difficulties;

Family advisory services;

Health related schemes;

Practical assistance such as community gardens or gardening with older people;

Volunteer bureaux;

Neighbourhood care projects.

The application should show evidence of the need for the service and assess realistically what measurable change can be achieved."

The fund is resourced with a grant from the Scottish office (£842,000 in 1994/95) to help projects in the first, second or third year of development in the Main Grants Programme. The maximum grant is currently £31,000 each year. In 1994/95, Main Grants Programme projects received grants totalling £731,000. Beneficiaries included: Caithness Deaf Care (£20,500), Voluntary Organisations North East Fife – Volunteer Bureau (£15,400) and Learning Difficulties Community Support Group in South Strathkelvin (£22,700).

There is also a Small Grants Scheme for projects without staff, in their preliminary stages. The maximum grant available from this scheme is £5,000. 13 such projects received grants totalling £22,100. Beneficiaries included Tak Tent Cancer Support (£3,000) and Aberdeen Action on Disability (£2,000).

About £290,000 is available to fund new schemes in the Main Grants Programme and the Small Grants Scheme each year.

Exclusions: Schemes which cannot be considered include: exhibitions, arts clubs and performances; business co-operatives; credit unions; food co-operatives; out-of-school care; housing and hostel welfare; formal educational or vocational courses and skills training; clean-ups and one-off projects; holidays and camps; conservation schemes; building projects, including playgrounds; social clubs; sports centres and sports activities; campaigning and political activities.

Applications: A detailed guidelines pack is available by writing or telephoning the Fund Office. Deadline dates for applications are: 30th June for the Main Grants Programme; decisions are made in December, and 31st March for the Small Grants Scheme; decisions to be made in June.

The David & Carole Walton Charitable Trust

£1,000 (1994/95)

Youth, education, medical, arts

4 Methven Road, Whitecraigs, Glasgow G46 6TG
0141-248 6033

Correspondent: David Walton

Trustees: David Walton; Carole Walton.

Beneficial area: Scotland with a preference for Glasgow.

Information available: Information was supplied by the trust.

General: In 1994/95, the trust had assets totalling about £25,000. Grants usually total about £1,000 and range between £25 and £100.

In 1994/95, the total amount awarded was £950 and grants ranged between £5 and £100. Beneficiaries included the Scottish Society for the Prevention of Cruelty to Animals, World Cancer Research, Youth Aliyah, British Heart Foundation, Jewish Blind Society – Scotland and Scottish Society for the Prevention of Cruelty to Animals. Only recognised charities are supported.

Exclusions: No grants to military organisations nor to government bodies.

Applications: In writing to the correspondent.

The Isidore & David Walton Foundation

£53,000 (1994)

Medical

Royal Exchange House, 100 Queen Street, Glasgow G1 3DL
0141-248 7333

Correspondent: David Walton

Trustees: D Walton; Mrs C Walton; Prof R A Lorimer; E Glen; Prof L Blumgart; M Walton; J R Walton.

Beneficial area: West of Scotland.

Information available: Accounts are available from Touche Ross & Co. Chartered Accountants, 39 St Vincent Place, Glasgow G1 2QQ.

General: In 1994, the foundation's total assets less liabilities totalled £1.8 million and its income totalled £90,000. Grants are awarded to charities in the West of Scotland concerned mainly with medical issues, although education, sport and the arts are also supported.

In 1994, grants totalled £53,000 with the largest including those to the Royal College of Physicians in Edinburgh (£5,000), Glasgow Royal Infirmary (£1,000) and Glasgow Leukaemia Trust (£25,000). Grants usually range between £100 and £25,000.

Exclusions: No grants to individuals or for political causes.

Applications: In writing to the correspondent, but note that unsolicited applications are not encouraged.

The Waterside Trust

Not known

Relief of disadvantage, Christian

56 Palmerston Place, Edinburgh EH12 5AY
0131 225 6366

Correspondent: R M W Clark

Trustees: Irvine Bay Trustee Company.

Beneficial area: UK and overseas.

Information available: The information for this entry is based on the trust's annual report and accounts, available from the correspondent.

General: Apart from existing commitments, grants typically range from £250 to £20,000 and are made to organisations which "provide adult Christian formation and pastoral care of the young, offer educational and recreational activities for disadvantaged young people, provide care and support for the elderly and deprived families, especially those with young children, engage in community development and the social rehabilitation of the unemployed, the homeless, the mentally ill, ex-offenders, refugees and those with a history of substance abuse."

Exclusions: No grants to individuals, environmental projects, arts organisations, conservation groups, endowment appeals, large capital appeals and major research projects.

Applications: In writing to the correspondent.

John Watson's Trust

£140,000 (1993) including individuals

Educational needs of children and young people

Signet Library, Parliament Square, Edinburgh EH1 1RF
0131-220 1640

Correspondent: J Penney, Administrator

Trustees: Six representatives of the Society of Writers to Her Majesty's Signet; two from Lothian Regional Council; one from the Merchant Company Education Board; one from the Lothian Association of Youth Clubs; and one additional member.

Beneficial area: Scotland, with a preference for Lothian.

Information available: Background notes are available from the trust.

General: Grants to children and young people under 21 who are physically or mentally disabled or socially disadvantaged, for education and training, private tutoring, Open University, equipment, travel, recreational and cultural activities.

Grants are given both to individuals and charitable organisations, with a preference for the Lothian region. There is provision for a limited number of boarding school grants.

The trust's assets in 1994, were £2.6 million, generating an income of £175,000. Donations totalled £140,000, of which £100,000 was given in grants to individuals.

173 grants were given to disabled or disadvantaged children and young people under 21. Grants to individuals included equipment for disabled people, in-school special expenses, living expenses for children forced to leave home, special school fees, post-school education for disadvantaged people, apprentice tools and equipment. Grants are one-off and range from £50 to £3,000, apart from boarding school grants which average £2,250 and may be recurrent.

66 grants totalling £40,000 were given to groups/organisations, most of which were based in the Lothian area. Grants included general funding for some important local organisations, funding of school projects, playschemes, after-school clubs, University of Edinburgh Special Entry Summer School, and research into improved special teaching of severely deprived children and other aspects of child educational welfare. Grants ranged from £50 to £5,750.

Exclusions: No grants to: people over 21, overseas causes or for medical purposes.

Applications: On a form available from the correspondent for individuals. By letter for organisations. Applications are considered in January, March, May, August and October.

The Lady Margaret Watt Charitable Trust

£28,000 (1993/94)

Relief of poverty, health, religion, education, local projects

KPMG, 24 Blythswood Square, Glasgow G2 4QS
0141-226 5511

Correspondent: John C Craig, Trustee

Trustees: J C Craig; R S Waddell; The Management Trust Company Ltd.

Beneficial area: Scotland.

Information available: Accounts were available for 1993/94.

General: In 1993/94, the trust's assets were £476,000 and grants totalled £25,000, although a total amount of £28,000 is available annually for charitable distribution. The trust's grant-making policy is very wide including support to organisations concerned with the relief of poverty and illness, the advancement of religion and education and organisations benefiting the community.

Grants ranged from £250 to £5,000. Beneficiaries included Rannoch School and Something for Romania (£2,500 each), Princess Royal Trust for Carers (£2,000), Glasgow Cathedral Organ Restoration Fund, KIDS Playgroup and RUKBA (£1,000 each), GSWS Federation of Boys' & Girls' Clubs, Salvation Army and Scottish Spina Bifida Association (£500 each) and Montrose YMCA (£250).

Exclusions: No grants for individuals.

Applications: In writing to the correspondent.

The James Weir Foundation

£153,000 (1993)

Health, social welfare, heritage, research

84 Cicada Road, London SW18 2NZ
0181-870 6233

Correspondent: Mrs L Lawson, Secretary

Trustees: Dr George Weir; Simon Bonham; William Ducas.

Beneficial area: UK, with a special interest in Scotland.

Information available: Full accounts are on file at the Charity Commission.

General: In 1993, the trust had assets of £3 million (up from £1.9 million in 1991) and an income of £176,000. Grants totalled £153,000.

The trust deed lists seven specific beneficiaries. In 1993, six of these received a grant: the Royal Society – Edinburgh and London (£28,000 and £2,000 respectively), University of Strathclyde Engineering Foundation (£2,500), RAF Benevolent Fund (£2,000) and Royal College of Physicians and Royal College of Surgeons (both £1,000). The British Association for the Advancement of Science did not receive a grant.

About 120 other grants were given of which 93 were for £1,000 and 14 for £500. The largest grant was £4,000 to South Ayrshire Hospitals NHS Trust, with £2,000 to each of the British American Education Foundation, Leonard Cheshire Foundation, National Galleries of Scotland, National Trust for Scotland and Prospect Foundation Appeal.

Most charities supported were in the fields of health, welfare and disability such as British Blind Sport, Childline, Disability Aid Fund, MIND, NACRO and Samaritans. A number of conservation and animal welfare charities also received support including International Fund for Animal Welfare, Scottish Wildlife Trust and World Wide Fund for Nature.

The trust has a special interest in Scotland, with beneficiaries in addition to those already mentioned including Age Concern Scotland, Association of Youth Clubs in Strathclyde, Buildings of Scotland Trust, Prison Fellowship Scotland and Riding for the Disabled Glasgow. About half the grants were recurrent.

Exclusions: Recognised charities only. No grants to individuals.

Applications: In writing to the correspondent. Distributions are made twice yearly in June and November.

The Western Recreation Trust

Not known

Recreation

Moores Rowland, 25 Bothwell Street, Glasgow G2 6NL
0141-221 6991

Correspondent: Ian Paterson

Beneficial area: West of Scotland.

Information available: No financial information was available.

General: The trust gives grants to organisations based in the West of Scotland working to improve recreational facilities for young people, elderly people and those who are unemployed. Grants are awarded towards the costs of equipment. No further information is available.

Applications: In writing to the correspondent. Applications are considered twice a year. This entry has not been confirmed by the trust. The address details are correct at time of giong to press.

The Whitehills Trust

£650 (1993)

General

Whitehills, Newton Stewart, Dumfries & Galloway DG8 6SL
01671-402049

Correspondent: C A Weston

Trustees: C A Weston; Mrs M S D Weston.

Beneficial area: UK with a preference for Scotland.

Information available: Information was supplied by the trust for this Guide.

General: This small family trust has a capital sum of £2,000. It was set up to respond to ad hoc appeals and is topped up each year by the trustees by means of an annual grant made under covenant.

In 1992/93, the trust awarded a total of £650 to voluntary organisations. Grants ranged between £10 and £50 and beneficiaries included Save the Children, RUKBA and the Children's Family Trust.

Applications: In writing to the correspondent.

The Edith & Isaac Wolfson (Scotland) Trust

£55,000 (1994)

General, particularly higher education

18–22 Haymarket, London SW1Y 4DQ
0171-930 1057

Correspondent: Dr B Rashbass, Secretary

Trustees: Lord Wolfson of Marylebone; Lord Quirk; Lord Quinton.

Beneficial area: Scotland.

Information available: Accounts are available from the trust.

General: In 1994, the trust's assets totalled £1 million generating an income of £83,000.

Grants totalled £55,000 and were mainly given to higher education institutions in Scotland. The following universities were funded: Aberdeen, Edinburgh, Dundee, Glasgow, Strathclyde and St Andrews.

Exclusions: No grants to individuals.

Applications: In writing to the correspondent.

The James Wood Bequest Fund

£53,000 (1994)

General

Messrs Mitchells Roberton, George House, 36 North Hanover Street, Glasgow G1 2AD
0141-552 3422

Correspondent: E H Webster

Trustees: E H Webster; Norman W McMillan; David A R Ballantine

Beneficial area: Glasgow and the "central belt of Scotland".

Information available: Accounts are available from the trust.

General: The trust gives to home and foreign missions of the Church of Scotland and other charitable organisations in the beneficial area. Grants totalled £53,000 in 1994; no further information is available.

Exclusions: Registered charities only.

Applications: In writing to the correspondent.

The Zeta Trust

£3,000 (1994/95)

Christian charities, alleviation of human suffering, education

Airlie Lodge, 5 Whitehouse Terrace, Edinburgh EH9 2EU
0131-447 4735

Correspondent: I A Nimmo

Trustees: I A Nimmo, sole trustee at present.

Beneficial area: Unrestricted, with a preference for Scotland.

Information available: Information was supplied by the trust.

General: In 1994/95, the trust had assets of £70,000 and an income of £3,500.

Grants for the same year came to £3,300 with beneficiaries including the Scottish Hospital Endowments Research Trust, Scottish Veterans' Garden City Association, Strathcarron Hospice, Multiple Sclerosis Society in Scotland, Royal Blind Asylum and School, Royal Caledonian Schools and Thistle Foundation. All received £150.

Exclusions: Grants are not awarded to organisations that are profit-making or under local or national government control.

Applications: In writing to the trustees by 1st May.

The Konrad Zweig Trust

About £10,000 a year

Ecological, social and economic projects

House with Arches, Ormiston Hall, Ormiston, East Lothian EH35 5NJ

Correspondent: Mrs Francesca Loening

Trustees: U Loening; Mrs F Loening; Prof A Manning; Ms A Mariand; Ms M Ashmore; Ms A Rookwood.

Beneficial area: UK with a preference for Scotland.

Information available: Information was supplied by the trust.

General: The trust funds organisations (and individuals) undertaking academic and/or practical work based on environmental concerns or on economic or social concerns which have an environmental dimension.

Exclusions: Organisations must be registered charities.

Applications: In writing to the correspondent, before August of each year.

Aberdeen & Perthshire

The Aberdeen Endowments Trust

£219,000 (1994) including grants towards bursaries

Education

19 Albert Street, Aberdeen AB9 1QF
01224-640194

Correspondent: William Russell, Clerk

Trustees: W J Hunter; Rev J C Stewart; N R D Begg; J Cameron; R Clark; W T Fraser; A C Kennedy; E A Leslie; I A McDonald; J M Macdonald; N Mackenzie; J A Porter; G S Stephen; J K A Thomaneck; G Thomson; Miss E F Torrance; M E Watt.

Beneficial area: Aberdeen, Grampian.

Information available: Guidance notes and an annual report are available from the trust.

General: The trust's assets at the end of 1994 were valued at £8.2 million, generating an income of £676,300. The vast majority of the trust's awards are given to Robert Gordon's College in Aberdeen in the form of bursaries to pupils and to other educational establishments. However, there is a provision for grants to be made to:

- Organisations providing sports facilities and other accommodation for sports for children and young people in Aberdeen;
- Clubs, societies or organisations undertaking work of an educational nature;
- Towards the costs of organising art exhibitions, lectures and demonstrations on any of the visual arts;
- Help establish, maintain and equip choirs, orchestras, bands and instrumental groups;
- Assist dramatic groups;
- Organisations undertaking educational experiments and research.

Applications: Contact the correspondent for further details.

The Aberdeenshire Educational Trust Scheme

Up to £45,000 a year

Education

Grampian Regional Council, Department of Education, Woodhill House, Westburn Road, Aberdeen AB9 2LU
01224-664664

Correspondent: The Assistant Director of Education (Finance)

Beneficial area: Aberdeenshire.

Information available: Guidelines for applicants are available from the Grants Section of Grampian Regional Council.

General: Grants may be made:

- To encourage the development of further education by helping those activities which are not usually provided by the education authority, and

- To help people to attend any institution or organised course of further education. Awards for individuals can be made for further education courses which would not normally be recognised for Further Education Bursaries, and in other special circumstances.

Grants can also be made to individuals to help them with educational trips in Great Britain or abroad, and to help individuals and bodies to undertake educational experiments and research which will be for the benefit of people belonging to Aberdeen County. Help may also be given towards "regional and national enterprises of an educational nature". All grants are seen as a minimal contribution towards the total cost of a project. Grants to individuals are usually for £50 to £150 depending upon need.

Applications: On a form available from the correspondent.

The Arbroath Improvement Trust

£7,000 (1993)

Arts, education, young people

11 Gallowden Road, Arbroath,
Angus DD11 3HL
01241-873598

Correspondent: Harry C Nicoll, Hon Secretary & Treasurer

Trustees: J J Whyte; Rev W G Beattie; A Smith; G McNicol; Dr R B Speirs; E Kear; A D Massie; A Carnegie; E F Gilbert; Mrs H G Cargill; R C Matthew; C S B Meldrum; A King; Mrs S Welsh.

Beneficial area: Arbroath Burgh.

Information available: 1993 accounts were provided by the trust.

General: In 1993, the trust's total income before expenses was £8,000, with grants approved by the trust totalling £7,000.

The objects of the trust are described as including "the improvement and beautifying of the town; acquiring works of art for the art gallery; purchasing books for the benefit of local students in supplement to those provided out of the library funds; encouragement of promising pupils from the town schools in any way not provided for by the educational authorities; encouragement of youth movements; in fact, anything on these or similar lines that will make the town a better place to live in, and tend to give the inhabitants a greater pride and produce a greater interest in their native town".

Grants in 1993 ranged between £125 and £1,000. Over half were for £125, with recipients including Arbroath Amateur Musical Society, Arbroath Male Voice Choir, Arbroath Choral Society, Arbroath Girls' Brigade, Arbroath Community Support Group, Arbroath Amateur Boxing Club and Angus Gilbert and Sullivan Society.

Larger amounts were awarded as follows: Arbroath & District Horticultural Society (£250), Arbroath & District Musical Festival Association (£400), Arbroath & District Athletics Club (£450), Arbroath Secondary Schools, Arbroath District Scout Council, Arbroath High School PTA, Arbroath United Cricket Club and Sea Cadets – T S Arbroath (£500 each), and Arbroath Primary Schools (£875). The largest grant of £1,000 was allocated to Locals Against Drug Abuse.

Exclusions: Organisations with liquor licences and churches are not considered.

Applications: In writing to the correspondent providing full details of the organisation, the scheme requiring funding, costings and details of other funds sought/received.

A G Bain's Trust

£66,000 (1993/94)

Elderly, disabled children and young people

2 Bon-Accord Crescent, Aberdeen AB1 2DH
01224-587261

Correspondent: J C Chisholm

Trustees: W S Crosby; C A B Crosby;
J C Chisholm

Beneficial area: Aberdeen.

Information available: Notes and audited accounts for 1993/94 were available from the correspondent.

General: The trust was set up in 1990 to work in the areas of care, maintenance, welfare and education of old people and disabled children and young people in homes, operated by Voluntary Service Aberdeen. Since then, the trustees have paid the free income of the trust to Voluntary Service Aberdeen with particular sums designated to particular areas of the organisation's work.

Applications: Contact the correspondent for further details.

The Banffshire Educational Trust Scheme

£8,500

Education

Grampian Regional Council, Department of Education, Woodhill House, Westburn Road, Aberdeen AB9 2LU
01224-664664

Correspondent: The Assistant Director of Education (Finance)

Beneficial area: Banffshire.

Information available: Guidelines for applicants are available from the Grants Section of Grampian Regional Council.

General: The trust awards grants to individuals as well as to Banff County Schools, further education centres, clubs and organisations operating for the benefit of people belonging to the county of Banff.

Apart from awarding a range of bursaries for study, the trust will help education centres with equipment, give grants to provide and maintain playing fields and other sports facilities for the benefit of children and young people resident in Banff County.

Additionally, grants are made to clubs, societies and organisations in Banff County which undertake work of an educational nature. The trust also awards grants to promote education in art, music and drama both through schools and organisations.

Grants total up to £8,500 a year.

Applications: On a form available from the correspondent.

The Ellis Campbell Charitable Foundation

£26,000 (1994)

Youth, education, heritage, conservation

The Steading, Shalden Park House, Shalden, Alton, Hampshire GU34 4DS
01252-722333

Correspondent: Michael Campbell

Trustees: Michael Campbell; Mrs Linda Campbell; Doris Campbell; Jamie Campbell; Alexandra Andrew; Trevor Aldridge.

Beneficial area: UK, with a preference for Perthshire and Hampshire.

Information available: Full accounts are on file at the Charity Commission.

General: "The foundation was established in 1989 by Michael Campbell, chairman of the Ellis Campbell Group of companies, and other members of his family who are also shareholders. Various companies within the group have covenanted £200,000 a year for four years to establish an endowment of £1 million.

"Special emphasis is placed upon donations towards youth, education and conservation (historical, architectural, and construction heritage including modes of transport) in Hampshire and Perthshire."

In the 1994 accounts, the chairman stated: "Since appearing in a number of Guides, we have received an enormously increased number of requests. This has enabled us to focus our giving more directly on the principal aims of the foundation although the 'other' category is still supported."

In 1994, the trust had assets of £858,000 and an income of £53,500. Grants totalling £26,000 were given in the categories: youth, education, conservation and other.

Youth: Eight grants totalling £6,600, including two each in Scotland and Hampshire. £3,000 went to Sir James Scott Memorial Appeal and £1,000 to Kintyre Tall Ships Youth Challenge and Understanding Industry.

Education: Eight grants totalling £3,300, including three in Scotland. These included £750 each to the Scottish Bobath Association and Workwise.

Conservation: Five grants totalling £11,800; three in Scotland and two in Hampshire. Beneficiaries included the Winchester Cathedral Trust (£10,000) and the Scottish Trust for Underwater Archaeology (£1,000).

Other: Ten grants totalling £2,800; four in Hampshire and six elsewhere.

Exclusions: No grants to individuals unless known by a trustee.

Applications: In writing to the correspondent. "Applicants should observe the areas of special interest and should not expect to receive an acknowledgement."

The A T Cathro Bequest

£1,000 (1995)

Children

The Finance Division, The City of Dundee District Council, 8 City Square, Dundee DD1 3BG
01382-434329

Correspondent: Professional Assistant, Charities Department

Trustees: Certain members of the City of Dundee District Council.

Beneficial area: Dundee.

Information available: The information for this entry was supplied by the City of Dundee Council.

General: The trust makes grants to organisations which provide holidays for disadvantaged children in Dundee. Grants range from £40 to £350.

Exclusions: No grants to individuals.

Applications: Applications should be made in writing to the Director of Finance. They should include the organisation's holiday plans and, if applicable, its latest set of audited accounts. The closing date for applications is 28th February.

The Dundee City Council Charities

Not known

Not known

Dundee City Council, 21 City Square, Dundee DD1 3BY
01382-434000

Correspondent: The Chief Executive's Department

Beneficial area: Probably the city of Dundee.

Information available: No financial information was available.

General: No information available. Administration of these charities may change following the reorganisation of local government after 31st March 1996.

Applications: In writing to the correspondent. This entry has not been confirmed by the trust.

The Melville Gray Charitable Trust

£1,000 (1993)

General

Miller Hendry Solicitors & Estate Agents, 10 Blackfriars Street, Perth PH1 5NS
01738-637311

Correspondent: Miller Hendry

Trustees: James K Cairncross; Dr Alice M Mathieson; Dr Isabelle M Donald; Alastair G Dorward; James S M Craig.

Beneficial area: Scotland, with a preference for Perth.

Information available: The information for this entry was taken from the trust's annual report and accounts.

General: In 1993, the trust made grants of £200 each to the following organisations: Royal Society for the Prevention of Cruelty to Children (Perth Branch); Samaritans (Perth Branch); National Society for Cancer Relief; Women's Aid, Perth Area, and Salvation Army Perth Citadel.

Applications: In writing to the correspondent.

The Mary Jamieson Hall & John F Hall Trust

£4,000 (1993/94)

Social welfare

c/o Gray & Kellas Solicitors, 11–12 Bon Accord Crescent, Aberdeen AB9 1XG
01224-586301

Correspondent: Mrs A Merson

Trustees: P G R Saxon; J H Gray; J Birnie; J P Grant.

Beneficial area: Aberdeen and surrounding area.

Information available: This entry is based on information supplied by the trust and its latest annual report and accounts.

General: This trust makes 30 to 40 twice yearly grants of £300 to £350 to ex-employees of Hall & Tawse Scotland Ltd in Aberdeen, or their families. Between two and three grants ranging between £500 and £1,000 are made twice a year to local Aberdeen charities such as the Salvation Army, the Samaritans and the Cyrenians.

In 1993/94, charitable organisations received a total of £3,500.

Applications: Apply in writing to the correspondent or to the Personnel Officer at Hall & Tawse, Granitehill Road, Northfield, Aberdeen AB9 2AW (01224-693155).

The Hannah Charitable Trust

£2,250 (1993/94)

Christian charities, poverty

58 Frederick Street, Edinburgh EH2 1LS
0131-225 8291

Correspondent: John M Hodge

Trustees: John M Hodge; Charles K Frampton.

Beneficial area: Perth.

Information available: Information was supplied by the trust.

General: This trust has a small annual income. It focuses on work of a Christian nature.

Grants, which totalled £2,250 in 1993/94, range between £250 and £1,000, with an average grant of £800. Christian organisations and occasionally cases of poverty are supported.

Applications: Unsolicited applications are not encouraged – grants are normally limited to causes known to the trustees.

William Harvey's Trust

£600 (1992)

Deafness, women

27 Hutchison Terrace, Aberdeen AB1 7NN
01224-315702

Correspondent: Alan Sharp

Trustees: Lord Provost James Wyness; C Massie; Rev Professor D Fergusson; Rev Professor W P Stephens; Rev J H A Dick; Rev J C Stewart; Rev J Watson.

Beneficial area: Scotland, with a preference for Aberdeen and Aberdeenshire.

Information available: The information for this entry was supplied by the trust's solicitors but we were unable to see the accounts.

General: The trust's deed specifies that one third of its free revenue should be spent on supporting deaf people, and two thirds on the protection of women. The trust solicitors value the trust's assets at about £15,000.

Organisations supported in 1992 include: Aberdeen & North East Society for the Deaf (£95), Grampian Women's AID (£50), and Voluntary Services, Aberdeen (£80). Grants ranged from £50 to £95.

Exclusions: No grants to individuals.

Applications: Contact the correspondent for further details.

The Anne Herd Memorial Trust

£24,000 (1993/94) – includes grants to individuals

Visual impairment

Messrs Bowman Gray Robertson & Wilkie, Solicitors, 27 Bank Street, Dundee DD1 1RP
01382-322267

Correspondent: B N Bowman

Trustees: B N Bowman; P M M Bowman; Mrs E N McGillivray.

Beneficial area: Scotland, with a preference for Tayside, the City of Dundee and Broughty Ferry.

Information available: Accounts were available from the trust.

General: The trust's assets totalled £564,000 in 1993/94. Grants totalling £24,000 and ranging between £200 and £19,200 were awarded to organisations concerned with visual impairment based in or connected with Broughty Ferry, Dundee or Tayside.

Grants were awarded to organisations such as Dundee Tape Newspaper for the Blind (£500). The trust provided £19,200 towards the creation of a tactile and sensory trail at Camperdown Country Park, Dundee.

Applications: In writing to the correspondent. This entry has not been confirmed by the trust, although the address details are correct.

The Kincardineshire Educational Trust Scheme

Variable

Education

Grampian Regional Council, Department of Education, Woodhill House, Westburn Road, Aberdeen AB9 2LU
01224-664664

Correspondent: The Assistant Director of Education (Finance)

Beneficial area: Kincardineshire.

Information available: Guidelines for applicants are available from the Grants Section of Grampian Regional Council.

General: The trust awards grants to individuals as well as to Kincardine County Schools, further education centres, clubs and organisations operating for the benefit of people belonging to the county of Kincardine. Apart from awarding a range of bursaries for study, the trust will help education centres and schools with equipment, give grants to provide and maintain playing fields and other sports facilities for the benefit of children and young people resident in Kincardine County.

Additionally, grants are made to clubs, societies and organisations in Kincardine County which undertake work of an educational nature. The trust also awards grants to promote education in art, music and drama both through schools and organisations.

No financial information was available.

Applications: Application forms are available from the correspondent. The closing date for applications is 30th September of each year.

The Mathew Trust

£154,000 (1994/95)

General

Royal Exchange, Dundee DD1 1DZ
01382-201234

Correspondent: KPMG, Secretaries

Trustees: Dr D B Grant; Lord Provost of Dundee; Professor G S Lowden; A F McDonald.

Beneficial area: Dundee and district.

General: The trust's net assets in 1994/95 were £4.4 million with a gross income of £191,000.

The organisation states: "the purpose of the trust is to provide financial assistance in any way or manner and to any extent the trustees may consider desirable for the recruitment, training and retraining of local male and female labour in industries in Dundee". The trustees consider requests for financial assistance on their merits.

Grants totalling £154,000 were awarded in 1994/95. Grants ranged between £100 and £40,000 and were awarded to organisations such as Dundee YMCA (£5,000) and Link Overseas Exchange (£2,400).

Applications: In writing to the correspondent.

The Patrick Mitchell Hunter Fund

£13,000 (1991)

General

Wilsone & Duffus, PO Box 81, 7 Golden Square, Aberdeen AB9 8EP
01224-641065

Correspondent: The Administrator

Trustees: J B Esslemont; J T C Gillan; W Howie.

Beneficial area: Aberdeen only.

Information available: 1991 accounts were available from the trust.

General: In 1991, the fund had assets totalling £203,000 and grants totalled £13,000.

The fund supports charities in Aberdeen only and grants range between £250 and £1,000. There are no further details about the type of beneficiary.

Exclusions: No grants to organisations which are not based in Aberdeen.

Applications: Contact the correspondent for further details. This entry has not been confirmed by the trust. The address details are correct.

The Mollison Fund

£6,000

Social welfare

Craigens Solicitors, 13 Bon Accord Crescent, Aberdeen AB9 1NQ
01224-588295

Correspondent: Mrs Joyce Simpson

Trustees: Melville Watson; Mrs Doris Meston; Laurence Reid.

Beneficial area: The city of Aberdeen.

Information available: The information for this entry was supplied by the trust. Accounts are available from the correspondent.

General: The trust's deed stipulates the trust must fund the Belmedie Eventide Home and the Endowment Fund for Cornhill Hospital. The remaining income is given to social welfare charities in Aberdeen. Grants total about £6,000 a year.

Exclusions: The trust does not give grants to charities which are supported by local or central government funding.

Applications: In writing to the correspondent.

The Northwood Charitable Trust

£317,000 (1993/94)

General

22 Meadowside, Dundee DD1 1LN
01382-201534

Correspondent: The Secretary

Trustees: B H Thomson; D B Thomson; A F Thomson; Professor A J McDonald; A McDougall.

Beneficial area: Dundee and Tayside.

Information available: The information for this entry is taken from the trust's latest annual report and accounts.

General: This trust is connected to the D C Thomson Charitable Trust, D C Thomson & Company and the Thomson family. It was established by Eric V Thomson in 1972 and has received additional funding from other members of the Thomson family.

In 1993/94, the trust's income was £873,000 and grants totalled £317,000, leaving a surplus of £460,000. The trustees planned to allocate £200,000 of this to two projects, one educational and the other medical, in the next financial year.

In 1993/94, most grants awarded are not listed in the annual report with the exception of a major donation of £58,600 to the University of Dundee Appeals. Grants range from £500 to £100,000.

Applications: The trust states that no applications will be considered or acknowledged.

Radio Tay – Caring for Kids (Radio Tay Listeners Charity)

£96,000 (1993/94)

Children and youth

PO Box 123, Dundee DD1 9UF
01382-200800

Correspondent: Lorraine Stevenson, Co-ordinator

Trustees: Lord J Elphinstone, Chairman; A Wilke; K Codognato; A Ballingall; M Naulty; M Laird.

Beneficial area: Tayside and North East Fife.

Information available: The information for this entry was supplied by the trust.

General: The fundraising appeal starts in August and continues until after Christmas. The main event is the station's charity auction, for which donated gifts usually include a new caravan. All the money raised is distributed within the community covered by the radio service. £96,000 was raised in 1993/94.

Allocations to individuals benefited 292 children and allocations to organisations benefited over 5,000 children either directly or indirectly. The largest grant of £7,000 went to Tayside Conductive Education Group to enable them to bring four conductors over from the Peto Institute.

Other beneficiaries included 2nd Montrose Scout Group and Tayside & Western Isles Association for the Deaf (£1,000 each), Perth Action on Autism (£600), and Auchtergaven Nursery and Peter Pan Playgroup Carnoustie (£100 each).

Applications: In writing to the correspondent. Grants are awarded in February and March.

John Mackie Spalding's Trust

£2,000 (1993/94)

Young people, general

1 East Craibstone Street, Bon-Accord Square, Aberdeen AB9 1YH
01224-581581

Correspondent: James & George Collie, Solicitors

Trustees: G F Collie; Mrs M C F Collie; D G Morgan; J I Collie.

Beneficial area: Scotland, with a preference for Aberdeenshire.

Information available: The information for this entry was supplied by the trust.

General: In 1992/93, the trust's assets were valued at £17,000 and generated a net income of £4,000 after expenses. Grants, which are awarded on a one-off basis, range between £200 and £1,000.

11 local charities each received grants of £250. These included Aberdeen Cyrenians, Nazareth House, Outward Bound and Newton Dee Village. One grant of £1,000 was awarded to a local scout troop to build a scout hut.

Applications: In writing to the correspondent.

The D C Thomson Charitable Trust

£21,000 (1993/94)

General

22 Meadowside, Dundee DD1 1LN
01382-201534

Correspondent: William Thomson & Sons

Trustees: D C Thomson & Co Ltd; W D C & F Thomson Ltd.

Beneficial area: Dundee and Tayside.

Information available: The information for this entry is taken from the trust's latest annual report and accounts.

General: This trust is connected to the Northwood Charitable Trust and was founded by DC Thomson & Company.

In 1993/94, the trust made grants ranging from £100 to £6,000 and totalling £21,000, mainly to organisations working in social welfare, the arts, youth and disability.

Beneficiaries included: Operation Shipshape, the RRS Discovery Appeal (£6,000); Talking Newspaper Association (£2,000); Scottish Fisheries Museum Trust, Scottish Commonwealth Games Youth Trust and British Blind Sport – Have a Go Day (£500 each).

Applications: The trust states that no applications will be considered or acknowledged.

Central

The Appletree Trust

£29,000 (1993/94)

Disability, sickness, poverty

The Royal Bank of Scotland plc, Private Trust
& Taxation, 2 Festival Square,
Edinburgh EH3 9SU
0131-523 2648

Correspondent: Mrs R Muirhead

Trustees: The Royal Bank of Scotland plc;
Rev W McKane; Rev Dr J D Martin.

Beneficial area: UK and overseas, with a
preference for the North East Fife district.

Information available: The information
for this entry is based on the trust's latest
annual report and accounts.

General: This trust was established by the
will of the late William Brown Moncour in
1982 to relieve suffering from disability,
sickness and poverty. The settlor
recommended that Action Research for the
Crippled Child, British Heart Foundation
and National Society for Cancer Relief
should receive funding from his trust,
particularly for their work in the North East
Fife district.

The trust generally makes grants ranging
from £1,000 to £10,000 and in 1993/94 the
following organisations were funded: Cancer
Relief Macmillan Fund for its Fife Project
and Rymonth Housing Society Ltd (£10,000
each), Fife Society for the Blind and North
East Continuing Care Service (£3,000 each),
and British Heart Foundation, Imperial
Cancer Research Fund and Royal
Commonwealth Society for the Blind
(£1,000 each).

Applications: In writing to the
correspondent.

The Bruce Charitable Trust

£7,000 (1994)

Community work

James Murray & Co, Chartered Accountants,
58 Bonnygate, Cupar, Fife KY15 4LD
01334-54044

Correspondent: G Lindsay

Trustees: P W Hutchison; G Lindsay;
Ms Elizabeth L Calderwood; Ms S A Clark.

Beneficial area: Cupar.

Information available: Information was
available from the trust.

General: In 1994, the trust had assets of
£226,000, generating an income of £9,000.
Grants to charities totalled £6,600.

Grants are given to community groups and voluntary organisations based within Cupar town boundary for the benefit of all age groups. Grants are also awarded to individuals within the specified area.

Applications: Contact the correspondent for further information.

The Callander Charitable Trust

Not known

General

Messrs A J & A Graham, 110 West George Street, Glasgow G2 1QA
0141-332 2441

Correspondent: A L Aitkenhead

Beneficial area: Falkirk and surrounding areas.

Information available: See below.

General: Grants are awarded to organisations in Falkirk and the surrounding areas for general charitable purposes. This trust offered to provide a copy of the accounts on payment of a fee. As the number of trusts in this book would have made payment on each set of accounts prohibitive, the offer was declined, and no further information is available on the activities of the trust.

Applications: Contact the correspondent for further details. This entry has not been confirmed by the trust.

The Carnegie Dunfermline Trust

£116,000 (1994)

Social, recreational or cultural facilities in Dunfermline

Abbey Park House, Abbey Park Place, Dunfermline, Fife KY12 7PB
01383-723638

Correspondent: William C Runciman, Secretary

Trustees: There are 16 life trustees, a further six appointed by Dunfermline District Council and three by Fife Regional Council.

Beneficial area: Dunfermline and its immediate environs. Applicants must be based in, or have a strong connection with, this area.

Information available: The trust publishes an annual report and guidance notes for applicants.

General: The trust was founded in August 1903. In Mr Carnegie's original instructions to the Gentlemen of the Commission, he said the endowment was "all to be used in attempts to bring into the monotonous lives of the toiling masses of Dunfermline more of sweetness and light ... some elevating conditions of life ... that the child of my native town, looking back in after years, however far from home it may have roamed, will feel simply by virtue of being such life has been made happier and better. If this be the fruit of your labours you will have succeeded; if not, you will have failed ... I have said your work is experimental ... If you can prove that good can be done you open new fields to the rich which I am certain they are to be more and more anxious to find for their surplus wealth ... Remember you are pioneers, and do not be afraid of making mistakes; those who never make mistakes never make anything. Try many things freely, but discard just as freely ...

As conditions of life change rapidly, you will not be restricted as to your plans or the scope of your activities."

Favoured applications

1. Schemes which are new and enterprising – ideas which will put Dunfermline or a Dunfermline club ahead of other comparable communities or clubs.
2. Schemes where people are helping others as well as themselves.
3. Schemes which result in attainment of an exceptionally high standard of accomplishment or excellence.
4. Schemes which would benefit young people so that in later life they feel they had an extra "something" simply because they came from Dunfermline.

Types of trust assistance available

1. Loans for major capital schemes, usually repayable over maximum of 5-7 years; usually interest-bearing (variable rate).
2. Grants usually only to organisations which are accepted by the Inland Revenue as having charitable status.
3. Provision of equipment – the trust will sometimes buy equipment and give it out on long loan.
4. Sponsorship eg. guarantee and grant-aid for training/coaching courses, sponsorship of courses arranged in Dunfermline by local groups.
5. Guarantees against loss on certain functions or events.

The trust's overall income in 1994 was £300,000 and grants totalled £116,000. It spent £15,000 on arts projects, £59,000 on community projects, £42,000 on international projects and set aside £49,000 towards special projects for the year 2000 and the trust's centenary in 2003.

Exclusions: No grants for:

1. Individuals (except in very special cases).
2. Closed clubs (ie. groups not open to the general public to join – this does not exclude minority groups catering for specialised interests).
3. Political organisations or causes, commercial enterprises, religious or sectarian bodies, or military or warlike pursuits.
4. Organisations which simply want help with maintenance and running costs; the trustees think these should be met out of subscription income. Exceptions might be made in special cases or for new bodies.
5. Projects which have already been started.

Applications: By letter at any time. "It is sometimes difficult for the trust to steer the correct course between helping a deserving group and sapping its initiative." Applicants are always expected to have applied to all relevant statutory bodies "and to show members' willingness to commit existing reserves or to embark on special fundraising activities".

The Murray Trust

£2,000 (1993/94)

General

Jardine Donaldson, Solicitors, 10 Bank Street, Tillicoultry
01259-750554

Correspondent: Mrs F E Dearing, Secretary

Trustees: Dr A I Ross; L J D Smith; A Gullen; J R Stalker.

Beneficial area: Tillicoultry.

Information available: Information was provided by the trust.

General: The trust's assets totalled £126,000 in 1993/94. Grants to charities totalled £2,400 and are awarded to churches, hospitals and hospices.

Applications: In writing to the correspondent.

Charities administered by North East Fife District Council

About £50,000

General

Department of Corporate Services, North East Fife District Council, County Buildings, St Catherine Street, Cupar, Fife KY15 4TA
01334-653722

Correspondent: E B Lawrie, Director of Corporate Services

Trustees: North East Fife District Council.

Beneficial area: North East Fife.

Information available: Information was provided by the trust.

General: North East Fife District Council administers between 50 and 60 local trusts which support individuals and organisations within the North East Fife region. Some of these trusts are very small and very specific in the beneficiaries they can support; one can help fisherman in a particular village for example.

Specific details of the individual trusts are available from the correspondent.

In 1994, the trusts had combined assets of £611,000, generating combined income for all the trusts of £56,000.

The various trusts give grants ranging between £50 and £5,000. As well as giving grants to individuals, local organisations such as Crime Prevention Panels, Boys Brigade and Scouts have been supported.

Applications: In writing to the correspondent.

Edinburgh & Lothians

The William Henry Arnott Trust

£2,000 (1993)

Religion, medical research

Bank of Scotland Trustee Department,
PO Box 41, 101 George Street,
Edinburgh EH2 3JH
0131-442 7777

Correspondent: The Secretary

Beneficial area: Crieff.

Information available: Accounts for 1993 were available from the trust.

General: In 1993, the trust's funds totalled £77,000 and grants amounted to £2,000.

The trust is committed to fund St Michael's Church in Crieff's Sunday School children's Christmas party and summer outing. Should the Church cease to be a Church of Scotland congregation, the grants will be given towards furthering medical research.

Applications: Contact the correspondent for further details. The trust stated that it did not want to appear in the Guide.

The Thomas Barclay Bequest

£640 (1994/95)

Social welfare

11 St Colme Street, Edinburgh EH3 6AG
0131-225 4606

Correspondent: Trust Fund Administrator

Trustees: Most Rev Richard Holloway; R Graeme Thom; Jean Malcolm; Maureen O'Neill, Geoffrey Lord.

Beneficial area: Edinburgh.

Information available: Information was available from the trust.

General: One-off grants up to £50 are given to charitable social welfare organisations working in the Edinburgh area. Grants totalled £640 in 1994/95)

Exclusions: No grants to individuals.

Applications: An application form is available from the correspondent.

The Miss J K Bertram Memorial Trust

£15,000 (1993)

Parkinson's disease

1 Darnaway Street, Edinburgh EH3 6DW
0131-226 2903

Correspondent: Mrs Joyce Hutchinson, Trustee and Secretary

Trustees: One representative of the Lothian Health Board; one Director of a public company (based in Edinburgh); one retired university lecturer; one retired administrative civil servant; one retired university professor.

Beneficial area: Scotland, with a preference for Lothian and a further preference for Edinburgh.

Information available: Information was provided by the trust.

General: At 1st April 1994, the trust's assets were valued at £64,000, generating, with grants received, an income of £16,500. Expenses amounted to £231, enabling the trust to make one exceptional grant of £15,000.

The trust supports the Parkinson's Disease Society by way of an endowment to the Lothian Health Board, which provides free use of one section of a hospital as an assessment centre. The endowment covers salary costs.

Grants are awarded only to organisations concerned with the welfare of people with Parkinson's Disease or undertaking research relating to the disease. The maximum amount awarded in any one year is usually £5,000.

Applications: Application forms are available from the correspondent.

Miss Beveridge's Trust

£48,000 (1993/94)

Children in Edinburgh

Edinburgh Voluntary Organisations Trusts, 11 Colme Street, Edinburgh EH3 6AG
0131-225 4606

Correspondent: The Trust Fund Administrator

Beneficial area: Lothian.

Information available: Information was provided by the trust.

General: In 1993/94, the trust had assets of £1 million and an income of £48,000, all of which was given in grants.

Support is given to organisations working with children in the Edinburgh area (generally taken to be Lothian).

Grants are awarded on a one-off basis and range from £500 to £1,000.

Exclusions: No grants for organisations concerned solely with the arts; churches for repairs; private schools or colleges; organisations not recognised as charities by the Inland Revenue nor affiliated to such an organisation; any organisation or individual for which statutory funding could be available for the same purpose; directly to individuals; organisations which in turn disburse money.

Applications: Application forms are available from the correspondent. Trustees meet quarterly, usually in March, June, October and December.

The Bruce Bequest Committee for Mentally Handicapped

£1,500 (1993/94)

Young people with learning difficulties

c/o Verandah Club, Royal Edinburgh Hospital, Morningside Terrace, Edinburgh EH10 5HF
0131-339 1048

Correspondent: Mrs V L Green

Trustees: Mrs M K Watt; J Briggs.

Beneficial area: Edinburgh City.

Information available: Information was available from the trust.

General: The committee's income after expenses amounted to £11,000 in 1994. Grants totalled £1,500.

The committee has supported adult training centres and respite homes to enhance the leisure activities of the trainees and other organisations offering social activities and group leisure for people with learning difficulties.

Exclusions: Carers' expenses/salaries are not covered.

Applications: Application forms are available from the correspondent.

The Buccleuch Place Trust

£5,000 (1995)

General

Edinburgh Voluntary Organisations Trusts, 11 Colme Street, Edinburgh EH3 6AG
0131-225 4606

Correspondent: The Trust Fund Administrator

Trustees: Bishop R Holloway; R G Thom; J Malcolm.

Beneficial area: Edinburgh only.

Information available: Information was provided by the trust.

General: The trust's assets totalled £90,000 in 1995, generating an income of £6,600. Grants amounted to £5,200 and were awarded to organisations based in Edinburgh. The trust gives grants to a wide range of organisations but especially to those working with older people.

Exclusions: No grants to organisations or individuals outside Edinburgh.

Applications: Applications for grants over £200 are considered quarterly – contact the correspondent for an application form. Applications for under £200 should be made in writing to the correspondent.

The Courant Fund for Needy Children

£4,000 (1994)

Children in need

25 Comely Bank Grove, Edinburgh EH4 1BS
0131-332 6928

Correspondent: Miss M S Normand, Hon. Secretary

Beneficial area: Edinburgh.

Information available: Information was provided by the trust.

General: The trust only supports underprivileged children. In 1994, the trust had assets of £56,000 generating an income of £4,000, all of which was given in grants.

Grants are awarded to organisations working with children and cover the costs of holidays, outings, clothing, equipment and entertainment. Organisations supported include local bodies such as the Salvation Army, Police Clothing Fund and children's hospitals.

Applications: In writing to the correspondent enclosing supporting information. Applications are considered at any time in spring and autumn.

The Darling Charitable Trust

£900 (1994/95)

General

16 Hermitage Drive, Edinburgh EH10 6BZ
0131-447 6369

Correspondent: T Y Darling

Trustees: T Y Darling; Mrs A M Darling.

Beneficial area: Unrestricted, but with a preference for Edinburgh.

Information available: Information was supplied by the trust.

General: The trust's income is about £1,000 a year and the trustees favour good causes in which they themselves are directly or indirectly involved. Grants, which totalled £930 in 1994/95, usually range between £25 and £100.

18 organisations benefited in 1994/95, including the British Red Cross, Scottish Council for Spastics, Rotary Jubilee Charitable Fund, Marie Curie Cancer and Royal Blind Asylum and School.

Applications: In writing to the correspondent.

The East Lothian Educational Trust

£32,000 (1994/95) to schools and individuals

Education

26 Clifford Road, North Berwick,
East Lothian EH39 4PP
01620-892314

Correspondent: George Russell, Clerk

Beneficial area: Former county of East Lothian.

Information available: Information was available from the trust.

General: The trust supports the education of those living in the beneficial area. Grants are given both to individuals and to schools. In 1994/95, about £15,000 was given in 40 grants to schools and about £15,000 in 30 grants to individuals. Grants range between £200 and £500.

Exclusions: No grants for the benefit of people not belonging to the former county of East Lothian.

Applications: On a form available from the correspondent. Applications are considered in October.

The Edinburgh Children's Holiday Fund

£51,000 (1994)

Holidays for children, children's welfare

Ernst & Young, Chartered Accountants,
Ten George Street, Edinburgh EH2 2DZ
0131-226 6400

Correspondent: R C Moore, Treasurer

Trustees: W G Waterston; Lady Clerk; Mrs P Balfour.

Beneficial area: Edinburgh and the Lothians.

Information available: Information was provided by the trust.

General: In 1994, the trust had assets totalling £990,000, generating an income of £53,000. Grants to charities totalled £51,000.

Grants are awarded to organisations providing holidays for disadvantaged children or helping with children's welfare in Edinburgh and nearby areas.

Grants range between £50 and £8,000. Beneficiaries included Family Care (£8,000), East Lothian Handicapped Children (£2,500) and Lothian Regional Council which received £10,000 to help individual families.

Applications: In writing to the correspondent by 30th November of each year.

The Edinburgh Old Town Charitable Trust

£17,000 (1993/94)

Education, social welfare

8 Advocates Close, 357 High Street, Edinburgh EH1 1PS
0131-225 8818

Correspondent: Mrs Linda Bettles, Administrator

Trustees: Anja Amsel; I Begg; Lorna J Blackie; Catherine Burns; A Burrell; Cllr R Cairns; Lady Dunpark; J A Eddison; Richard Ewing; Nigel Fordyce; Gordon Izatt; Cllr G Kerevan; A Kerr; Dr D Lyddon; J McFarlane; A H B Mitchell; Mrs L Nicholsby; Rev Charles Robertson; G T Ross; Rev Dr D Shaw; Dr D Smith; R Smith;

Sir Jamie S Darling; J Swanson; J Thomson; Mrs M Whitfield; Lt Col D J Wickes.

Beneficial area: Edinburgh Old Town.

Information available: Information was supplied by the trust. Audited accounts for 1993/94 were available.

General: This trust was set up in 1987 to provide a channel for private funding to social welfare projects in Edinburgh Old Town. As a fundraising trust its income varies considerably from year to year.

In 1993/94, grants ranged from £100 to £4,000 and totalled £17,000. A variety of social welfare projects received support including St Ann's Mothers' and Toddlers' Group (£120), Southside Community Centre (£500), St Catherine's Convent (£4,000), and Old Town Gala (£1,750).

Exclusions: Profit-making organisations, organisations without charitable status and individuals are excluded.

Applications: Application forms are available from the correspondent.

Trusts Administered by Edinburgh Voluntary Organisations' Council

£159,000 (1994/95) to individuals and organisations

General

Ainslie House, 11 St Colme Street, Edinburgh EH2 4EQ
0131-225 4606

Correspondent: E A Matthews, Secretary

Trustees: Most Rev Richard Holloway; Jean Malcolm; Graeme Thom.

Beneficial area: Edinburgh and Lothian.

Information available: Written information is available on request.

General: Edinburgh Voluntary Organisations Council administers various trusts including The Beveridge Trust, The William Thyne Trust and The Kenneth Young Bequest Fund. They include general trusts supporting organisations in the beneficial area such as the Kenneth Young Bequest Fund, and specific trusts such as the Edinburgh Night Shelter Trust (organisations helping the homeless) and the Edinburgh Discharged Prisoner's Aid Society.

A total of £159,000 was awarded in grants to local organisations and individuals in 1994/95. The largest grants were to Edinburgh Voluntary Organisations Council (£26,800); Scottish Refugee Council (£4,800); Stevenson College (two grants totalling £4,500); Bosnia Now (£4,000); Edinburgh Central CAB and SOAPA (£3,000); British Red Cross (£2,000) and Milan (£1,500). Grants of £1,000 went to EAMH, ECSH, Garvald Centre, Lothian Association of Youth Clubs, Nucleus, St Clair Playgroup, Scotland Yard Adventure Playground and YWCA Runabout Centre.

Grants of under £1,000 totalling £29,700 were also made to organisations. A further £71,900 was given in grants to individuals.

Exclusions: The trusts do not help with church maintenance, private schools and colleges, organisations concerned solely with the arts, payments directly to individuals and trusts which disburse money.

Applications: In writing to the Trust Fund Administrator.

The Alice Hamilton Trust

£600 (1992/93)

Preservation and improvement of the environment, recreation

c/o West Linton Community Council, West Linton, Peebleshire EH46

Correspondent: The Chair

Beneficial area: West Linton and surrounding areas.

Information available: Accounts for 1992/93 are available from the trust.

General: The trust had funds totalling £52,000 in 1992/93, with an income of £2,700.

Grants amounting to £550 were awarded to charitable organisations for the preservation and improvement of the environment of the village of West Linton and for recreational facilities for residents.

Applications: In writing to the correspondent. This entry has not been confirmed by the trust.

The Lindsays Charitable Trust

Not known

General

Lindsays WS, 11 Atholl Crescent, Edinburgh EH3 8HE
0131-229 1212

Correspondent: The Secretary

Beneficial area: Scotland, mainly the Edinburgh area.

Information available: No financial information was available.

General: No information is available other than that the trust supports charities in Scotland, especially in the Edinburgh area.

Applications: In writing to the correspondent. The trustees meet once a year.

The Peter Lothian Newtongrange Charitable Trust

£2,000 (1992/93)

General

c/o Grange Estates (Newbattle) Ltd, Old Laboratory Building, Newtongrange, Midlothian EH22 4QN
0131-660 5311

Correspondent: Miss G Lesley Graham

Trustees: Rev J L McPake; Mrs E Swinton; A Storrie; I Nicholson; Miss G L Graham; Rev Paul Kelly; Mrs J Donaldson.

Beneficial area: Newtongrange.

Information available: Annual accounts for 1993/94 were available from the trust.

General: Most of the grants are given to help with the cost of transporting incapacitated people to hospital. A very small number of grants are given to organisations in Newtongrange which provide education, welfare or recreation facilities for the benefit of those living in Newtongrange.

Exclusions: No grants outside Newtowngrange.

Applications: Contact the correspondent for further details.

The Nancie Massey Charitable Trust

£152,000 (1994/95)

Education, medicine, the arts, children and elderly people

3 Albyn Place, Edinburgh EH2 4NQ
0131-225 7515

Correspondent: J G Morton

Trustees: J G Morton; C A Crole; E K Cameron.

Beneficial area: Edinburgh and Leith.

Information available: Full accounts are on file at the Charity Commission.

General: The trust was established in 1989 to help organisations supporting elderly people, children, medical research, education and the arts. Assistance is primarily given to projects established in the Edinburgh and Leith areas. In 1994/95, the trust gave grants totalling £152,000 from an income of £170,000, but no information was available on the beneficiaries.

The latest year for which a grant list was available was 1991/92 when 50 grants were made totalling £189,000. The largest were to the University of Edinburgh MRI Unit (£25,000), National Gallery of Scotland (£15,000) and the Scottish National Portrait Gallery (£12,500).

Grants of £10,000 went to the Royal Lyceum Theatre, Royal Infirmary of Edinburgh, Scottish International Disaster Relief Agency, Edinburgh International Festival, Scottish Wildlife Trust, Buildings of Scotland Trust and the Edinburgh Festival.

Other grants ranged from £100 to £5,000 to Scottish charities, local charities in Scotland and Scottish branches of UK charities.

Exclusions: Grants are not given to individuals.

Applications: In writing to the correspondent setting out in detail why the application is being made, how the donation will be spent and the overall cost of the project. Applications will be acknowledged, confirming whether they will be considered further.

The Pleasance Trust

£20,000 (1994)

Disadvantaged young people in Edinburgh

James Ivory, 45 Charlotte Square,
Edinburgh EH2 4HW
0131-226 3271

Correspondent: The Secretary

Trustees: N Campbell; F Ivory;
J Henderson; S Marshall.

Beneficial area: Edinburgh.

Information available: Accounts for 1994
were available from the trust.

General: In 1994, the trust had assets
totalling £400,000, generating an income of
about £20,000 all of which was given in
grants.

The trust gives grants to voluntary
organisations such as youth clubs working
with disadvantaged young people in
Edinburgh.

Exclusions: No grants to individuals or to
national organisations (except occasionally
for specific local projects).

Applications: No application form is
required. Applicants should contact the
correspondent for further details, although
they should note that the trust already
receives more applications than it can
support.

The Ponton House Trust

£39,000 (1994)

Young people, disadvantaged groups, elderly people

11 Atholl Crescent, Edinburgh EH3 8HE
0131-229 1212

Correspondent: David S Reith, Secretary

Trustees: G Gemmell; Hon. Lord Grieve;
Mrs G Russell; Mrs J Gilliat; Rev J Munro;
Mrs F Meikle; A Dobson.

Beneficial area: Lothian.

General: Grants are given mainly to
charities working with people in the 16 to 25
age range, with disadvantaged groups and
those providing training. The trustees are
also keen to help charities "where help from
Ponton House can make all the difference to
their financial viability".

Grants usually range between £250 and
£2,000 and totalled £39,000 in 1994.

The trust also operates a "Donate-a-Duvet
Scheme" providing free bedding to elderly
people on referrals from medical practices.

Applications: In writing to the
correspondent.

The Lord Rosebery Charitable Settlement

£5,000 (1993/94)

General

Coopers & Lybrand, Erskine House,
68 Queen Street, Edinburgh EH2 4NH
0131-226 4488

Correspondent: Mrs Jane Clark

Trustees: Rt Hon The Seventh Earl of
Rosebery; Countess of Rosebery;
D M Henderson.

Beneficial area: Mainly Edinburgh and
Lothians.

Information available: Accounts for
1993/94 were available from the trust.

General: The settlement's assets amounted
to £52,000 at April 1994, generating an
income of £4,500 in the same year. Grants
totalled £5,000.

30 charities, predominantly in the Edinburgh and Lothians area, covering a broad range of activities were supported. Grants did not exceed £1,000.

Exclusions: No grants to individuals.

Applications: Contact the correspondent for further information.

The Row Fogo Charitable Trust

£52,000 (1993/94)

Medical research, general

Messrs Brodies WS, 15 Atholl Crescent, Edinburgh EH3 8HA
0131-228 3777

Correspondent: Evan J Cuthbertson

Trustees: E J Cuthbertson; A W Waddell; Dr C Brough.

Beneficial area: Edinburgh, Lothians and Dunblane.

Information available: The information for this entry comes from the annual report and accounts available from the correspondent.

General: In 1994, the trust's assets were valued at £1.3 million. Grants are made for research into medical matters, with particular emphasis on the neurosciences.

In 1993/94, an exceptional grant of £500,000 (comprised of the trust's capital as well as income) was awarded to the Molecular Medicine Centre at the Western General Hospital in Edinburgh, with other grants totalling £52,000.

The trustees have adopted a policy of accumulating part of the income to reimburse the capital. In general, the trustees intend to utilise 50% of the income for medical research and connected problems; between 35% and 40% of available income

for specific projects undertaken by local charities and 10% to 15% for smaller charities.

Exclusions: No grants to individuals.

Applications: In writing to the correspondent. The trustees meet annually, although decisions regarding grant-making are made throughout the year.

The Russell Bequest

£10,000 (1993/94)

Sport

Lyle Crawford & Co, 15 Glenorchy Road, North Berwick EH39 4PE
01620-892090

Correspondent: R S Wotherspoon

Trustees: J B Macnair; G Wanless; R B R Walker.

Beneficial area: North Berwick.

Information available: Information is available from the correspondent.

General: The bequest had total assets of £495,000 in 1993/94 and grants totalling £10,000 were awarded to charitable organisations concerned with sport. Provision has been made for future charitable expenditure amounting to £300,000.

In 1993/94, grants were awarded to Thistle Archers (£456) and East Lothian Community Development Trust (£1,268). Sums approved were an additional £3,867 for East Lothian Community Development Trust and £4,250 for North Berwick High School.

Exclusions: Grants are only awarded to sports organisations in North Berwick.

Applications: Contact the correspondent for further details at: Minaki, York Road, North Berwick.

The Save & Prosper Educational Trust

£1,155,000 (1994/95)

Education

Finsbury Dials, 20 Finsbury Street,
London EC2Y 9AY
0171-417 2332

Correspondent: Duncan Grant, Director

Trustees: The trustee is Save & Prosper Group Ltd who appointed the following managing committee for the year under review: C J Rye (Chairman); D Grant; I W Lindsey; P J Rowney.

Beneficial area: UK with a special interest in the London borough of Havering and Edinburgh and the surrounding areas of both.

Information available: Accounts are on file at the Charity Commission.

General: The trust makes grants to organisations concerned with education and training in the inner cities; with education for disabled people; arts education and scholarships and bursaries for disadvantaged pupils (which are not made directly to individuals). Grants generally range between £100 and £30,000 and support is provided for up to two years.

The trust was established in 1974 in conjunction with the launch of a school fees planning service run by Save & Prosper Group Ltd. The trust gets its income from this scheme but is managed as a separate entity with its own staff.

The trust supports educational projects "which generally fit into one of the following categories:

- Support for primary and secondary schools, tertiary educational establishments such as universities as well as research bodies and museums.

- Community projects, particularly those relating to children and young people in inner-cities. We aim to improve the education and training of these people, particularly in information technology and to widen the opportunities open to them, giving them prospects of a more rewarding adult life.

- Arts education, with the emphasis on helping more people gain access to the arts and to better appreciate them. Support for performing, fine and decorative arts is usually directed at school-age children and students.

- Education for the disadvantaged. This covers special needs, inner cities, ethnic minorities, rural disadvantage, and youngsters in trouble or at risk.

- Scholarships and bursaries to organisations for educational fees and maintenance. Generally, direct support is not given to individuals.

- New and innovative ways of advancing education in the UK."

It is the usual policy of the trust to establish, where possible and appropriate, a relationship with successful applicants, particularly those receiving larger grants.

Although the general policy of the trust is not to make firm commitments for longer than two years, support can be continued in exceptional cases on a year to year basis without a commitment to any definite period.

In 1994/95, the trust's total net assets were £172,000 with income available for distribution totalling £1.2 million. 251 grants were given totalling £1.16 million (£1.36 million in 1993/94).

Beneficiaries in Scotland included Museum of Scotland (£33,000), Scottish Opera (£10,000 in two grants in 1994/95 and 1993/94), Scotvec (£8,000 in 1994/95 and £8,000 in 1993/94), Garvald Centre Edinburgh (£4,000), Edinburgh Common Purpose (£2,330), Highland Society for the Blind,

Highland and Islands Educational Trust and Scottish Youth Dance Festival (£1,000), Heriot-Watt University (Dundee Health Care) (£650), Scottish International Children's Festival (two grants of £500 each in 1994/95 and 1993/94), as well as a number of primary schools and colleges which received smaller grants of about £250.

Exclusions: The trust does not support open appeals from national charities, building appeals, charity gala nights and similar events, anniversary appeals, appeals by individuals for study grants, travel scholarships or charity sponsorships.

Applications: The initial approach should be addressed in writing to the correspondent. It should preferably be in the form of a brief letter (not exceeding two A4 sides) setting out the reason for the application and enclosing any relevant publicity material and accounts.

Applications are always acknowledged. If an application is unsuccessful, organisations should wait at least a year before re-applying. The trustees meet in March, May, July, September and December.

Mrs Rhoda Nina Scott's Trust

£10,000 (1994/95)

See below

Messrs Mackenzie & Wilson, Solicitors, 77 Crown Street, Aberdeen AB9 2AN 01224-589421

Correspondent: Robert Leslie May

Trustees: A R Carle; R L May.

Beneficial area: Edinburgh.

General: The trust's assets in 1994/95 were valued at £199,000, generating an income of £11,000. Grants totalled £10,000.

Grants are only awarded to three charities – the Scottish Society for the Prevention of Cruelty to Animals, Cancer Research Campaign and the Royal National Lifeboat Institution.

Applications: In writing to the correspondent, although applicants should note the above.

The Ernest Shering Evangelistic Trust

£1,000 (1992/93)

Christianity, social welfare

Balfour & Manson Nightingale & Bell, 58 Frederick Street, Edinburgh EH2 1LS 0131-225 8291

Trustees: D M Shering; Ruth Shering; S L Bannister;

Beneficial area: UK with a preference for Edinburgh.

Information available: An annual report and accounts are available from the trust.

General: The trust's income in 1993 was £7,750, of which £4,200 was donated by Shering Weighing Limited, a manufacturing company. The trustees are the chairman and directors of the company. As well as supporting the Christian religion, the trustees' report states that the trust may also support cultural, educational, religious or welfare work.

In 1992/93, the trustees made one donation of £1,000 to an Edinburgh church to be used to make gifts to people in need at Christmas time.

Applications: In writing to the correspondent. The trust did not wish to be included in the Guide.

The Tekoa Trust

£4,000 (1993/94)

Special needs, homelessness, wildlife

11 Nelson Street, Edinburgh EH3 6LF

Correspondent: William Balfour

Trustees: W H S Balfour; S J Balfour; M S Balfour.

Beneficial area: Lothian.

Information available: Accounts are available on request.

General: This is a small family trust and grants are normally awarded to organisations in which the trustees have a particular interest or in which they are involved.

Grants range between £250 and £500 and in 1993/94 a total of £4,000 was awarded to organisations such as Artlink, the Woodlands Trust, the Rock Trust, Scottish Wildlife Trust and the Big Issue.

Applications: In writing to the correspondent, although new applicants are unlikely to be considered as funds are already committed.

The John Wilson Bequest Fund

£46,000 (1994)

Poverty, health, missionary work

Messrs J & R A Robertson WS, 15 Great Stuart Street, Edinburgh EH3 7TS
0131-225 5095

Correspondent: A D Shepherd

Trustees: A M Bradley; Dr A Currie; A G D Johnston; Dr G M McAndrew; Dr H M MacLeod; D M Nicolson; C F Sleigh; Councillor J C Wilson.

Beneficial area: City of Edinburgh, Midlothian and East Lothian.

Information available: Accounts for 1994 were available from the trust.

General: The trust awarded grants totalling £45,350 in 1994 distributed as follows:

20% to charities

70% to individuals

10% to missionaries working overseas

Typical grants range between £250 and £2,250, with beneficiaries including Edinburgh Society for the Relief of Indigent Old Men, Leith Aged Mariners Fund and Bethany Christian Trust.

Applications: In writing to the correspondent, enclosing a recent set of accounts, by 31st January of each year.

Glasgow & West of Scotland

The Balmore Trust

£17,000 (1994)

Social welfare, young people, women's projects, third world

Viewfield, Balmore, Torrance,
Glasgow G64 4AE
01360-620742

Correspondent: The Secretary

Trustees: J Riches; Ms R Jarvis;
Ms O Beauvoisin; C Brown; Ms J Brown;
Ms M Brown; J Eldridge; S Hamilton; Ms R
Riches.

Beneficial area: Third world and UK with
a preference for Strathclyde.

Information available: The trust
produces an annual newsletter available free
in its shop, The Coach House Charity Craft
Shop in Balmore or by sending an SAE to the
Company Secretary at the above address.

General: The trust's assets consist of the
stock of its shop, The Coach House Charity
Craft Shop, and a small investment. The
figure for the trust's total income for 1994 is
not available but is roughly in line with its
grant total of £17,000.

Two thirds of the trust's grant total is
awarded to projects overseas, with the
remainder given in the UK. The trust favours
schemes which are in areas of greatest social
need and with which the trust has a personal
link. Projects are also supported by
importing and wholesaling high quality
crafts from co-operatives and women's
groups in the third world through the trust's
trading arm, "Just Trading Balmore".
Projects in the third world are also
supported in kind.

In 1994, grants were awarded on a one-off
basis to organisations such as the Diocese of
Namibia (£2,000), Scott Hospital, Lesotho
(£2,000), Child in Need Institute, Calcutta
(£400), Church House, Bridgeton, Glasgow
(£800), Strathkelvin Women's Aid (£800) and
Braendam Family House, Gargunnock
(£150).

The trust gives grants to local community
projects working with young people and
women.

Exclusions: No grants to individuals.

Applications: The trust is run entirely
voluntarily and unless the applicant is
known to the trust or has a connection with
The Coach House and could be categorised
as being in great social need, applications are
unlikely to succeed.

Applications should be made in writing to
the correspondent at the very beginning of
the year (disbursement is made annually in
February). The following information should
be provided:

- Details of the project for which funding is
  sought

- The amount requested
- Details of past and current funders
- An outline of the background and experience of key staff
- A copy of the organisation's recent accounts
- References
- Details of other funders the organisation is approaching
- Any other relevant information.

Applications are only acknowledged if an sae is enclosed.

The Bellahouston Bequest Fund

£92,000 (1994)

Protestant religion, church restoration

Messrs Mitchells Roberton, George House, 36 North Hanover Street, Glasgow G1 2AD
0141-552 3422

Correspondent: E H Webster

Trustees: Sir T Dunlop; B G Hardie; D H Galbraith; W Bowie; N W McMillan; E H Webster.

Beneficial area: Within five miles of the City of Glasgow boundary.

Information available: The fund's annual report is available from the correspondent.

General: The fund states its objectives are to help build, expand and repair Protestant Evangelical churches or places of religious worship, as well as supporting the clergy of these churches, to give grants to charities for the relief of poverty or disease and to support organisations concerned with promoting the Protestant Evangelical religion, education and conservation of places of historical and artistic significance. All organisations should be within the parliamentary boundaries of the City of Glasgow or within a five mile radius of the Glasgow district.

Grants which totalled £92,000 in 1994, ranged between £40 and £5,000. Churches benefiting included Strathbungo Parish Church (£5,000), St Marks Church, Drumchapel (£3,000), St Thomas' Church, Gallowgate (£1,000), Colston Wellpark Parish Church (£750) and the United Free Church, Knightswood (£500).

Other charitable organisations supported include Glasgow Cathedral Organ Restoration Project (£2,500), The Pearce Institute (£1,500), Epilepsy Association of Scotland, Prince and Princess of Wales Hospice, Royal Highland Fusiliers, Scottish Council on Alcohol and SENSE Scotland (£1,000 each), Ibrox Safe Play Group, Lorne Street Primary School, Mental Health Institute, Rehab Scotland and Scottish Prison Mission (£500 each) and City of Glasgow Society of Social Service (£450).

Exclusions: No grants to organisations or churches whose work does not fall within the geographical remit of the fund. The fund only gives to registered charities.

Applications: In writing to the correspondent.

The Charities Aid Fund of the City of Glasgow Society of Social Service

£30,000 (1994/95)

General

The City of Glasgow Society of Social Service, 30 George Square, Glasgow G2 1EG
0141-248 3535

Correspondent: James Smillie, Secretary

Beneficial area: Glasgow.

Information available: Information was provided by the trust.

General: In 1994/95, the fund's income was £39,000. £30,000 was distributed to charities in the beneficial area. No further information was available.

Applications: In writing to the correspondent.

The Chrimes Family Charitable Trust

£15,000 (1994)

Social welfare

Northfield, Upper Raby Road, Neston, South Wirral L64 7TZ
0151-336 4959

Correspondent: Mrs Anne Williams

Trustees: Mrs A Williams; H Kirkham-Prosser.

Beneficial area: Priority to Merseyside, Strathclyde, Newcastle-upon-Tyne and North Wales.

Information available: Information was supplied by the trust.

General: In 1994, the trust's assets totalled £253,000 and the income amounted to £114,000. A total of £15,000 was awarded in grants. The trust gives grants for general charitable purposes and prefers to support community welfare on Merseyside.

Work elsewhere is supported if it focuses on community welfare, is original or of "outstanding excellence".

Exclusions: No grants to individuals for educational purposes.

Applications: In writing to the correspondent.

The Peter Coats Trust

Not known

Not known

152 Bath Street, Glasgow G2 4TB
0141-332 9988

Correspondent: David McRobert

Beneficial area: Paisley.

Information available: No financial information was available.

General: No information available.

Applications: In writing to the correspondent. This entry has not been confirmed by the trust. The address details are correct.

The Common Good Fund of the District Council

Not known

General

Bearsden and Milngavie District Council, Municipal Buildings, Boclair, 100 Milngavie Road, Bearsden, Glasgow G61 2TQ
0141-942 2262

Correspondent: The Chief Executive

Beneficial area: Bearsden.

Information available: No financial information was available.

General: The fund gives grants towards the costs of work undertaken by organisations based in Bearsden. Grants are not awarded to organisations which raise money through house-to-house collections or flag days.

Applications: On a form available from the correspondent which must be returned by 31st December of each year. Applications are considered annually in January.

Charities Administered by Dumfries & Galloway Council

Not known

General

Dumfries and Galloway Council, Council Offices, English Street, Dumfries DG1 2DD
01387-261234

Correspondent: Chief Executive's Department

Beneficial area: Former burghs of Sanquhar and Dumfries.

Information available: Information was provided by the trust.

General: These charities were formerly administered by Nithsdale District Council, which ceased to exist on 31st March 1996. At the time of writing the administration of the charities was likely to be managed by Dumfries and Galloway Council.

The two common good funds were valued at £328,000 in 1994/95. This would presumably generate an income of about £20,000 to £25,000. Grants are given to local organisations for general charitable purposes. No further details were available.

Exclusions: Organisations outside the beneficial area are not supported.

Applications: Contact the correspondent for further details. Potential applicants should note that contact details were unconfirmed at the time of writing, owing to the changes in local government.

The Dumfriesshire Educational Trust

£18,000 (1992/93) including grants to individuals

Education

Regional Council Offices, English Street, Dumfries DG1 2DD
01387-61234

Correspondent: James M Smith, Clerk

Beneficial area: The former county of Dumfriesshire.

Information available: Accounts were available for 1992/93.

General: The trust had assets of £198,000 in 1992/93, generating an income of £7,000. Grants totalled £18,000 and are given for educational purposes. This includes grants to clubs, as well as organisations promoting education in music, drama, the arts and sport. Grants range from £20 to £200.

In 1992/93, £125 was given for sports facilities and £1,100 to promote education in the visual arts.

Exclusions: No grants to organisations or individuals based outside Dumfriesshire.

Applications: On a form available from the correspondent.

The Ferguson Bequest Fund

£117,376 (1994) to individuals and churches

Maintenance and repair of church buildings

182 Bath Street, Glasgow G2 4HG
0141-332 0476

Correspondent: Angus Sutherland, Secretary

Beneficial area: South West Scotland.

Information available: Accounts are available from the trust.

General: The trust was established in 1869 to maintain and repair church buildings and to help educational activities in the churches of Ayr, Kirkcudbright, Wigtown, Lanark, Renfrew and Dumbarton.

In 1994, the trust's assets totalled £1.5 million, generating an income of £134,000. Grants totalled £117,000.

A number of beneficiaries were individuals receiving education or relief-in-need grants. Grants to churches totalled £111,950, although this included retirement gifts, stipends and grants to probationers. The accounts record that £67,400 was spent on church repairs, and named beneficiaries in addition to this general category were: Congregational Church College, United Free Church and Free Church College (£850 each) and Church House (£750).

Exclusions: Churches outside the beneficial area are not supported.

Applications: In writing to the correspondent.

The Gaul Trust

£4,000 a year

Health

Clydebank District Council, District Council Offices, Clydebank G81 1TG
0141-941 1331

Correspondent: Chief Executive's Department

Beneficial area: Clydebank.

Information available: Information was supplied by the trust.

General: The trust supports charities in the Clydebank area concerned with health. It makes grants totalling about £4,000 a year.

Applications: In writing to the correspondent.

The Gemmell Bequest Fund

£8,000 (1995)

General

Bishop and Robertson Chalmers Solicitors, 2 Blythswood Square, Glasgow G2 4AD
0141-248 4672

Correspondent: The Secretary

Trustees: M S L Thomson; I L Dunsmore.

Beneficial area: Glasgow and the Parish of Sorn, Ayrshire.

Information available: Information was provided by the trust.

General: The trust's assets totalled £151,000 in 1995, generating an income of £10,000. Grants totalled £8,000 and were awarded for general charitable purposes. Many grants are awarded on an annual recurrent basis, but one-off grants ranging between £50 and £100 can be made.

Exclusions: No grants to individuals nor to charities outside the stated beneficial area.

Applications: In writing to the correspondent.

The Glasgow-Kilmun Charitable Society

£15,000 (1994/95) to individuals and organisations

Relief-in-need

The City of Glasgow Society of Social Service, 30 George Square, Glasgow G2 1EG
0141-248 3535

Correspondent: James Smillie, Secretary

Beneficial area: Glasgow.

Information available: Information was provided by the trust.

General: In 1994/95, the trust had an income of £13,000, and gave £15,000 in grants to individuals and organisations. The society supports recuperative holidays for those who may be unable to afford the cost, and supports the work of convalescent homes and other charitable organisations which provide holidays for those in need.

Applications: In writing to the correspondent.

The Glendoune Charitable Trust

Not known

Forces charities

Messrs A J & A Graham, 110 West George Street, Glasgow G2 1QA
0141-332 2441

Correspondent: A L Aitkenhead

Beneficial area: Ayrshire.

Information available: See below.

General: The trust supports forces charities. This trust offered to provide a copy of the accounts on payment of a fee. As the number of trusts in this book would have made payment on each set of accounts prohibitive, the offer was declined, and no further information is available on the activities of the trust.

Applications: Contact the correspondent for further information.

The Dora Hay Charitable Trust

£2,700 (1994)

General

Bannerman, Johnstone Maclay, Tara House, 46 Bath Street, Glasgow G2 1HG
0141-332 2999

Correspondent: G J Johnstone

Trustees: J G L Robinson; G J Johnstone.

Beneficial area: Moffat.

Information available: Information was provided by the trust.

General: In 1994, the trust had assets totalling £51,000, generating an income of £2,700 all of which was given in grants. Organisations based in Moffat are given preference.

Applications: Contact the correspondent for further details.

The Holywood Trust

£72,000 (1993/94)

Disadvantaged young people

Mount St Michael, Craigs Road, Dumfries DG1 4UT
01387-269176

Correspondent: Peter Robertson, Director

Trustees: C A Jencks; Mrs C Wagg; Capt A E Weatherall; Lady C Keswick; J J G Brown; A M Macleod.

Beneficial area: Dumfries and Galloway.

Information available: A leaflet about the trust is available.

General: Grants to charities in 1993/94 totalled £72,000 and ranged between £10 and £10,000. Support is given to organisations concerned with young people between the ages of 15 and 25 who are disadvantaged, particularly self-help groups and organisations involving the wider community.

In 1993/94, organisations benefiting included Dumfries YMCA, Boys Brigade, BBC Children in Need in Dumfries & Galloway, and Duke of Edinburgh's Award Scheme Regional Committee.

Exclusions: Grants are not given to political parties, as a substitute for statutory funding, for landlord's deposits, nor for retrospective applications.

Applications: In writing to the correspondent, outlining the project on no more than two A4 sheets. Applications are considered every six to eight weeks.

The Hoover Foundation

£261,000 (1993/94)

Education, health, welfare

Pentrebach, Methyr Tydfil, Mid-Glamorgan CF48 4TU
01685-721222

Correspondent: Mrs Marion Heaffey

Trustees: D J Hunt; S West.

Beneficial area: National, but with a special interest in South Wales, Glasgow and Bolton.

Information available: Accounts, but without details of donations made, are on file at the Charity Commission.

General: The trust is "primarily committed to supporting children and locally based charitable works in and around the immediate areas of our employee locations".

In 1993/94, the trust had assets of £2 million generating an income of £200,000. Grants totalled £261,000 and are categorised as follows in the accounts (1992/93 figures in brackets):

Education	£48,000	(£70,000)
Medical and welfare	£125,500	(£76,300)
Youth organisations	£5,000	(£9,000)
Other activities	£82,100	(£84,100)

Although in 1993/94, donations exceeded income, future policy is that donations will be no more than income in any year.

Exclusions: Few grants for individuals.

Applications: In writing to the correspondent. The trustees review quarterly the financial donations to be made.

The George Hunter Trust

£1,000 (1994)

Social welfare

Annandale & Eskdale District Council, District Council Chambers, High Street, Annan DG12 6AQ
01461-203311

Correspondent: Mrs Delna Weston, District Solicitor

Trustees: James Gordon; Rev Jack Owen; Tom Russell; Anthony Turner.

Beneficial area: Lochmaben.

Information available: Information was provided by the trust.

General: In 1994, the trust had assets totalling £7,000 and an income of £1,000, all of which was given in grants.

Grants range between £50 and £400 and are awarded to community groups and voluntary organisations promoting the well-being of the local community of Lochmaben.

Applications: Contact the correspondent for further details.

The Islay Campbell Trust

Not known

General

c/o The Highland Fund Ltd, 56 Kirkintilloch Road, Bishopbriggs, Glasgow
0141-204 3570

Correspondent: D MacDonald, Secretary

Beneficial area: Islay.

Information available: No financial information available.

General: Grants are awarded to charities benefiting the residents of Islay.

Applications: Contact the correspondent at the above address for further details. This entry has not been confirmed by the trust.

The Kennyhill Bequest Fund

£12,000 (1994)

Deprived people

Messrs Mitchells Roberton, George House, 36 North Hanover Street, Glasgow G1 2AD
0141-552 3422

Correspondent: J A M Cuthbert

Trustees: W S Henderson; P C Paisley; Mrs Gillian Weir; J A M Cuthbert.

Beneficial area: Glasgow only.

Information available: Information was provided by the trust.

General: The trust's income totalled £12,000 in 1994. Funds are awarded to charitable organisations in Glasgow working for deprived people.

Exclusions: No grants are given to organisations outside Glasgow.

Applications: In writing to the correspondent. The trustees meet annually in December.

Lamb's Bequest

£5,500 (1994)

General

City Chambers, 285 George Street, Glasgow G2 1DU
0141-227 4042/4044/4068

Correspondent: The Director of Finance

Trustees: Glasgow District Council Finance Committee.

Beneficial area: Glasgow.

Information available: Information was provided by the trust.

General: In 1993/94, the trust's assets totalled £74,000, generating an income of £5,540, all of which was distributed in grants. Three quarters of the total is given in equal amounts to Glasgow Royal Infirmary, Glasgow Royal Workshops for the Blind and Glasgow & West of Scotland Society for the Deaf and Dumb. The remaining quarter is distributed "for the benefit of the poor of the city". Amounts vary according to income.

Exclusions: No grants to individuals.

Applications: Contact the correspondent for further details.

The McCallum Bequest Fund

£15,000 a year

Relief of poverty and illness

Macdonalds, Solicitors, 1 Claremont Terrace, Glasgow G3 7UQ
0141-248 6221

Correspondent: The Secretary

Trustees: G G Morris; Mrs G E Morris.

Beneficial area: Glasgow.

Information available: Information was provided by the trust.

General: Assets total around £225,000 and generate an annual income of £15,000 which is distributed in grants.

Grants are awarded to organisations based in Glasgow which benefit Glasgow residents and which are concerned with the relief of poverty and illness. The fund also gives grants for bursaries and scholarships for law students at Glasgow University.

Exclusions: No grants to individuals, organisations of a purely religious, educational or sporting nature or organisations outside Glasgow.

Applications: In writing to the correspondent. However, few new applications are likely to succeed as funds are already committed.

The Agnes McGallagley Bequest

£30,000 (1993/94)

Religion, education, social welfare

196 Clyde Street, Glasgow G1 4JY

Correspondent: The Chancellor

Trustees: Cardinal T J Winning.

Beneficial area: Glasgow.

Information available: The bequest's accounts for 1993/94 were available.

General: The bequest's assets in 1993/94 totalled £203,000 with an income of £39,000 (£34,000 in 1992/93). Grants totalled £30,000 in the same year (£22,000 in 1992/93).

The bequest takes care of the upkeep of the Archbishop of the Archdiocese of Glasgow's residence.

However, funds are also awarded to charities concerned with education and religion (particularly Roman Catholicism) and social welfare. In 1993/94, all grants were towards the maintenance of the Archbishop's residence.

Applications: Contact the correspondent for further details.

MacGregor's Bequest

£9,000 (1994/95)

Social welfare, general

City of Glasgow District Council, PO Box 19, 285 George Street, Glasgow G2 1DU
0141-227 4044/4068

Correspondent: The Director of Finance

Beneficial area: City of Glasgow.

Information available: Information was provided by the trust.

General: The trust's income over the period 1992-1994 ranged between £8,000 and £9,000 a year.

In 1994/95, £8,750 was given in grants which generally range from £100 to £1,000. Beneficiaries included Shelter Scotland (£800), Fairbridge in Scotland (£400), SENSE in Scotland (£500) and PARC (£350).

Exclusions: No funds for religious organisations, for organisations based outside the City of Glasgow, nor for individuals.

Applications: In writing to the correspondent by December of each year, including details of the organisation's work, a set of annual accounts and an outline of the project for which funding is requested. Grants are disbursed in January of each year.

The McGregor's Trust

£9,000 (1993/94)

General

Glasgow District Council, City Chambers, Glasgow G2 1DU
0141-227 4044/4068

Correspondent: The Director of Finance

Beneficial area: Glasgow.

Information available: Information was provided by the trust.

General: In 1993/94, the trust had assets of £119,000 generating an income of £9,000 all of which was given in grants.

The trust gives grants to organisations based in Glasgow for general charitable purposes. Grants range between about £100 and £1,000 and beneficiaries include the Glasgow Simon Community (£1,000); Barnardos (£700); RSSPCC (£500); Riding for the Disabled (£100) and Shelter (£800).

Exclusions: No grants to religious organisations.

Applications: Contact the correspondent for further details.

The Merchants House of Glasgow

Not known

General

7 West George Street, Glasgow G2 1BA
0141-221 8272

Correspondent: The Collector

Beneficial area: Glasgow and the West of Scotland.

Information available: No financial information available.

General: Grants are awarded to registered charities based in the beneficial area for general charitable purposes. No further information is available about the size of grants or the beneficiaries. The Merchants House of Glasgow is one of a number of Merchants Houses found in the major Scottish cities.

Exclusions: No grants are given to individuals.

Applications: Contact the correspondent for further details.

Middleton's Bequest

£1,900 (1993/94)

General

Glasgow District Council, City Chambers, 285 George Street, Glasgow G2 1DU
0141-227 4044/4068

Correspondent: The Director of Finance

Beneficial area: Glasgow.

Information available: Information was provided by the trust.

General: In 1993/94, the trust had assets totalling £25,000 generating an income of

£1,875. Grants to charities totalled £1,900 in the same year.

The bequest gives grants to organisations undertaking general charitable work in the city of Glasgow. Grants range between £200 and £900 and beneficiaries included the Open Close Community, Glasgow City Mission and the Salvation Army.

Applications: Contact the correspondent for further details.

The Thomas Wharrie Morrison Bequest Fund

£10,000 (1994)

Ex-services, illness and poverty connected with the armed services

Mitchells Roberton, George House, 36 North Hanover Street, Glasgow G1 2AD
0141-552 3422

Correspondent: W Grant

Trustees: A J B Agnew; D C Prior; J R Findlay; W F C Forbes; W M C Grant.

Beneficial area: Glasgow and district.

General: The fund's assets totalled £105,000 in 1994, generating an income of £10,000 all of which was distributed in grants. The Princess Louise Scottish Hospital, Erskine received £3,600 and Soldiers', Sailors' and Airmen's Families Association and Forces Help Society, Glasgow received £1,500.

All the other grants were for £600 and were given to: Bridge of Weir, British Limbless Ex-Services Men's Association, City of Glasgow Society of Social Services Inc, Ex-Services Mental Welfare Society, Glasgow Old People's Welfare Committee, National Playing Fields Association (Scottish Branch), Prince and Princess of Wales Hospice, Quarrier's Homes and Society for the Blind in Glasgow and West of Scotland.

Grants are usually awarded on a one-off basis and are to fund a specific project. Grants are not usually awarded to cover core costs.

Exclusions: No grants to individuals. Registered charities only.

Applications: In writing to the correspondent, enclosing details of the project and an outline of the costings.

James & John Napier's Trust

£16,000 (1994/95)

Disabled young people, elderly people, maritime, medical research

Headrick Inglis Glen & Co, 48 West Regent Street, Glasgow G2 2QR
0141-332 3341

Correspondent: Neil M Headrick

Trustees: A S Headrick; N M Headrick; I Bruce.

Beneficial area: Glasgow and the West of Scotland.

Information available: Accounts are available from the correspondent.

General: The trust had assets of £173,000 in 1994/95. A total of £16,000 was given to charities (£14,000 in 1993/94).

The trust states that grants are awarded to smaller local organisations and charities in Glasgow and the West of Scotland. Grants are awarded to a wide range of organisations and in 1994/95 all beneficiaries received £1,000 each (grants ranged between £500 and £750 in 1993/94).

Beneficiaries were the County of the City of Glasgow Girl Guides; Community Central Hall; Glasgow and West of Scotland Society for the Blind; Beatson Oncology Centre;

Shipwrecked Fishermen and Mariners Benevolent Society; Salvation Army; Cancer Relief Macmillan Fund; Scottish Council for Spastics; Association of Youth Clubs in Strathclyde; Scottish Campaign for Homeless People; YWCA, Riding for the Disabled Association – Glasgow group; NSF Scotland; Scottish Foundation for Kidney Disease; Glasgow City Mission and Glasgow and West of Scotland Outward Bound Association.

Applications: In writing to the correspondent.

The Night Asylum Fund

£19,500 (1994/95)

Young people in Glasgow

City of Glasgow Society of Social Services, 30 George Square, Glasgow G2 1EG
0141-248 3535

Correspondent: James Smillie, General Secretary

Beneficial area: Glasgow.

Information available: Information was provided by the trust.

General: In 1994/95, the trust had assets totalling £ 411,000 generating an income of £21,500. Grants totalled £19,500.

The fund gives grants to organisations concerned with young people which work to prevent vagrancy, homelessness, delinquency and the breakdown of the family unit.

Applications: In writing to the correspondent.

The John Primrose Trust

£7,800 (1993/94)

Welfare, education

92 Irish Street, Dumfries DG1 2PF
01387-67316

Trustees: J Wyllie Irving; Matthew J Pumphrey; John C Burn.

Beneficial area: Dumfries and Maxwelltown.

Information available: Accounts for 1993/94 were available from the trust.

General: The trust was established in 1925 for the benefit of the poor of Dumfries and Maxwelltown. It gives grants to help with rent or educational needs of young people, both to individuals and organisations.

In 1993/94, the trust had assets of £213,000 and an income of £10,000. Grants totalled nearly £8,000 including £4,125 to individuals and £3,707 to institutions.

Applications: In writing to the correspondent.

Radio Clyde – Cash for Kids at Christmas

£480,000 (1994)

Children in the Strathclyde area

Clyde Action, 236 Clyde Street, Glasgow G1 4JH
0141-204 1025; Fax: 0141-248 2148

Correspondent: Robert Caldwell, Trustee

Trustees: Alex Dickson; John R Bowman; Robert F Caldwell.

Beneficial area: West and Central Scotland ie. the Radio Clyde broadcasting area.

Information available: Accounts and guidelines for applicants are available from Clyde Action.

General: This fund is administered by Clyde Action, the media wing of CSV (Community Service Volunteers). Every Christmas, Clyde Action, the community broadcasting arm of Radio Clyde, organises a massive appeal on behalf of children in West Central Scotland. On-air events such as radio auctions are combined with fundraising events organised by listeners all over the region. In its conditions of grant, Clyde Action states that "the appeal, which runs for six weeks until Christmas, depends on the goodwill of the listening public and, to maintain their level of donations, we have found it extremely helpful in the past to interview representatives of organisations who benefit from the appeal. If asked to help in this way, we hope that you will be cooperative."

The Cash for Kids at Christmas appeal is designed to raise money to provide Christmas treats for sick and underprivileged children whose families are unable to do so from their own resources and who would otherwise miss out. Examples of how the appeal has helped include Christmas presents, food and clothing, pantomime trips etc. Beneficiaries are selected by Clyde Action in conjunction with the Social Work Department of Strathclyde Regional Council.

Both groups and individuals can apply; however, individual children not known to the department must be nominated by a head teacher, parish priest or minister who is aware of the family circumstances and who will take responsibility for the cashing of the cheque. Community or voluntary groups applying to the appeal do not have to be registered charities, but they must obtain a covering letter of support from a local authority officer such as a community social worker. After the grant has been received, a report must be submitted detailing how that money was spent.

In 1994, grants totalled £480,000.

Exclusions: Grants are not available for salaries, equipment or summer or Easter trips. Grants are only available for children in the age range 0 to 16 years.

Applications: Clyde Action states in its conditions of grant that it "welcomes applications from all bona-fide sources to ensure that children living in the west of Scotland who need assistance from the appeal actually receive it". Application forms (which are short and simple) are available from Clyde Action.

The Renfield Street Trust

£9,200 (1994)

Maintenance and repair of Scottish churches in Glasgow, general

182 Bath Street, Glasgow G2 4HG
0141-332 0476

Correspondent: Angus Sutherland, Secretary

Beneficial area: Glasgow.

Information available: Accounts are available from the trust.

General: The trust's principle object is to maintain Renfield St Stephen's Church and Centre in Glasgow which received £378,000 in 1994. It also gives a number of grants for the building and repair of Scottish churches in the beneficial area.

The trust's general fund had an income of £87,000 in 1994. £13,000 was spent on administration and £9,200 was given in grants. Beneficiaries receiving £500 each were: Boys Brigade; Girls Brigade; BLESMA (Scotland); Christian Aid; Scottish Institute for the War Blinded; YMCA and YWCA. All but one of these were recurrent from the previous year.

Applications: In writing to the correspondent. The trust states that it has heavy commitments at present, and is currently declining new applications.

The Russell Trust

Not known

General

Hamilton, Burns and Moore, 3 Carmunnock Road, Mount Florida, Glasgow G44 4TZ
0141-632 2248

Correspondent: The Secretary

Beneficial area: Glasgow.

Information available: No financial information available.

General: No information available.

Applications: In writing to the correspondent.

The Rosemary Scanlan Charitable Trust

£51,000 (1993/94)

General

Messrs Grant Thornton, Chartered Accountants, 112 West George Street, Glasgow G2 1QF
0141-332 7484

Trustees: Cardinal T J Winning; K Sweeney; Rosemary McKenna.

Beneficial area: Glasgow.

Information available: Accounts for 1993/94 are available from the trust.

General: The trust's assets in 1993/94 totalled £550,000 and income amounted to £76,000.

A total of £51,000 was given in the following grants: Linacre Centre (£10,000); Shelter (£5,000); Archdiocese of Glasgow, Pastoral Education (£12,000); St Aloysius College (£20,300).

Applications: Contact the correspondent for further details.

The Templeton Goodwill Trust

£95,000 (1994)

General

12 Doon Street, Motherwell, Lanarkshire ML1 2BN
01698-262202

Correspondent: W T P Barnstaple

Trustees: A D Montgomery; J H Millar; Mrs A A Hannah; W T P Barnstaple.

Beneficial area: Glasgow and the West of Scotland.

Information available: Information was supplied by the trust.

General: In 1994, the trust's assets totalled £800,000. Grants totalling £95,000 were given to charities in Glasgow and the West of Scotland.

Organisations benefiting included youth organisations, medical research charities, churches and other organisations concerned with social work and providing caring services for all age groups.

Exclusions: Registered charities only.

Applications: Contact the correspondent for further details.

The Trades House of Glasgow

£300,000 (1994/95)

Social welfare, general

310 St Vincent Street, Glasgow G2 5QR
0141- 228 8000

Correspondent: The Clerk

Trustees: Incorporated by Act of Parliament.

Beneficial area: Glasgow.

Information available: A report and accounts are available. These do not include a list of grants.

General: The Trades House of Glasgow manages a wide range of trust funds, each bound to its separate trust deed. It works in close association with Glasgow's 14 Incorporated Trades which are Scottish equivalents of the craft guilds and livery companies which developed in European cities in the middle ages. They include the Hammermen, Barbers and Masons whose members now may be electronic engineers, brain surgeons or surveyors, or civil engineers. Most of the trusts of the Incorporated Trades are tied to precise objects and beneficial areas. The majority are concerned with various aspects of social welfare and individual need particularly in Glasgow. The House's staff of five includes two social workers.

In May 1995, the total assets of the combined trusts under the control of the House was around £8.5 million which generated an income of about £500,000 from which grants totalling £300,000 were made. Disbursements were made in 1994/95 as follows:

Bursaries and educational grants	£15,000
Individual beneficiaries	£138,000
Other charitable grants	£150,000

Lists of grants were not given with the annual accounts. In its booklet the Trades House describes its work as concerned with "numerous good causes; helping those in need, encouraging promising youngsters at college or in industry, and many other worthwhile projects. In addition, when particular causes are put forward the Trades House seeks to respond by raising new funds to support them."

The example quoted in its booklet was its support to a conservation and research expedition led by Glasgow University to Papua New Guinea in 1987. Other initiatives included the Glasgow Schools Craft Work Competition and Exhibition, and the Glasgow Schools Craft Project.

One of its major trusts is the Commonweal Fund which had assets of over £2.5 million in 1994/95. Its work is described as support for "good and pious uses tending to the advancement of the Commonweal of the Burgh".

Schemes which will be of benefit to citizens of Glasgow may receive consideration even when the schemes are not exclusively based in the city. Grants over recent years have been made to a variety of projects from medical research at Glasgow University to Cancer Relief, prizes for the Scottish Motor Neurone Disease Association, gifts for geriatric wards, projects for disabled people, holidays for disabled children, help for the elderly and disadvantaged, projects to help with work experience for the young unemployed, chaplaincy costs for overseas students, conservation in Glasgow, adventure holiday equipment for youth clubs, aid to deep sea fishermen and numerous other worthwhile activities.

Prospective applicants should contact the correspondent for further information.

Applications: In writing to the correspondent but only after obtaining details about the grant-making practices of the trusts to ensure that a relevant approach is made.

The Murray Usher Foundation

£3,500 (1993/94)

General

Cally Estate Office, Gatehouse-of-Fleet,
Dumfries & Galloway DG7 2HX
01557-814361

Correspondent: The Administrator

Trustees: J Murray Usher, Chairman

Beneficial area: Former burgh of
Gatehouse-of-Fleet and the parishes of
Girthon and Anwoth.

Information available: Accounts are
available from the trust.

General: The trust's first object is to support
charitable organisations working for the
benefit of people living in the beneficial area.

In 1993/94, grants to Gatehouse-of-Fleet
amenities totalled £2,300, and other charities
received grants totalling £1,160.

Applications: In writing to the
correspondent.

Highlands & Islands

The Brownies Taing Pier Trust

Not known

Community groups

Tait & Peterson, Bank of Scotland Buildings, Lerwick, Shetland Islands ZE1 0EB
01595-693010

Correspondent: George S Peterson

Beneficial area: Sandwick and Levenwick.

Information available: No financial information was available.

General: Grants are given to community projects in Sandwick and Levenwick. Projects which receive part of their funding from the local community are given preference.

No further information is available about recent beneficiaries or the size of grants.

Applications: Contact the correspondent for further details. This entry has not been confirmed by the trust. The address details are correct at time of going to press.

The Common Good Fund

Not known

General

Highland Council, Regional Buildings, Glenurquhart Road, Inverness IV3 5NX
01463-702000

Correspondent: The Chief Executive's Department

Beneficial area: The former Royal Burgh of Inverness.

Information available: No financial information was available.

General: Grants are awarded to organisations based only in the beneficial area for general charitable purposes. The fund was previously administered by the Inverness District Council which ceased to exist on 31st March 1996. At the time of writing details of the future administration of the fund were still uncertain.

Exclusions: Organisations outside the beneficial area will not be supported.

Applications: Contact the correspondent for further details. Potential applicants should note that contact details were unconfirmed at the time of writing.

The Cromarty Trust

£15,000 (1994)

Preservation of buildings, conservation, education

Wormshill Court, Sittingbourne,
Kent ME9 0TS
01622-884235

Correspondent: Michael Nightingale of Cromarty

Trustees: M Nightingale of Cromarty; Miss E V de B Murray; J Nightingale.

Beneficial area: UK, with a preference for the parish of Cromarty.

Information available: Information was provided by the trust.

General: Grants totalled £15,000 in 1994 and were awarded to organisations mainly in the parish of Cromarty concerned with preservation of buildings of historical or architectural interest, conservation and education of the public in the history, character and wildlife of the parish of Cromarty.

Exclusions: Unsolicited appeals other than those from the parish of Cromarty will not receive a response.

Applications: Applications are not invited.

The Howard Doris Trust

£83,000 (1994)

General

Brodies, 15 Atholl Crescent,
Edinburgh EH3 8HA
0131-228 3777

Correspondent: The Secretary

Beneficial area: Lochcarron, South West Ross.

Information available: Information is available from the trust.

General: The trust's annual income amounts to £28,000, a small proportion of which is awarded to individuals. Owing to the large number of appeals it receives, the trust is spending considerably more than its income. Grants to charities totalled £83,000 in 1994.

Grants are usually one-off and for general charitable purposes to organisations based in the districts of Lochcarron and South West Ross. Grants (or loans) are given to encourage new employment and for educational purposes.

Applications: In writing to the correspondent.

Mrs A M Garnett's 1973 Charitable Trust

£16,000 (1995)

Medical, education, environment

Chiene & Tait, 3 Albyn Place,
Edinburgh EH2 4NQ
0131-225 7515

Correspondent: J G Morton

Trustees: E Drysdale; J Drysdale; J A Findlay.

Beneficial area: UK, with a preference for the Highlands of Scotland.

Information available: A set of accounts is available from the trust on payment of £25 to cover administration.

General: The trust's total assets in 1995 amounted to £290,000, generating an income of £19,000. Grants totalled £16,000 in the same year and ranged between £50 and £2,000. The trust aims to assist medical, educational and environmental charities.

Exclusions: No grants to individuals.

Applications: In writing to the correspondent. Applications will not be acknowledged unless they fall within the trust's criteria outlined above.

The Hamarslea Trust

£1,700 (1994)

Christian

86 St Olaf Street, Lerwick, Shetland ZE1 0ES
01595-693504

Correspondent: The Secretary

Beneficial area: Preference for Shetland.

Information available: Accounts for 1994 were available from the trust.

General: The trust gives grants for furthering Christian teaching and spreading the Christian gospel. Preference is given to the Shetland Islands area.

In 1994, grants totalled £1,700 with no grant exceeding £200. Beneficiaries included Shetland Aid Trust, Child Evangelism Fellowship, SASRA and LUCHO Valez, Bolivia.

Applications: In writing to the correspondent.

Highland Regional Council Charities

Not known

General

Highland Regional Council, Regional Buildings, Glenurquhart Road, Inverness IV3 5NX
01463-663830

Correspondent: A C Gilchrist, Director of Education

Beneficial area: Highland region.

Information available: Information was provided by the trust.

General: The council runs a number of grant-making trusts which support community projects locally. The trusts operate through divisional offices. These are:

Caithness: J H Edgar, Divisional Education Officer, Rhind House, West Banks Avenue, Wick (01955-602362).

Inverness: N W Murray, Divisional Education Officer, 13 Ardross Street, Inverness (01463-663800).

Lochaber: J McCabe, Divisional Education Officer, Montrose Avenue, Inverlochy, Fort William (01397-702466).

Ross and Cromarty: A G Forsyth, Divisional Education Officer, The Education Centre, Castle Street, Dingwall (01349-63441).

Sutherland: J S Metcalfe, Divisional Education Officer, Education Offices, Brora (01408-621382).

Applications: Contact the appropriate division for further information.

The Isobel Parker Charitable Fund

£1,000 (1993)

Relief of hardship

100 High Street, Linlithgow EH49 7AQ
01506-845144

Correspondent: Robert Alexander

Trustees: R Alexander.

Beneficial area: Newtonmore Community Council area.

Information available: Information was supplied by the trust.

General: The fund had an income of £2,700 in 1992. Grants may be up to £500. In 1992, six grants totalling £1,000 were made.

Beneficiaries were the Village Hall Fund (£360), First Newtonmore Brownies (£200), Newtonmore Shinty Club (£125), and Newtonmore Friendship Club and Newtonmore Playgroups (£100 each).

Exclusions: Voluntary organisations outside the specified geographical area.

Applications: The trust invites applications on an annual basis by advertising in the local press.

James Paton's Charitable Trust

£11,000 (1993/94)

General

7 Muirfield Road, Inverness IV2 4AY
01463-231025

Correspondent: R M Murray

Trustees: R M Murray; J W Mackintosh.

Beneficial area: Inverness.

Information available: Accounts for 1993/94 are available.

General: The trust had assets of £276,000 in 1993/94. Grants totalled £11,000, with the same amount awarded in 1992/93.

The trust has given two grants in each of the last two years. Highland Regional Council's Social Work Department received £1,000 in both years. The other £10,000 went to Isobel Fraser Home of Rest in 1992/93 and Highland Society for the Blind in 1993/94.

Exclusions: The trust does not normally fund national charities.

Applications: The trust states that it "prefers to operate anonymously and does not solicit applications".

The Ross & Cromarty District Council Charities

£10,500

Education and training in the Isle of Lewis

Education & Leisure Services, Western Isles Council, Council Offices, Stornoway, Isle of Lewis HS1 2BW
01851-703773

Correspondent: The Director of Education & Leisure Services

Trustees: Highland Council, Inverness.

Beneficial area: The Isle of Lewis.

Information available: Information was provided by the trust.

General: The trust gives grants and bursaries to students for education and training. It supports educational trips and travel, and helps with sports facilities and local clubs.

Exclusions: The trust only supports people living on the Isle of Lewis.

Applications: Contact the correspondent for further information.

The Ross & Cromarty Educational Trust

£8,800 (1994/95)

Education

Education & Leisure Services, Western Isles Council, Council Offices, Sandwick Road, Stornoway, Isle of Lewis HS1 2BW
01851-703773

Correspondent: The Director of Education & Leisure Services

Beneficial area: The former county of Ross & Cromarty (including the Isle of Lewis, now part of the Western Isles Islands Area).

Information available: Information was available from the trust.

General: In 1994/95, the trust had an income of £10,500. £1,700 was given in education grants to individuals, and the remaining share of the income was given for school trips, education projects, clubs and societies, sports facilities, adult education and the promotion of education in music, art and drama.

Exclusions: Organisations not benefiting people living in the beneficial area.

Applications: In writing to the correspondent. Applications are considered in April and October.

The Sandison Trust

£2,000 (1993/94)

General in Shetland

Tait & Peterson, Bank of Scotland Buildings, Lerwick, Shetland ZE1 0EB
01595-693010

Correspondent: George S Peterson, Trustee

Trustees: G S Peterson; P J Thomson; E E Sandison; C G D Sandison; V E Owers.

Beneficial area: Shetland, with a preference for the Island of Unst.

Information available: 1993/94 accounts were available from the trust.

General: The trust's total assets were £53,000 in 1993/94. Grants are given for general charitable purposes in Shetland and in Unst in particular.

A total amount of £2,000 was awarded in 1993/94 and grants ranged between £50 and £1,500. Beneficiaries included the Methodist Church, Haroldswick, St John's Church,

Baltasound, Uyeasound Hall and St John's Kirk for Hardship Fund.

Exclusions: No grants to organisations outside the Shetland Islands.

Applications: In writing to the correspondent.

The Shetland Islands Council Charitable Trust

£10,620,000 (1993/94)

General in Shetland

Breiwick House, 15 South Road, Lerwick, Shetland ZE1 0RB
01595-744681

Correspondent: The Chief Executive

Trustees: Twenty-seven trustees, being the elected Shetland councillors (acting as individuals), the Lord Lieutenant and the Headmaster of the Anderson High School.

Beneficial area: Shetland.

Information available: Model reports and accounts are available from the trust for £2.

General: This exemplary body was established from "disturbance" payments negotiated by the local council with the developers of Sullom Voe oil terminal.

The trust is a charity but it is administered by Shetland Islands Council staff and the trustees have chosen for the time being to make grants on the recommendations, not necessarily always accepted, of the appropriate council committees. "The council ... provides an existing and democratic structure through which the trustees may hear the views of the Shetland community."

By 1993, capital of £94 million had been accumulated, generating a high income of £9 million. Capital growth continues, both from the increasing value of internal investments and from the on-going disturbance payments of £3.5 million a year at present. The trust employs the independent WM Company to appraise regularly and publicly the performance of the trust's investment managers. This is a measure which more trusts might well imitate.

"The trustees set out to:

(a) Improve the quality of life for Shetlanders, especially in the areas of:

Social need

Leisure

Environment

Education

(b) Support traditional industries, in ways where a charity might usefully assist, particularly:

Agriculture

Fishery

Knitwear

(c) Maintain flexibility for the trust's funds, in order to be able to meet new situations and priorities, but to do so against the background of a published framework of plans."

The trust produces an admirable narrative report. The following excerpts give a flavour of the range of the trust's work:

"About £337,000 was allocated to the Property Improvement Grant Scheme, to assist the infirm and/or elderly to retain a measure of independence and remain in their own homes ...

"There are many local action and self-help groups formed and run by members of the public ... often to support a particular group of sick or disabled people ... Nearly £417,000 was spent via these groups ...

"The charitable trust also supports the Shetland Arts Trust ... and the Shetland Amenity Trust, for its various environmental initiatives such as the anti-litter campaign, the development of local museums and the employment of a full-time archaeologist ..."

Methods of working: The trust is very open about its procedures, and has clear policies of long-term planning and publicising its decisions. For example, each year the trustees adopt a budget for the incoming financial year, based on a rolling five-year plan. Inclusion of a project in the plan does not guarantee that funds will be made available, but does indicate that it is likely ...

"The trustees usually debate the five-year plan and the annual budget in public. Most charitable disbursements are also considered in public. The main exceptions are grants to specific individuals ..."

The minutes of all meetings are public and, where items of business have been transacted in private, a press release summarising the decisions taken is issued the next day.

Exclusions: The trust only supports charitable purposes.

Applications: "External grant applications are not entertained."

The Stornoway Trust

Not known

General

Perceval Square, Stornoway, Isle of Lewis

Correspondent: D M Smith

Beneficial area: The area of the Stornoway Trust Estate.

Information available: No financial information available.

General: No information available.

Applications: In writing to the correspondent. We have been unable to confirm the details of this trust.

Sutherland District Council Charities

Not known

General

Sutherland District Council, District Offices, Golspie, Sutherland KW10 6RB
01408-633033

Correspondent: J Allison, Director of Administration

Beneficial area: Sutherland District.

Information available: No financial information was available.

General: Grants are awarded for general charitable purposes to local charitable organisations. There is no further information about the size of grant or the type of beneficiary.

Applications: Contact the correspondent for further details.

W Stuart Sutherland's Trust Fund

£8,000 to £10,000

Research into chest-related diseases

26 Church Street, Inverness IV1 1HX
01463-225165

Correspondent: David J Hewitson, Solicitor

Trustees: I S Smith; J Stewart; D J Hewitson.

Beneficial area: Preference for the Highland region of Scotland.

Information available: Information was provided by the trust.

General: The assets of the trust originate from a bequest of a share of residue of the estate of the late W Stuart Sutherland whose executry has just completed and the amount of the bequest determined. It is about £164,000. Grants in the future may therefore total about £8,000 to £10,000 a year.

The objects of the trust are "the treatment of and research into asthma and other chest-related diseases and complaints".

Applications: In writing to the trustees.

Urras an Eilean

Not known

Cultural activities, the promotion of Gaelic, education

Eilean Iarmain, Isle of Skye IV43 8QR
01471-833266

Correspondent: The Secretaries

Beneficial area: The Isle of Skye.

Information available: No financial information available.

General: Grants are given to organisations based on the Isle of Skye which run cultural activities or small projects connected with Gaelic. Educational projects are also considered, particularly Gaelic play groups. No further information is available.

Applications: Contact the correspondent for further details. This entry has not been confirmed by the trust. The address details are correct.

Index

Aberdeen: The Aberdeen Endowments
Trust   131

Aberdeenshire: The Aberdeenshire
Educational Trust Scheme   131

Adams: Miss S E Adams Charitable
Trust   27

Adamson: The Adamson Trust   27

Age: The Age Concern Scotland
Enterprise Fund   27

Aitken: The Sylvia Aitken Charitable
Trust   28

Alexander's: Edward Alexander's Trust   28

AMW: The AMW Charitable Trust   29

Anderson: The James & Grace Anderson
Trust   29

Anderson's: Miss Agnes Anderson's
Trust   29

Appletree: The Appletree Trust   141

Arbroath: The Arbroath Improvement
Trust   132

Archer: The John M Archer Charitable
Trust   30

Arnott: The William Henry Arnott Trust   145

Bain's: A G Bain's Trust   133

Baird: The Baird Trust   30

Balcraig: The Balcraig Foundation   30

Balfour: The Balfour Aitnoch Charitable
Trust   31

Balfour's: H D Balfour's Trust   31

Balmore: The Balmore Trust   157

Banffshire: The Banffshire Educational
Trust Scheme   133

Barclay: The Thomas Barclay Bequest   145

Barge: The Kenneth Barge Memorial
Trust   32

Bartholomew: The Bartholomew
Christian Trust   32

Baxter: The Ian & Margaret Baxter
Charitable Trust   33

BBC: BBC Children in Need Appeal   33

Beauchamp: The Beauchamp Trust   34

Bell's: Bell's Nautical Trust   34

Bellahouston: The Bellahouston
Bequest Fund   158

Bertram: The Miss J K Bertram
Memorial Trust   146

Bethesda: The Bethesda Charitable
Trust Fund   34

Beveridge's: Miss Beveridge's Trust   146

Bhan: The Mairi Bhan Trust   35

Birnie: The Birnie Trust   35

Blackstock: The Blackstock Trust   36

Bourne-May: The Bourne-May
Charitable Trust   36

Boyd's: Miss Margaret Boyd's Charitable
Trust   36

Boyle's: James Boyle's Trust   37

Broughton's: Miss Marion Broughton's
Charitable Trust   37

Brown: The Brown Charitable Trust   37

Brownies: The Brownies Taing Pier
Trust   173

Bruce: The Bruce Bequest Committee
for Mentally Handicapped   141

Bruce: The Bruce Charitable Trust   147

Buccleuch: The Buccleuch Place Trust   147

Calders: John J Calders Charitable Trust
and Trust for Guides & Scouts   38

Caledonian: The Caledonian Foundation   38

Callander: The Callander Charitable
Trust   142

Campagnat: The Campagnat Trust   39

Campbell: The Ellis Campbell
Charitable Foundation   133

Cancer: The Cancer Relief Macmillan
Fund   39

Cargill:

The W A Cargill Charitable Trust   39

The D W T Cargill Fund   40

The W A Cargill Fund   40

Carnegie:

The Carnegie Dunfermline Trust   142

The Carnegie Trust for the
Universities of Scotland   40

The Carnegie United Kingdom Trust   42

Cathro: The A T Cathro Bequest   134

Cattanach: The Cattanach Charitable
Trust   45

Cephas: The Cephas Trust   45

Challenge: The Challenge Trust   46

Charities: The Charities Aid Fund
of the City of Glasgow Society of
Social Service   158

Chest: Chest Heart & Stroke Scotland   46

Chrimes: The Chrimes Family
Charitable Trust   159

Claremont: The Claremont Trust   46

Coats: The Peter Coats Trust   159

Coila: The Coila Charitable Trust   47

Combe: The Combe Trust   47

Common:

The Common Good Fund   173

The Common Good Fund of
the District Council   159

Connell: The Martin Connell Charitable
Trust   48

Courant: The Courant Fund for Needy
Children   147

Craignish: The Craignish Trust   48

Cray: The Cray Trust   48

Crichton's:

Mrs Doris M Crichton's
Charitable Trust   49

Hamish Crichton's Charitable Trust   49

Cromarty: The Cromarty Trust   174

Cross: The Cross Trust   49

Cunningham: The Cunningham Trust   50

Darling: The Darling Charitable Trust   148

Dickson: The Dickson Minto Charitable
Trust   50

Doris: The Howard Doris Trust   174

Douglas: The Douglas Charitable Trust   51

Drake: The Jack Drake Charitable Trust   51

Drummond: The Drummond Trust   52

Dumfries: Charities Administered by
Dumfries & Galloway Council   160

Dumfriesshire: The Dumfriesshire
Educational Trust   160

Dundee: The Dundee City Council
Charities   134

Dunn's: Mrs J C Dunn's Trust   52

Earl: The Earl of Perth Charitable Trust   52

East: The East Lothian Educational
Trust   148

Eckford: The Christina Mary Eckford
Estate   53

Edinburgh:

The Edinburgh Children's Holiday
Fund   148

The Edinburgh Old Town Charitable Trust 149

Trusts administered by Edinburgh Voluntary Organisations' Council 149

Edinvar: The Edinvar Trust 53

Erskine: The Erskine Cunningham Hill Trust 53

Falkland: The Falkland Community Trust 54

Ferguson: The Ferguson Bequest Fund 160

Fleming: The J & C Fleming Trust 54

Foreman: The Russell & Mary Foreman 1980 Charitable Trust 55

Fraser:

The Emily Fraser Trust 55

The Gordon Fraser Charitable Trust 55

The Hugh Fraser Foundation 56

Fyfe: The J G Fyfe Charitable Trust 57

Gamma: The Gamma Trust 57

Gannochy: The Gannochy Trust 57

Garnett's: Mrs A M Garnett's 1973 Charitable Trust 174

Gateway: The Gateway Exchange Trust 59

Gaul: The Gaul Trust 161

Gemmell: The Gemmell Bequest Fund 161

Gillman: The Helen & Horace Gillman Trusts 59

Glasgow-Kilmun: The Glasgow-Kilmun Charitable Society 162

Glendoune: The Glendoune Charitable Trust 162

Goodacre: The Goodacre Benevolent Fund 60

Gough: The Gough Charitable Trust 60

Gray: The Melville Gray Charitable Trust 135

Gray's: The Very Reverend Dr John R Gray's Trust 61

Green:

The Elizabeth Green Trust 61

The Ann Jane Green Trust 62

Guy: The Susan H Guy Charitable Trust 62

Guy-Lockhart: The Guy-Lockhart Charitable Trust 62

Haldane's: J M Haldane's Charitable Trust 63

Hall: The Mary Jamieson Hall & John F Hall Trust 135

Hamarslea: The Hamarslea Trust 175

Hamilton: The Alice Hamilton Trust 150

Hannah: The Hannah Charitable Trust 135

Harbinson: The Roderick Harbinson Charitable Trust 63

Harbinson's: Miss K M Harbinson's Charitable Trust 63

Harbour: The Harbour Trust 64

Harryhausen's: Mrs D L Harryhausen's 1969 Trust 64

Harvey's: William Harvey's Trust 136

Hay:

The Dora Hay Charitable Trust 162

The Douglas Hay Trust 65

Hayward: The Hayward Foundation 65

Henderson: The A Sinclair Henderson Trust 66

Hendrie: The Christina Mary Hendrie Trust for Scottish & Canadian Charities 66

Herd:

The Herd Charitable Trust 67

The Anne Herd Memorial Trust 136

Highgate: The Highgate Charitable Trust 67

Highland: Highland Regional Council Charities 175

Hilden: The Hilden Charitable Fund 67

Hill: The L E Hill Memorial Trust 68

Hill's: L S Hill's Charitable Trust 68

Hillhouse: The M V Hillhouse Trust 69

Holywood: The Holywood Trust 162

Hoover: The Hoover Foundation 163

Hope: The Hope Trust 69

Housing: The Housing Associations
Charitable Trust 70

Howat: The James Thom Howat
Charitable Trust 71

Howman: The Howman Charitable
Trust 71

Hunter:

The Patrick Mitchell Hunter Fund 137

The George Hunter Trust 163

Hunter's: Miss Agnes H Hunter's Trust 72

Imries: The Mrs E Y Imries Trust 72

Inchrye: The Inchrye Trust 73

Innes: The Gilbert Innes Trust 73

Inverclyde: The Inverclyde Bequest
Fund 73

Ireland's: The P M Ireland's Charitable
Trust 74

Islay: The Islay Campbell Trust 164

Jardine: The Lady Eda Jardine
Charitable Trust 74

Jeffrey: The Jeffrey Charitable Trust 74

K: The K C Charitable Trust 75

Kaye's: Robert Kaye's Trust 75

Kennyhill: The Kennyhill Bequest
Fund 164

Keymer: The Ronald & Mary Keymer
Trust 75

Kincardineshire: The Kincardineshire
Educational Trust Scheme 137

Kinpurnie: The Kinpurnie Charitable
Trust 76

Kintore: The Kintore Charitable Trust 76

Laing:

The Hon. Mark Laing Charitable Trust 77

The Lord & Lady Laing of Dunphail
Charitable Trust 77

The Robert Laing Charitable Trust 77

The Timothy & Charlotte Laing
Charitable Trust 78

Lamb's: Lamb's Bequest 164

Landale: The Landale Charitable Trust
(formerly the D & G Charitable Trust) 78

Lane: The Allen Lane Foundation 78

Lankelly: The Lankelly Foundation 79

Larg: The R J Larg Family Trust 80

Leggat's: Duncan Campbell Leggat's
Charitable Trust 80

Lethendy: The Lethendy Trust 81

Lindsay's: Lindsay's Charitable Trust 81

Lindsays: The Lindsays Charitable
Trust 150

Liston's: John Liston's Scottish
Charitable Trust 81

Little: The Andrew & Mary Elizabeth
Little Charitable Trust 82

Logie: The Logie Charitable Trust 82

Lothian:

The Marquess of Lothian's
Charitable Trust 83

The Peter Lothian Newtongrange
Charitable Trust 151

Low: The Low & Bonar Charitable
Fund 83

Lumsden's: Mrs M A Lumsden's
Charitable Trust 84

Lynch: The Anne Lynch Memorial
Fund 84

McCallum: The McCallum Bequest
Fund 165

McCrone: The McCrone Charitable
Trust 84

MacDonald: The R S MacDonald
Charitable Trust 85

MacFarlane: The N S MacFarlane
Charitable Trust 85

McGallagley: The Agnes McGallagley
Bequest 165

MacGregor's: MacGregor's Bequest 165

McGregor's: The McGregor's Trust 166

McKenzie: The Elspeth McKenzie
Memorial Fund 86

Maclay:

The Maclay Charitable Trust 86

The Maclay Murray & Spens
Charitable Trust 86

MacLennan: The MacLennan Trust 87

MacLeod: The George MacLeod
Charitable Trust 87

MacRobert: The MacRobert Trusts 87

MacTaggart: The Ian MacTaggart Trust ... 89

Massey: The Nancie Massey Charitable
Trust 151

Mathew: The Mathew Trust 137

MEB: The MEB Charitable Trust 90

Melville: The Melville Trust for Care
& Cure of Cancer 90

Merchants: The Merchants House of
Glasgow 166

Mester: Mrs Henni Mester Will Trust ... 90

Mickel: The Mickel Fund 91

Middleton's: Middleton's Bequest 166

Millar: Andrew Millar Charitable Trust ... 91

Miller:

The Miller Foundation 91

The Hugh & Mary Miller Bequest Trust ... 92

The Roy Miller Charitable Trust 92

Mollison: The Mollison Fund 138

Mongomerie: The Agnes C
Mongomerie Charitable Trust 92

Moray: The Moray & Nairn
Educational Trust Scheme 93

Morrison:

The Thomas Wharrie Morrison
Bequest Fund 167

The Stanley Morrison Charitable Trust ... 93

Morriston: The Morriston Davies Trust ... 94

Murray:

The James & Elizabeth Murray
Charitable Trust 94

The Murray Trust 143

Nairn's: Sir George Nairn's Charitable
Trust 94

Nairne:

The Nairne Trust 95

The Stanley Nairne Memorial Trust ... 95

Napier's: James & John Napier's Trust ... 167

Netherdale: The Netherdale Trust 95

Network: The Network Foundation 96

New: The New Horizons Trust 96

Nicol: The Bill & Margaret Nicol
Charitable Trust 97

Night: The Night Asylum Fund 168

1970: The 1970 Trust 97

North:

The North British Hotel Trust 97

Charities administered by
North East Fife District Council 144

Northwood: The Northwood
Charitable Trust 138

Oil: The Oil Industry Community Fund ... 98

Oppenheim:

The Harold Oppenheim Charitable
Trust 98

The Meyer Oppenheim Trust 98

P: The P F Charitable Trust 99

Parker: The Isobel Parker Charitable
Fund 175

Paterson's: Miss M E S Paterson's
Charitable Trust 100

Paton's:

Andrew Paton's Charitable Trust 101

James Paton's Charitable Trust 176

Phillips: The Hyman Phillips Trust for
Charities 101

Pilkington's: A M Pilkington's
Charitable Trust 101

Pleasance: The Pleasance Trust 152

Ponton: The Ponton House Trust 152

Primrose: The John Primrose Trust 168

Prince's: The Prince's Scottish Youth
Business Trust   102

Radio:

Radio Clyde – Cash for Kids at
Christmas   168

Radio Tay – Caring for Kids
(Radio Tay Listeners Charity)   139

Reid: The Reid Charitable Trust   102

Renfield: The Renfield Street Trust   169

Riddon: The Riddon Trust   103

Robertson:

The Robertson Charitable Trust   103

The Robertson Trust   103

Robertson's: Miss Elizabeth T
Robertson's Charitable Trust   105

Rosebery: The Lord Rosebery
Charitable Settlement   152

Rosemount: The Rosemount Trust   106

Ross:

The Ross & Cromarty District
Council Charities   176

The Ross & Cromarty Educational
Trust   176

Row: The Row Fogo Charitable Trust   153

Russell:

The Russell Bequest   153

The Russell Trust   170

The Hector Gordon Russell Trust   106

Salvesen: The Andrew Salvesen
Charitable Trust   106

Salvesen's:

Mr & Mrs John Salvesen's Charitable
Trust   107

The Mrs M H Salvesen's
Charitable Trust   107

Sandison: The Sandison Trust   177

Save: The Save & Prosper Educational
Trust   154

Scanlan: The Rosemary Scanlan
Charitable Trust   170

Scott: The John Scott Trust   107

Scott's:

Mrs Elizabeth Scott's Charitable Trust   108

Mrs Rhoda Nina Scott's Trust   155

Scottish:

The Scottish Chartered Accountants'
Trust for Education   108

The Scottish Churches Architectural
Heritage Trust   109

The Scottish Disability Foundation   109

The Scottish Homoeopathic Research
& Education Trust   109

The Scottish Hospital Endowments
Research Trust   110

The Scottish Housing Associations
Charitable Trust (SHACT)   110

The Scottish International Education
Trust   111

The Scottish Slimmers Charitable
Trust   112

Sharp: The Charles Neil Sharp Charity
Trust   112

Shering: The Ernest Shering
Evangelistic Trust   155

Shetland: The Shetland Islands Council
Charitable Trust   177

Sinclair: The George Sinclair Charitable
Trust   113

Society: The Society in Scotland for
Propagating Christian Knowledge   113

Souter: The Souter Foundation   113

Spalding's:

Miss D R Spalding's Charitable Trust   114

John Mackie Spalding's Trust   139

Sportsman's: The Sportsman's Charity   114

Springboard: The Springboard
Charitable Trust   115

Spurgin: The Spurgin Charitable Trust   115

Stenhouse:

The Hugh Stenhouse Foundation   115

The Rennie Stenhouse Foundation   116

Stephen's: Miss Margaret J Stephen's
Charitable Trust   116

Stewart:

The Govan Stewart Trust   116

The Sir Ian Stewart Foundation   117

Stone: The Alexander Stone
Foundation   117

Stornoway: The Stornoway Trust   178

Strang's: Mr & Mrs W G Strang's
Charitable Trust   117

Strutt: The Joan Strutt Charitable Trust   118

Sunflower: The Sunflower Trust   118

Sutherland: Sutherland District
Council Charities   179

Sutherland's: W Stuart Sutherland's
Trust Fund   179

Sykes: The Verden Sykes Trust   118

T: The T C Charitable Trust   119

Talteg: Talteg Ltd   119

Tarnie: The Tarnie Trust   119

Tay: The Tay Charitable Trust   120

Tekoa: The Tekoa Trust   156

Templeton: The Templeton Goodwill
Trust   170

Tenovus: Tenovus-Scotland   120

Thomson:

The D C Thomson Charitable Trust   139

The Len Thomson Charitable Trust   121

The Scott Thomson Charitable Trust   121

Tibbermore: The Tibbermore
Charitable Trust   121

Tillyloss: The Tillyloss Trust   122

Trades: The Trades House of Glasgow   171

Trinafour: The Trinafour Trust   122

TSB: The TSB Foundation for Scotland   122

Tunnell: The John Tunnell Trust   124

Turnberry: The Turnberry Trust   124

Unemployed: The Unemployed
Voluntary Action Fund   124

Urras: Urras an Eilean   179

Usher: The Murray Usher Foundation   172

Walton:

The David & Carole Walton
Charitable Trust   125

The Isidore & David Walton
Foundation   126

Waterside: The Waterside Trust   126

Watson's: John Watson's Trust   127

Watt: The Lady Margaret Watt
Charitable Trust   127

Weir: The James Weir Foundation   128

Western: The Western Recreation Trust   129

Whitehills: The Whitehills Trust   129

Wilson: John Wilson Bequest Fund   156

Wolfson: The Edith & Isaac Wolfson
(Scotland) Trust   129

Wood: The James Wood Bequest Fund   130

Zeta: The Zeta Trust   130

Zweig: The Konrad Zweig Trust   130

Other books from DSC

A Guide to the Major Trusts Volume 1 1995/96 Edition

Our best-selling guide gives the most detailed information on grant-making trusts anywhere in print. Volume 1 covers 300 major trusts, all making grants of over £200,000 a year. The editors include each trust's own guidelines and advice for applicants, give examples of the actual donations that have been made, and provide a diary of trustees' meetings so that applicants can target their applications successfully. Essential! *"Compulsory reading for anyone involved in raising money from grant-making trusts."* (Growthpoint)

A4, 272 pages, 5th edition, 1995. ISBN 1 873860 49 8 £15.95

A Guide to the Major Trusts Volume 2 1995/96 Edition

Volume 2 covers a further 700 trusts, each with a potential to make grants of at least £45,000, and contains hitherto unpublished details of over 50 trusts. A guide no charity can afford to be without.

A4, 304 pages, 2nd edition, 1995. ISBN 1 873860 64 1 £15.95

A Guide to Company Giving 1995/96 Edition

Another best-selling title, this standard reference guide covers the charitable donations and community contributions of 1,400 companies, totalling over £300 million a year. Includes information on sponsorship, Business in the Community, staff secondments, joint promotions, the Per Cent Club, and employee giving. *"...invaluable to charitable organisations ... a bargain."* (Reference Reviews)

A4, 292 pages, 6th edition, 1995. ISBN 1 873860 50 1 £15.95

The Major Companies Guide 1996/97 Edition

The most detailed information in print on the charitable giving of the UK's top 400 companies, listing financial details; charitable giving policy and practice, including information on company trusts; types of grants made and more.

A4, 272 pages, 4th edition, 1995. ISBN 1 873860 89 7 £16.95

The Central Government Grants Guide 1995/96 Edition

Central government is a key funding source for charities. This book will help you tap the available resources. It covers grants, loans and payments for services available to voluntary bodies from central government departments and other official sources.

205x145mm, 272 pages, 3rd edition, 1995. ISBN 1 873860 73 0 £13.95

The Complete Fundraising Handbook

A book no fundraiser can afford to be without! Offers clear and down to earth advice on raising money for charity, covering the range of funds available and techniques that can be employed, marketing, PR, and much more. Published with ICFM.

246x189mm, 256 pages, 2nd edition, 1993. ISBN 1 873860 21 8 £12.95

Writing Better Fundraising Applications

Packed with information, advice, worked examples and exercises, this handbook will help you get your applications right. Published with ICFM.

A4, 80 pages, 1992. ISBN 0 907164 66 8 £9.95

Organising Local Events

A local event can raise awareness of issues, draw crowds, bring in money and attract publicity – or it can be a disaster. Including advice on licences and liabilities, and fully revised and up-dated, this is the book to help you get it right first time.

256x189mm, 144 pages, 2nd edition, 1995. ISBN 1 873860 88 9 £9.95

Tried and Tested Ideas for Raising Money Locally

Packed to the hilt with money-spinning ideas and practical tips for success, this lively book is ideal for community groups, local charity projects, schools and any small-scale fundraisers.

246x189mm, 144 pages, 1994. ISBN 1 873860 36 6 £8.95

Good Ideas for Raising Serious Money

A detailed examination of five adaptable events for crowds of between 4,000 and 40,000. This is a book for the non-professional that will give anyone the skills to make a big event work.

246x189mm, 160 pages, 1995. ISBN 1 873860 72 2 £9.95

The Complete Guide to Business and Strategic Planning for Voluntary Organisations

This practical guide will help you draw up realistic plans and implement them effectively. *Don't forget that the National Lottery Charities Board now calls for all big applications to be supported with a business plan!*

246x189mm, 106 pages, 1994. ISBN 1 873860 61 7 £10.95

Managing Quality of Service

This excellent guide addresses the ways in which voluntary sector funding contracts now emphasise measurement and accountability, and sheds new light on the potentially fraught process of quality assurance.

246x189mm, 104 pages, 1995. ISBN 1 873860 86 2 £10.95

How to order

These are just a few of the books available from DSC. Orders can be made by fax (0171-209 5049), through the post, or by telephone with a credit card. If you would like a current DSC Booklist, please ring us on 0171-209 5151, or at:

Directory of Social Change, 24 Stephenson Way, London NW1 2DP
Tel: 0171-209 5151; Fax: 0171-209 5049